MTV's

SIC TELEVISION®

BEAVIS AND B -HEAD's GREATEST HITS™

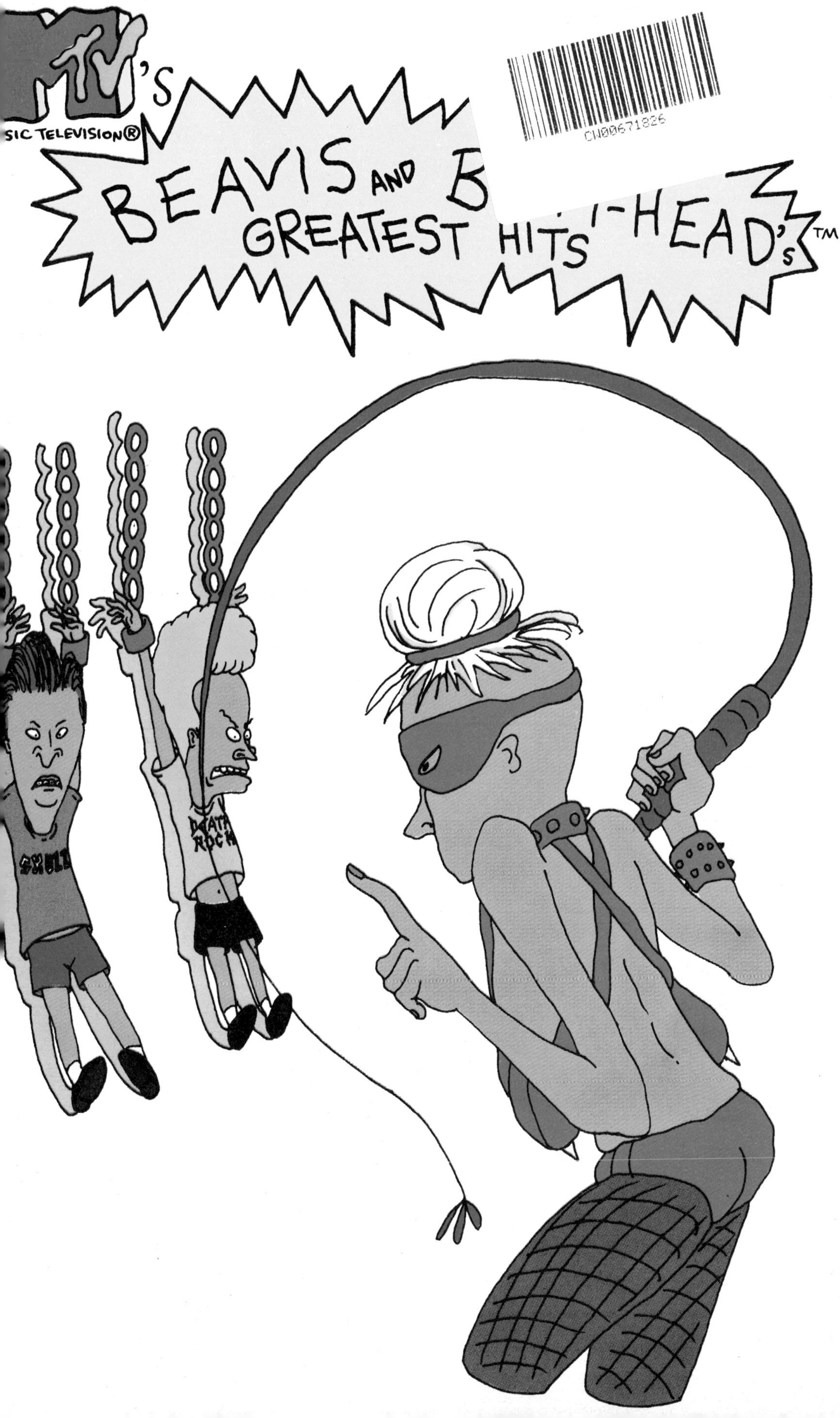

DENTAL HYGIENE DILEMMA

5

HUH, HUH, HUH!

DON'T MAKE ME KICK YOUR ASS!

THAT'S COOL!

YOU WUSS!

DEAD FROM THE NECK UP

28

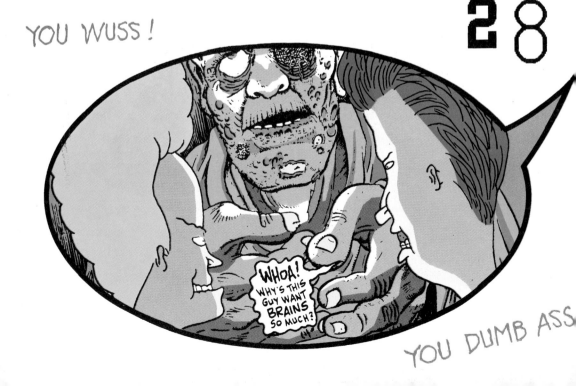

YOU DUMB ASS

BREAK OUT AT BURGER WORLD

51

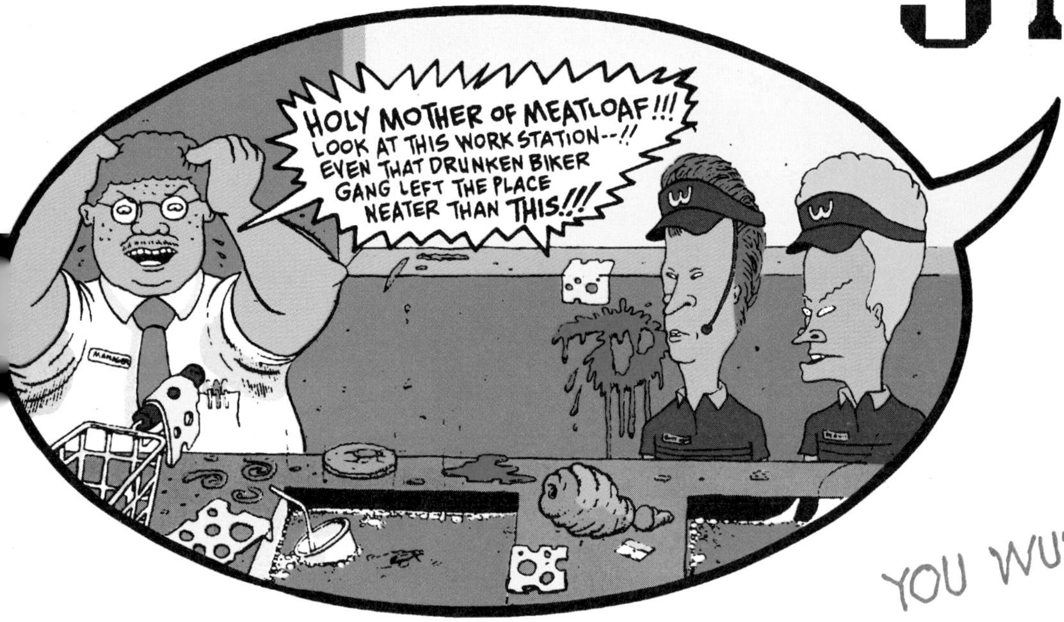

HOLY MOTHER OF MEATLOAF!!! LOOK AT THIS WORK STATION--!! EVEN THAT DRUNKEN BIKER GANG LEFT THE PLACE NEATER THAN THIS!!!

YOU WUSS!

BREAKIN' THE LAW, BREAKIN' THE LAW!

TATTOO PARLOR

74

I DON'T LIKE STUFF THAT SUCKS!

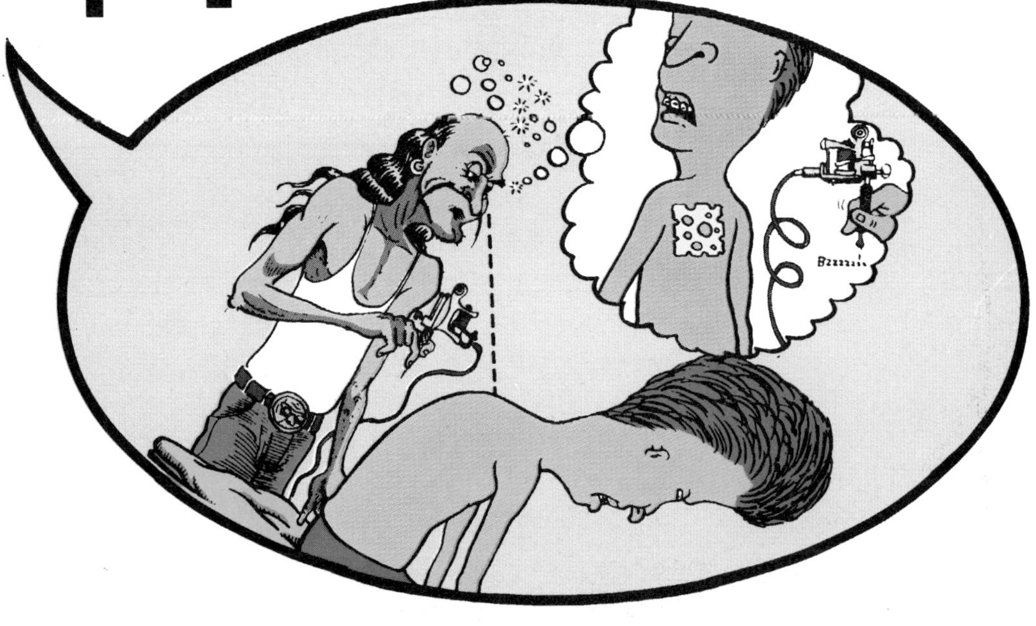

Bzzzzz

The dorks who helped us with this stuff

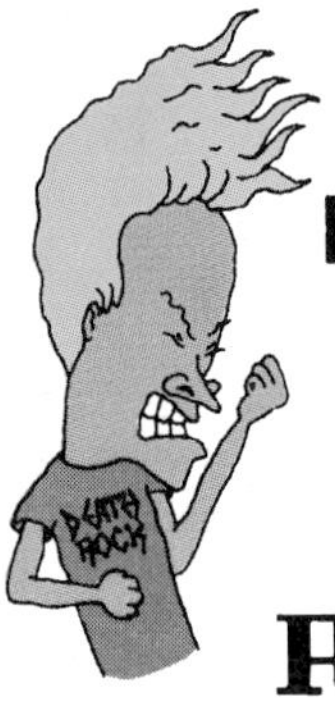

MIKE LACKEY
writer

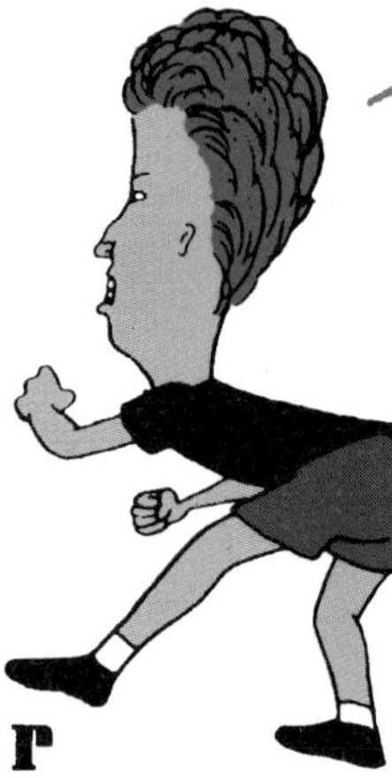

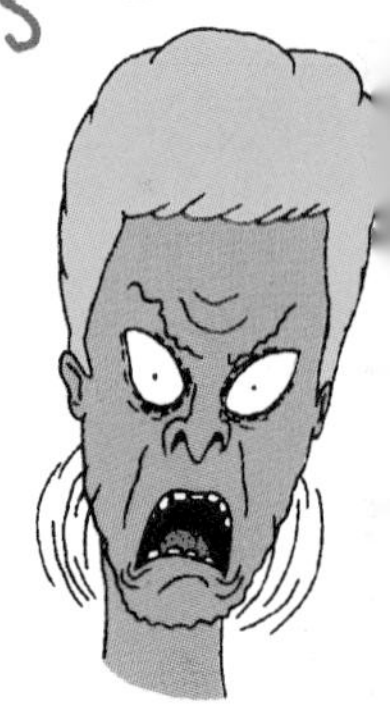
THAT'S COOL!

RICK PARKER
artist and letterer

I DON'T LIKE STUFF
THAT SUCKS!
YOU DUMB A

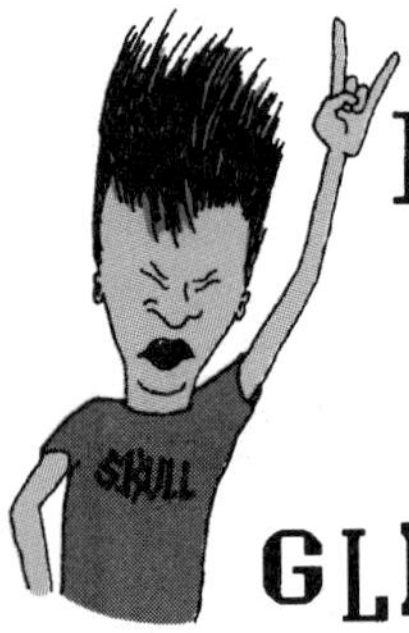

BOB SHAREN
colorist

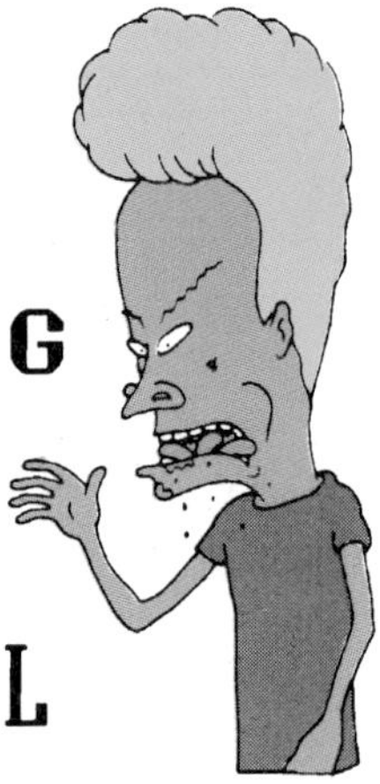

GLENN HERDLING
editor

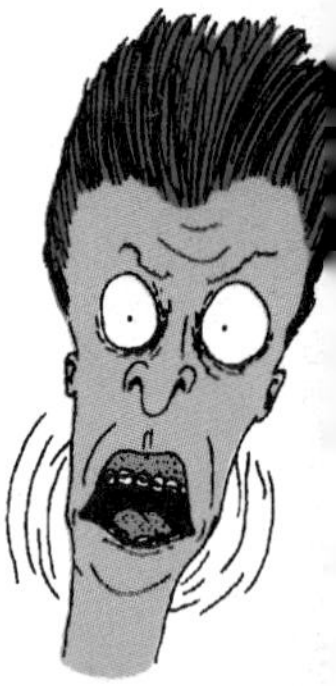

SCOTT MARSHALL
assistant editor

HUH, HUH, HUH!

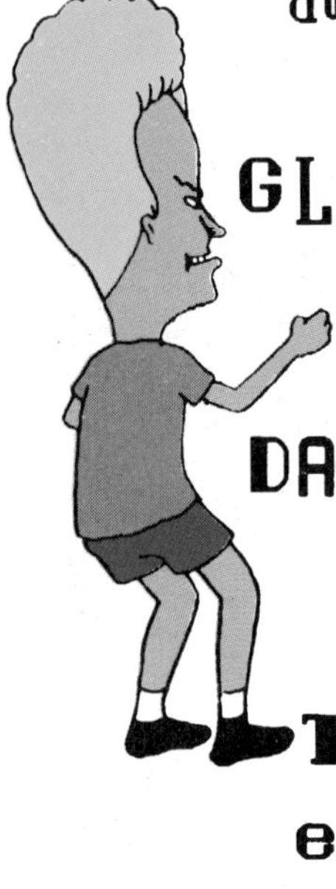

GLENN EICHLER
consultant

DON'T MAKE ME KICK
YOUR ASS!

DAWN GEIGER
designer

TOM DeFALCO
editor in chief

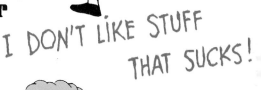

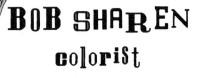

BEAVIS & BUTT-HEAD™: GREATE
Published by Titan Books, 42-44 Dolben St, London S
ISBN 1 85286 591 1 First UK edition: Septem
1 2 3 4 5 6 7 8 9 10 Printed

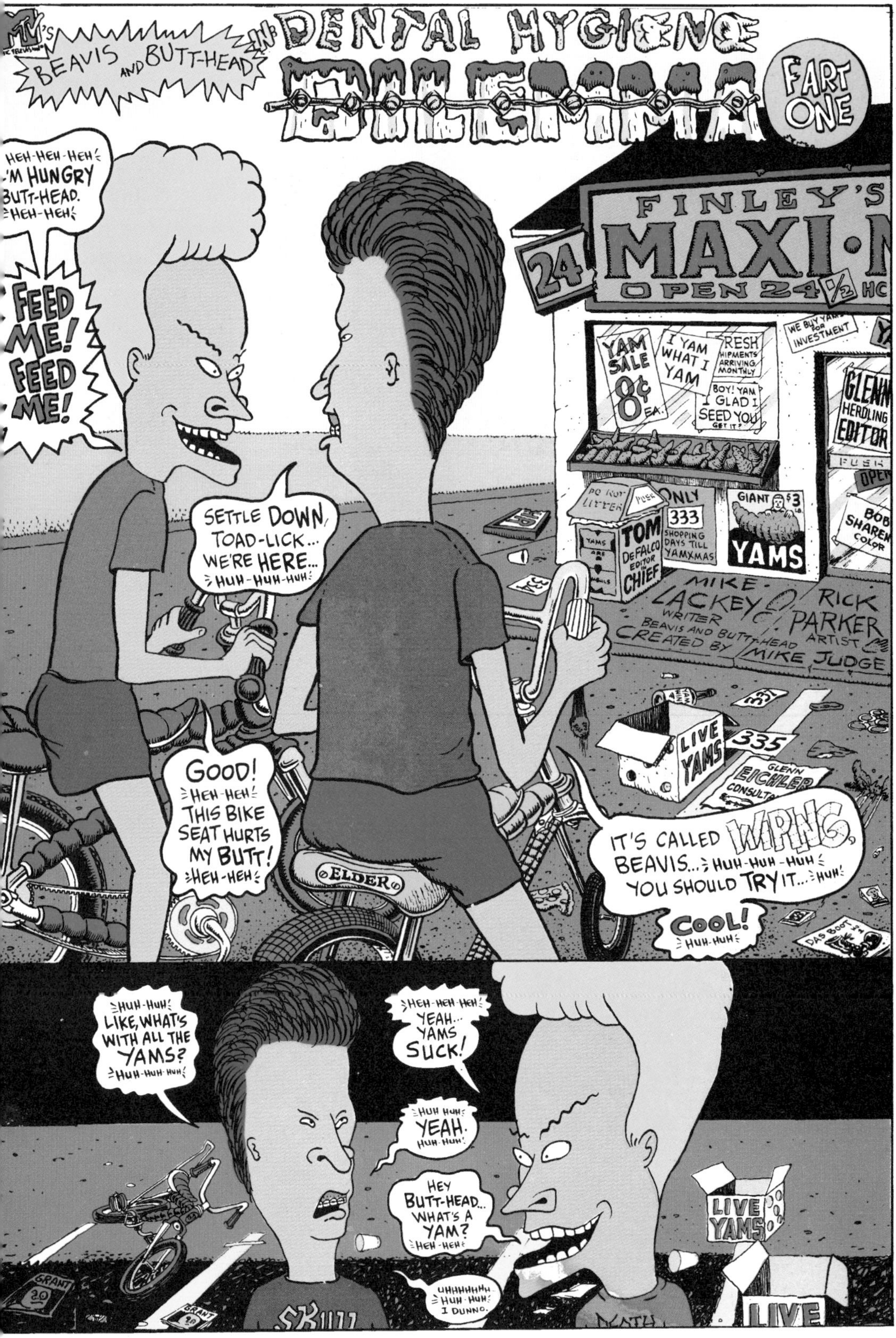
MTV's
BEAVIS AND BUTT-HEAD
in DENTAL HYGIENE DILEMMA
FART ONE
HEH-HEH-HEH I'M HUNGRY BUTT-HEAD. HEH-HEH
FEED ME! FEED ME!
FINLEY'S MAXI-M
24
OPEN 24½ HO
YAM SALE 8¢ EA.
I YAM WHAT I YAM
FRESH SHIPMENTS ARRIVING MONTHLY
BOY! YAM GLAD I SEED YOU GET IT?
WE BUY YAMS FOR INVESTMENT
GLENN HERDLING EDITOR
PUSH
OPEN
DO NOT LITTER
PUSH
ONLY 333 SHOPPING DAYS TILL YAMXMAS
GIANT $3 LB. YAMS
TOM DeFALCO EDITOR IN CHIEF
BOB SHAREN COLOR
SETTLE DOWN, TOAD-LICK... WE'RE HERE... HUH-HUH-HUH
MIKE LACKEY WRITER
RICK PARKER ARTIST
BEAVIS AND BUTT-HEAD CREATED BY MIKE JUDGE
LIVE YAMS
335
GLENN EICHLER CONSULTANT
GOOD! HEH-HEH THIS BIKE SEAT HURTS MY BUTT! HEH-HEH
ELDER
IT'S CALLED WIRING, BEAVIS... HUH-HUH-HUH YOU SHOULD TRY IT... HUH
COOL! HUH-HUH
DAS BOOT
HUH-HUH LIKE, WHAT'S WITH ALL THE YAMS? HUH-HUH-HUH
HEH-HEH-HEH YEAH... YAMS SUCK!
HUH HUH YEAH. HUH-HUH
HEY BUTT-HEAD... WHAT'S A YAM? HEH-HEH
UHHHHHHH HUH-HUH I DUNNO.
GRANT
LIVE YAMS
LIVE
SKULL

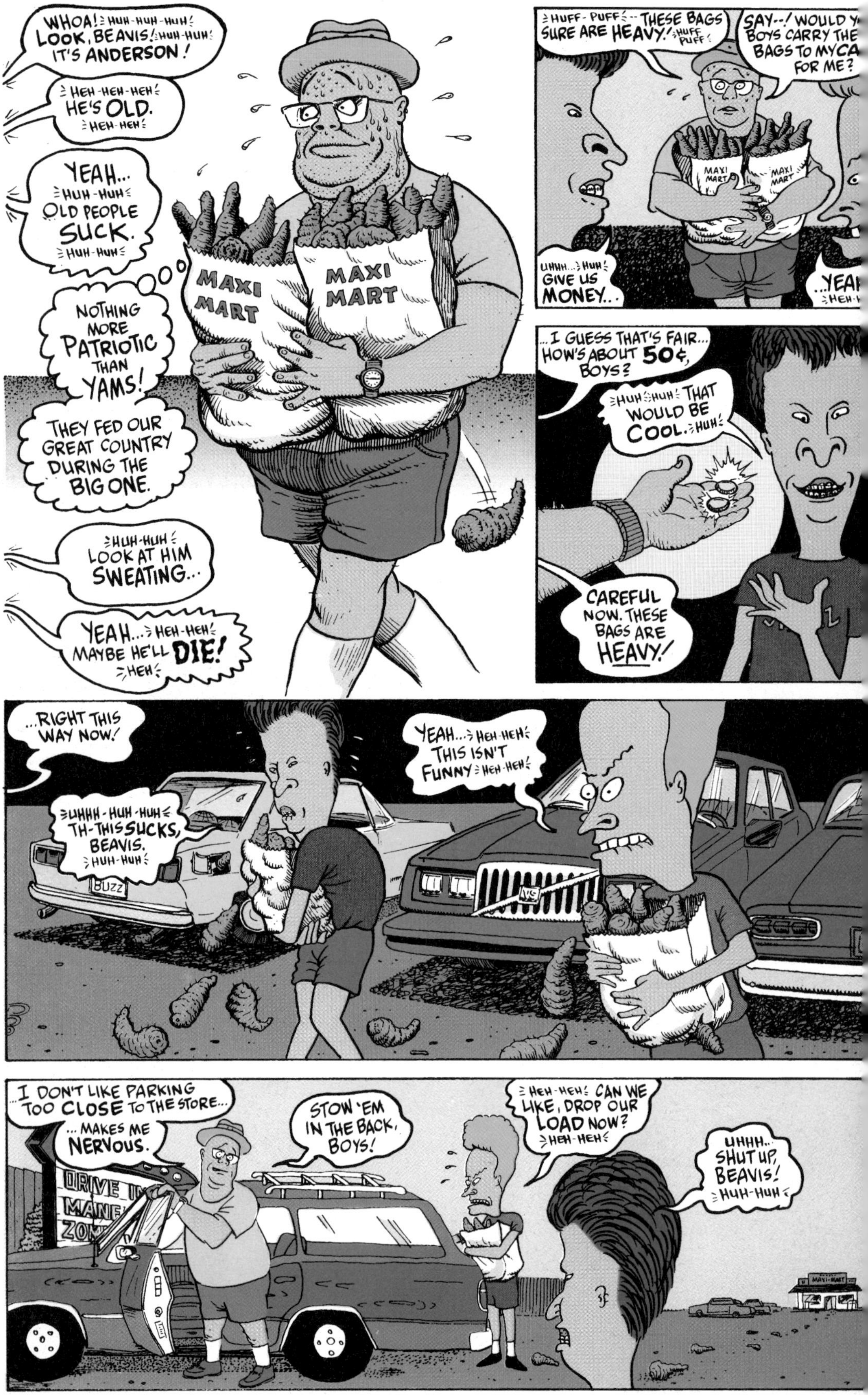
WHOA! HUH-HUH-HUH LOOK, BEAVIS! HUH-HUH IT'S ANDERSON!
HEH-HEH-HEH HE'S OLD. HEH-HEH
YEAH... HUH-HUH OLD PEOPLE SUCK. HUH-HUH
NOTHING MORE PATRIOTIC THAN YAMS!
THEY FED OUR GREAT COUNTRY DURING THE BIG ONE.
MAXI MART
MAXI MART
HUH-HUH LOOK AT HIM SWEATING...
YEAH... HEH-HEH MAYBE HE'LL DIE! HEH
HUFF-PUFF -- THESE BAGS SURE ARE HEAVY! HUFF PUFF
SAY--! WOULD Y BOYS CARRY THE BAGS TO MY CA FOR ME?
MAXI MART
MAXI MART
UHHH... HUH GIVE US MONEY...
...YEA HEH
...I GUESS THAT'S FAIR... HOW'S ABOUT 50¢, BOYS?
HUH HUH THAT WOULD BE COOL. HUH
CAREFUL NOW. THESE BAGS ARE HEAVY!
...RIGHT THIS WAY NOW!
UHHH-HUH-HUH TH-THIS SUCKS, BEAVIS. HUH-HUH
BUZZ
YEAH... HEH-HEH THIS ISN'T FUNNY HEH-HEH
I DON'T LIKE PARKING TOO CLOSE TO THE STORE... ...MAKES ME NERVOUS.
STOW 'EM IN THE BACK, BOYS!
HEH-HEH CAN WE LIKE, DROP OUR LOAD NOW? HEH-HEH
UHHH.. SHUT UP, BEAVIS! HUH-HUH
DRIVE IN MANE ZOM
MAXI-MART

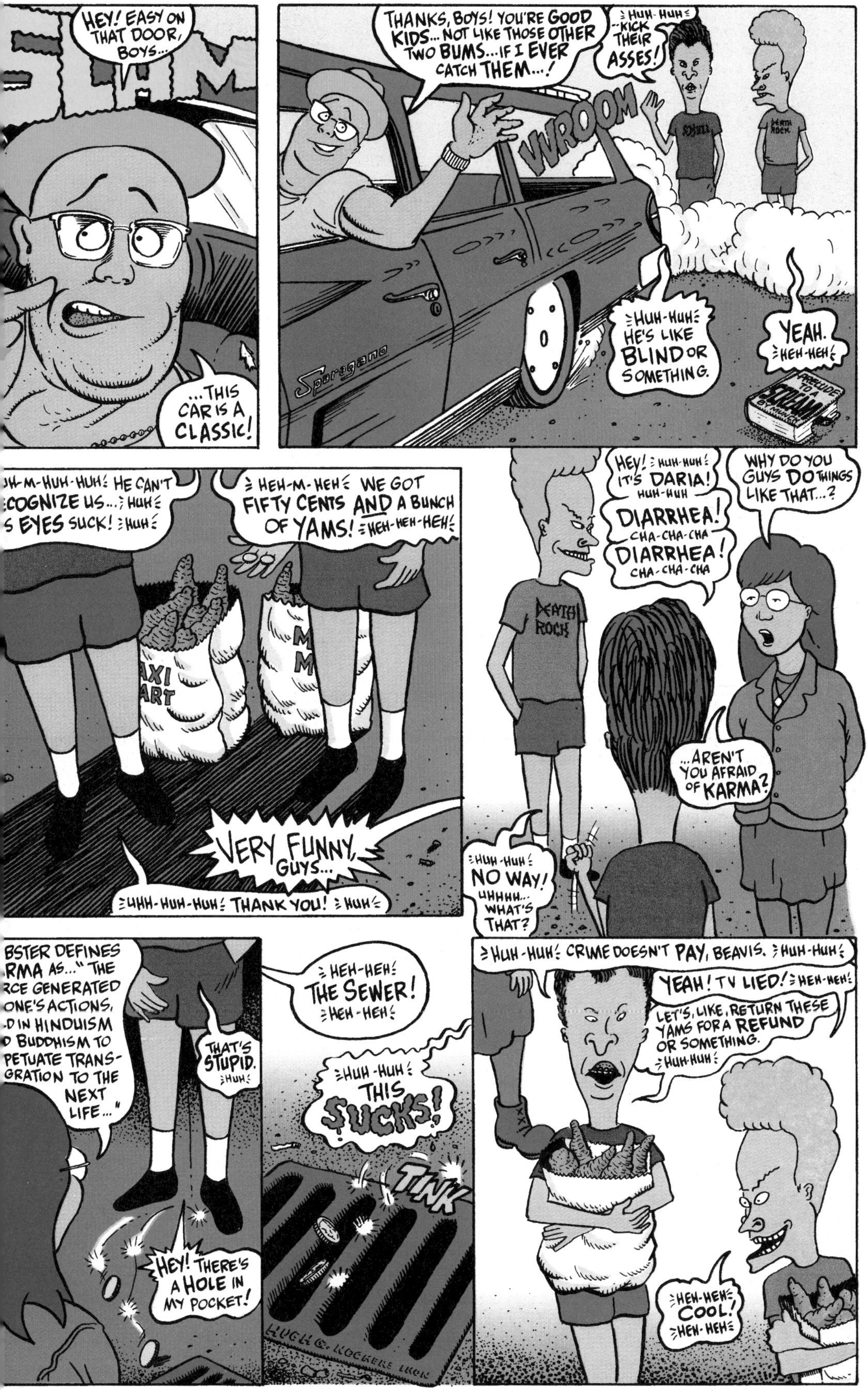
SLAM
HEY! EASY ON THAT DOOR, BOYS...
...THIS CAR IS A CLASSIC!
THANKS, BOYS! YOU'RE GOOD KIDS... NOT LIKE THOSE OTHER TWO BUMS... IF I EVER CATCH THEM...!
HUH-HUH ...KICK THEIR ASSES!
VVROOM
HUH-HUH HE'S LIKE BLIND OR SOMETHING.
YEAH. HEH-HEH
PRELUDE TO A SCREAM BY MUNCH
H-M-HUH-HUH HE CAN'T ECOGNIZE US... HUH S EYES SUCK! HUH
HEH-M-HEH WE GOT FIFTY CENTS AND A BUNCH OF YAMS! HEH-HEH-HEH!
VERY FUNNY, GUYS...
UHH-HUH-HUH THANK YOU! HUH
HEY! HUH-HUH IT'S DARIA! HUH-HUH
DIARRHEA! CHA-CHA-CHA DIARRHEA! CHA-CHA-CHA
WHY DO YOU GUYS DO THINGS LIKE THAT...?
...AREN'T YOU AFRAID OF KARMA?
HUH-HUH NO WAY! UHHHH... WHAT'S THAT?
BSTER DEFINES RMA AS..." THE RCE GENERATED ONE'S ACTIONS, D IN HINDUISM D BUDDHISM TO PETUATE TRANS-GRATION TO THE NEXT LIFE..."
THAT'S STUPID. HUH
HEY! THERE'S A HOLE IN MY POCKET!
HEH-HEH THE SEWER! HEH-HEH
HUH-HUH THIS SUCKS!
TINK
HUGH G. ROCKERE IRON
HUH-HUH CRIME DOESN'T PAY, BEAVIS. HUH-HUH
YEAH! TV LIED! HEH-HEH!
LET'S, LIKE, RETURN THESE YAMS FOR A REFUND OR SOMETHING. HUH-HUH
HEH-HEH COOL! HEH-HEH

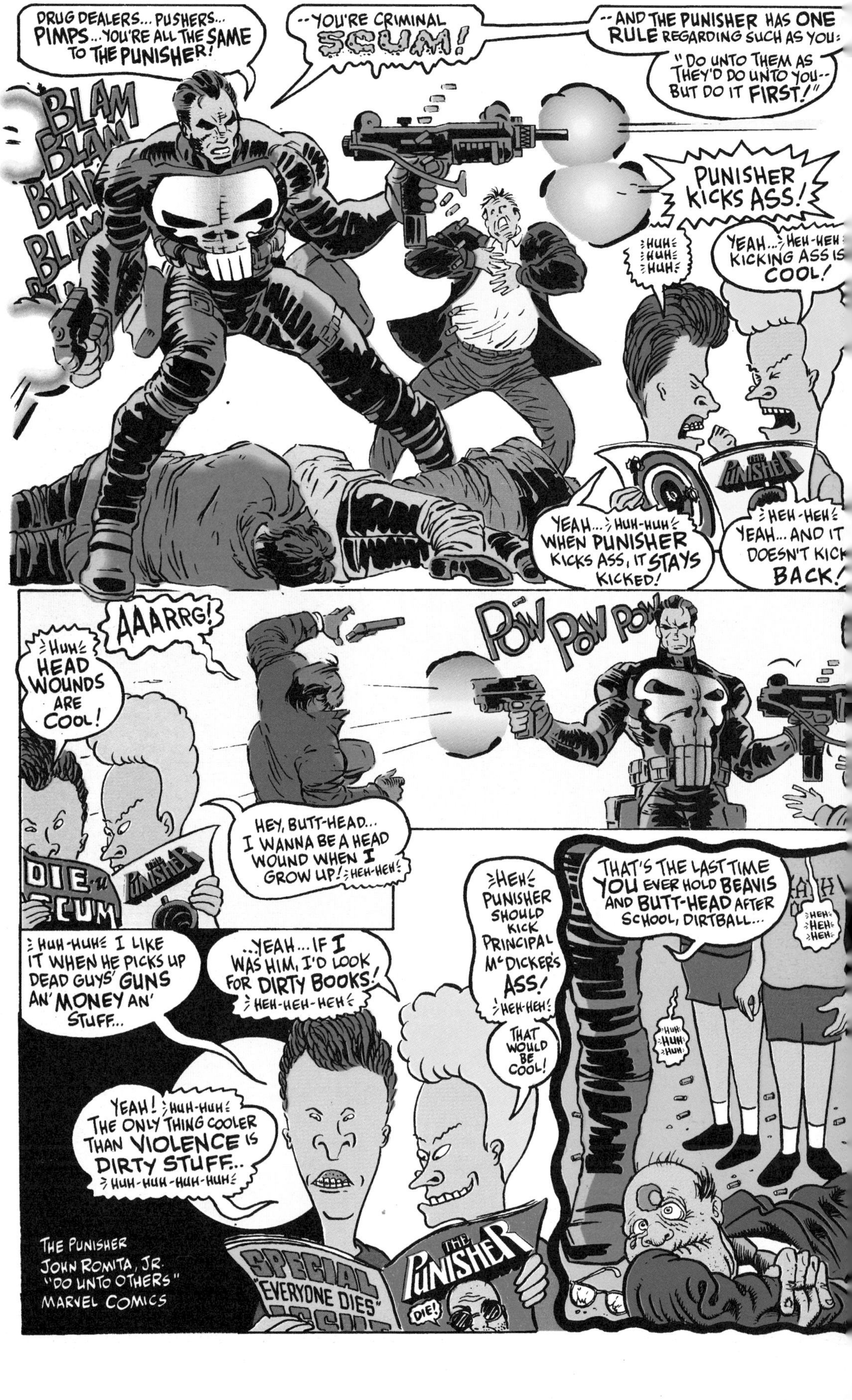
DRUG DEALERS... PUSHERS... PIMPS... YOU'RE ALL THE SAME TO THE PUNISHER!
--YOU'RE CRIMINAL SCUM!
--AND THE PUNISHER HAS ONE RULE REGARDING SUCH AS YOU:
"DO UNTO THEM AS THEY'D DO UNTO YOU-- BUT DO IT FIRST!"
BLAM BLAM BLAM BLAM BLAM
PUNISHER KICKS ASS!
HUH HUH HUH
YEAH... HEH-HEH KICKING ASS IS COOL!
YEAH... HUH-HUH WHEN PUNISHER KICKS ASS, IT STAYS KICKED!
HEH-HEH YEAH... AND IT DOESN'T KICK BACK!
AAARRG!
HUH HEAD WOUNDS ARE COOL!
POW POW POW
HEY, BUTT-HEAD... I WANNA BE A HEAD WOUND WHEN I GROW UP! HEH-HEH
DIE SCUM
THE PUNISHER
HEH PUNISHER SHOULD KICK PRINCIPAL M^cDICKER'S ASS! HEH-HEH
THAT WOULD BE COOL!
THAT'S THE LAST TIME YOU EVER HOLD BEAVIS AND BUTT-HEAD AFTER SCHOOL, DIRTBALL...
HEH HEH HEH
HUH-HUH I LIKE IT WHEN HE PICKS UP DEAD GUYS' GUNS AN' MONEY AN' STUFF...
..YEAH... IF I WAS HIM, I'D LOOK FOR DIRTY BOOKS! HEH-HEH-HEH
HUH HUH HUH
YEAH! HUH-HUH THE ONLY THING COOLER THAN VIOLENCE IS DIRTY STUFF... HUH-HUH-HUH-HUH
SPECIAL "EVERYONE DIES" ISSUE
THE PUNISHER
DIE!
THE PUNISHER
JOHN ROMITA, JR.
"DO UNTO OTHERS"
MARVEL COMICS

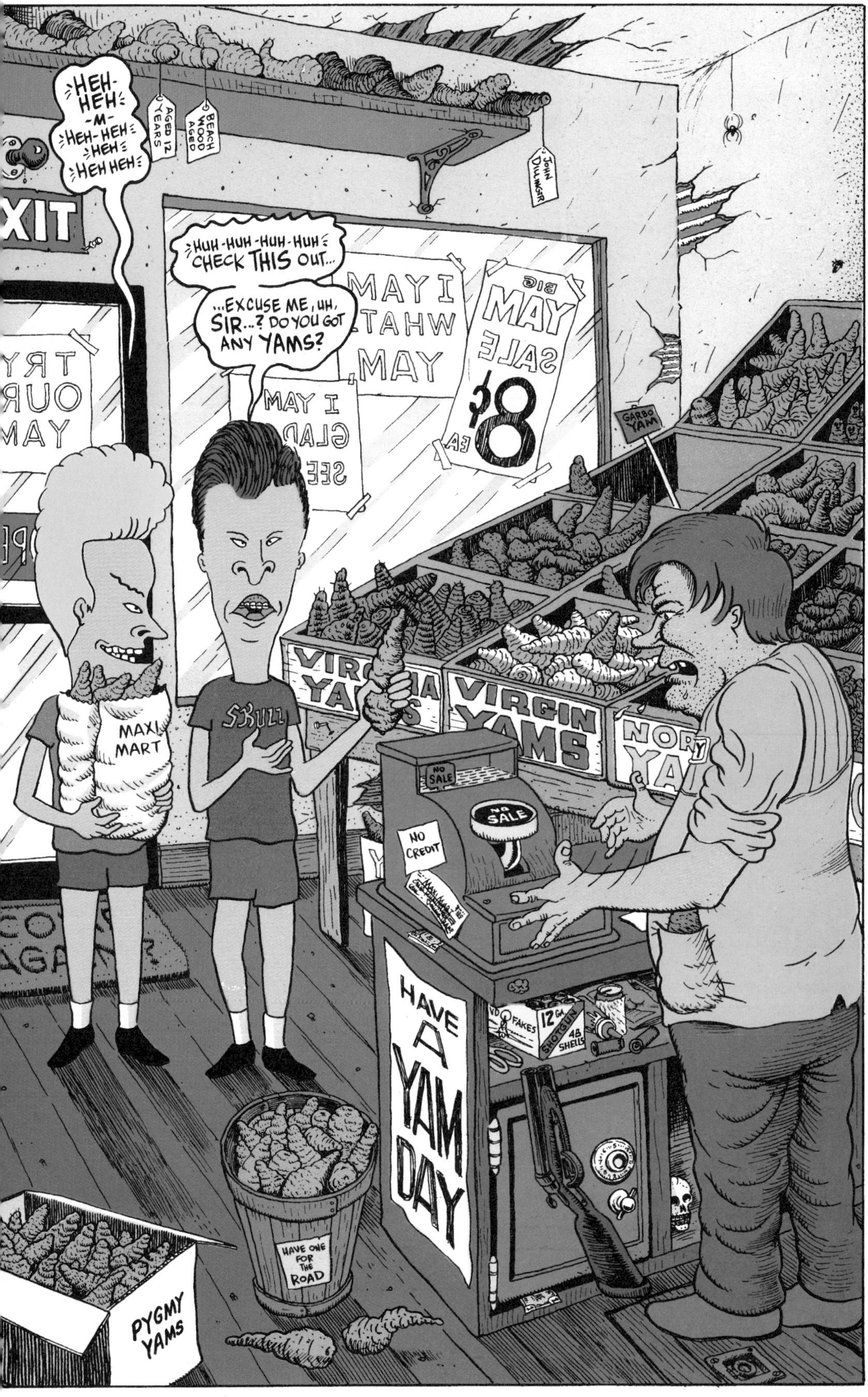
HEH-HEH -M- HEH-HEH HEH HEH HEH
AGED 12 YEARS
BEACH WOOD AGED
JOHN DILLINGER
EXIT
HUH-HUH-HUH-HUH CHECK THIS OUT...
...EXCUSE ME, UH, SIR...? DO YOU GOT ANY YAMS?
TRY OUR YAM
MAY I YAM WHAT I MAY
BIG YAM SALE 8¢ EA.
GARBO YAM
MAXI MART
SKULL
VIRGINIA YAMS
VIRGIN YAMS
NO SALE
NO CREDIT
HAVE A YAM DAY
12 GA SHOTGUN 48 SHELLS
HAVE ONE FOR THE ROAD
PYGMY YAMS

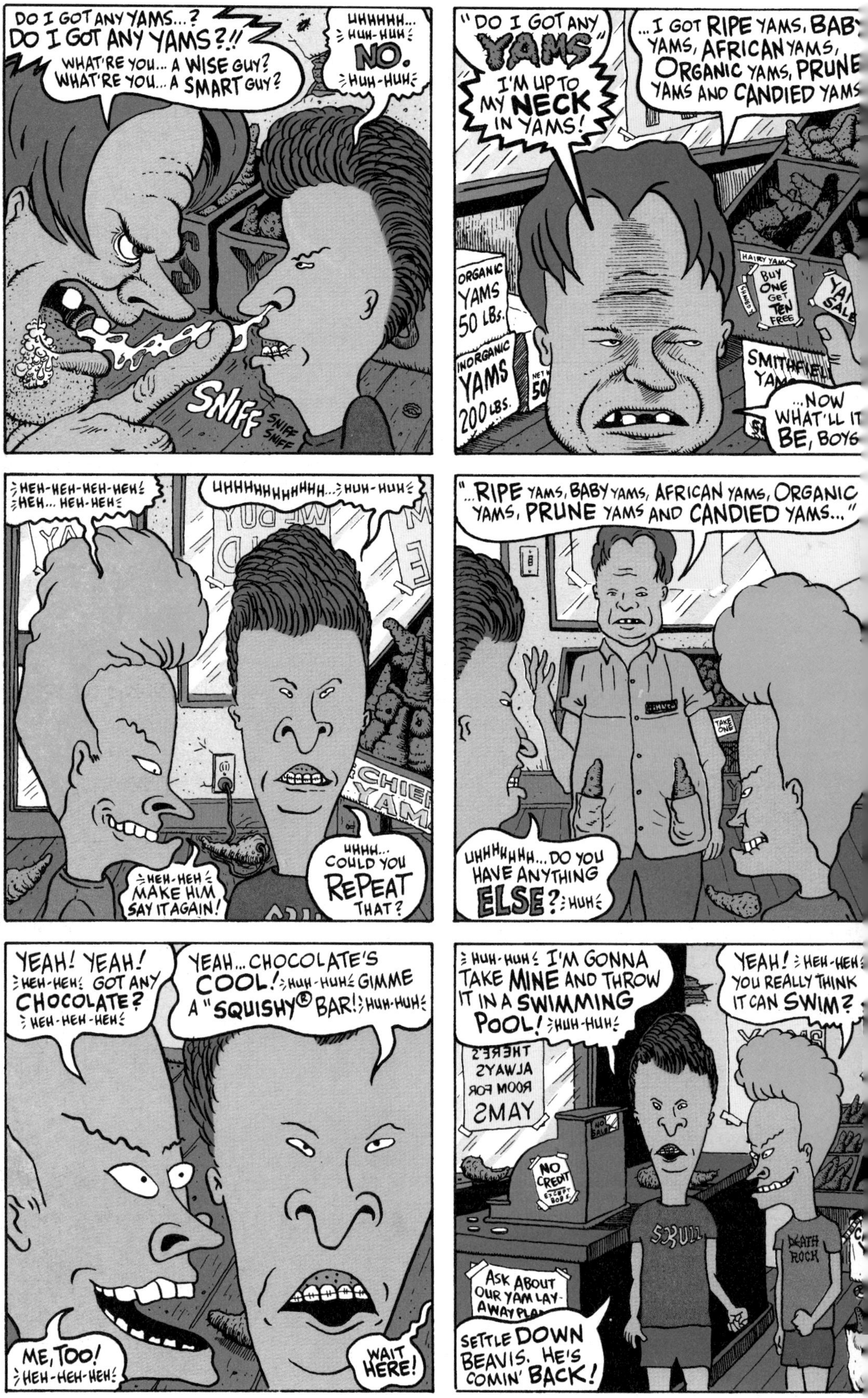
DO I GOT ANY YAMS...?
DO I GOT ANY YAMS?!!
WHAT'RE YOU... A WISE GUY? WHAT'RE YOU... A SMART GUY?
UHHHHH... HUH-HUH NO. HUH-HUH
SNIFF SNIFF SNIFF
"DO I GOT ANY YAMS"
I'M UP TO MY NECK IN YAMS!
...I GOT RIPE YAMS, BABY YAMS, AFRICAN YAMS, ORGANIC YAMS, PRUNE YAMS AND CANDIED YAMS
ORGANIC YAMS 50 LBs.
INORGANIC YAMS 200 LBS.
HAIRY YAMS
BUY ONE GET TEN FREE
SMITHFIELD
...NOW WHAT'LL IT BE, BOYS
HEH-HEH-HEH-HEH HEH... HEH-HEH
UHHHHHHHHHHH... HUH-HUH
CHIEF YAMS
HEH-HEH MAKE HIM SAY IT AGAIN!
UHHH... COULD YOU REPEAT THAT?
"...RIPE YAMS, BABY YAMS, AFRICAN YAMS, ORGANIC YAMS, PRUNE YAMS AND CANDIED YAMS..."
TAKE ONE
UHHHHHHH... DO YOU HAVE ANYTHING ELSE? HUH
YEAH! YEAH! HEH-HEH GOT ANY CHOCOLATE? HEH-HEH-HEH
YEAH... CHOCOLATE'S COOL! HUH-HUH GIMME A "SQUISHY® BAR! HUH-HUH
ME, TOO! HEH-HEH-HEH
WAIT HERE!
HUH-HUH I'M GONNA TAKE MINE AND THROW IT IN A SWIMMING POOL! HUH-HUH
YEAH! HEH-HEH YOU REALLY THINK IT CAN SWIM?
THERE'S ALWAYS ROOM FOR YAMS
NO SALE
NO CREDIT EXCEPT BOB'S
SKULL
DEATH ROCK
ASK ABOUT OUR YAM LAY-AWAY PLAN
SETTLE DOWN BEAVIS. HE'S COMIN' BACK!

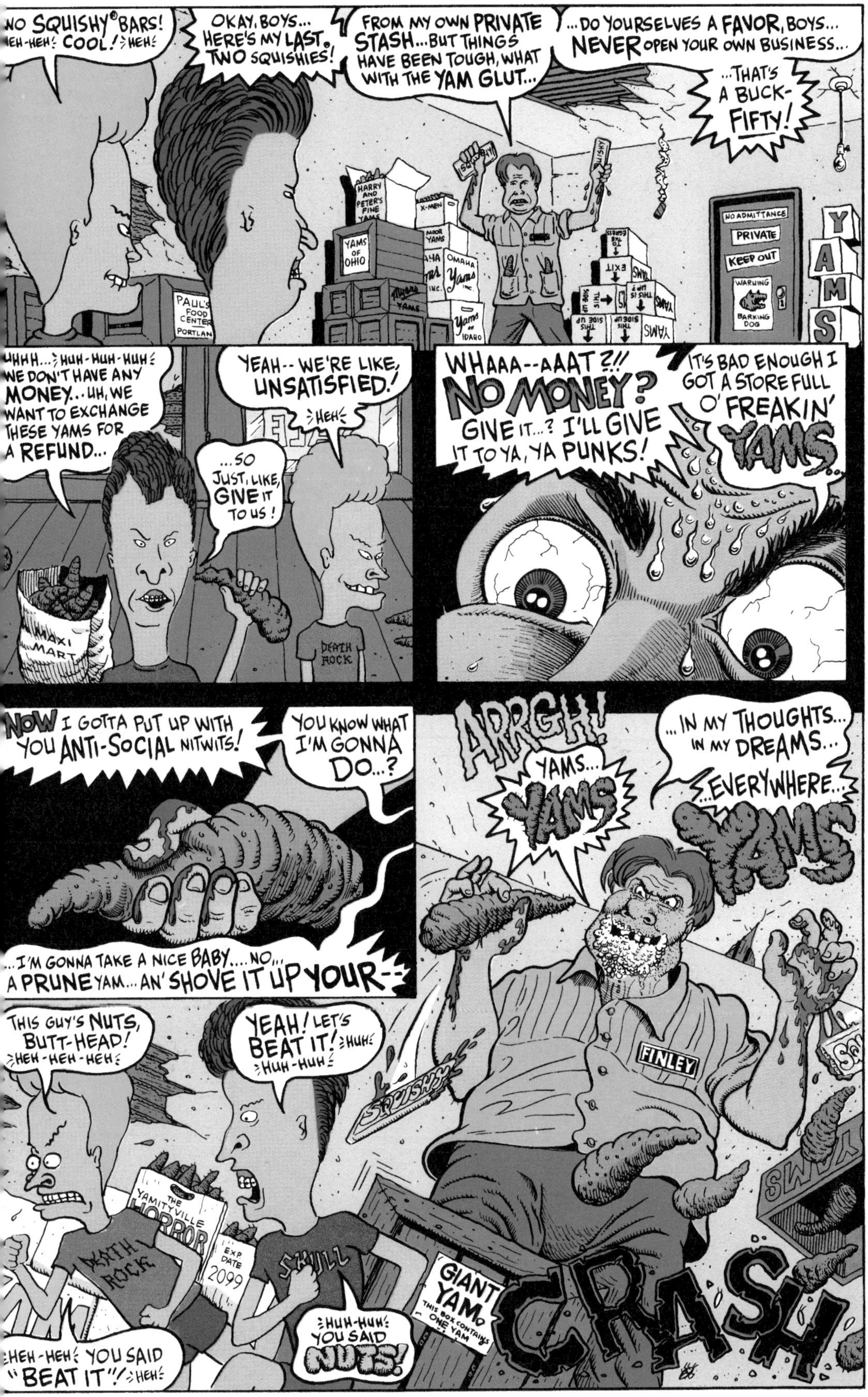
NO SQUISHY® BARS! HEH-HEH COOL! HEH
OKAY, BOYS... HERE'S MY LAST® TWO SQUISHIES!
FROM MY OWN PRIVATE STASH...BUT THINGS HAVE BEEN TOUGH, WHAT WITH THE YAM GLUT...
...DO YOURSELVES A FAVOR, BOYS... NEVER OPEN YOUR OWN BUSINESS...
...THAT'S A BUCK-FIFTY!
HARRY AND PETER'S FINE YAMS
X-MEN
YAMS OF OHIO
OMAHA Yams INC.
Yams OF IDAHO
PAUL'S FOOD CENTER PORTLAN
THIS SIDE UP
EXIT
NO ADMITTANCE
PRIVATE
KEEP OUT
WARNING
BARKING DOG
YAMS
UHHH... HUH-HUH-HUH WE DON'T HAVE ANY MONEY... UH, WE WANT TO EXCHANGE THESE YAMS FOR A REFUND...
YEAH-- WE'RE LIKE, UNSATISFIED! HEH
...SO JUST, LIKE, GIVE IT TO US!
MAXI MART
DEATH ROCK
WHAAA--AAAT?!! NO MONEY? GIVE IT...? I'LL GIVE IT TO YA, YA PUNKS!
IT'S BAD ENOUGH I GOT A STORE FULL O' FREAKIN' YAMS...
NOW I GOTTA PUT UP WITH YOU ANTI-SOCIAL NITWITS!
YOU KNOW WHAT I'M GONNA DO...?
...I'M GONNA TAKE A NICE BABY.... NO... A PRUNE YAM... AN' SHOVE IT UP YOUR--
ARRGH!
YAMS... YAMS
...IN MY THOUGHTS... IN MY DREAMS... ...EVERYWHERE... YAMS
FINLEY
SQUISHY
THIS GUY'S NUTS, BUTT-HEAD! HEH-HEH-HEH
YEAH! LET'S BEAT IT! HUH HUH-HUH
THE YAMITYVILLE HORROR
EXP. DATE 2099
DEATH ROCK
SKULL
HUH-HUH YOU SAID NUTS!
GIANT YAM THIS BOX CONTAINS ONE YAM
CRASH
YAMS
HEH-HEH YOU SAID "BEAT IT"! HEH

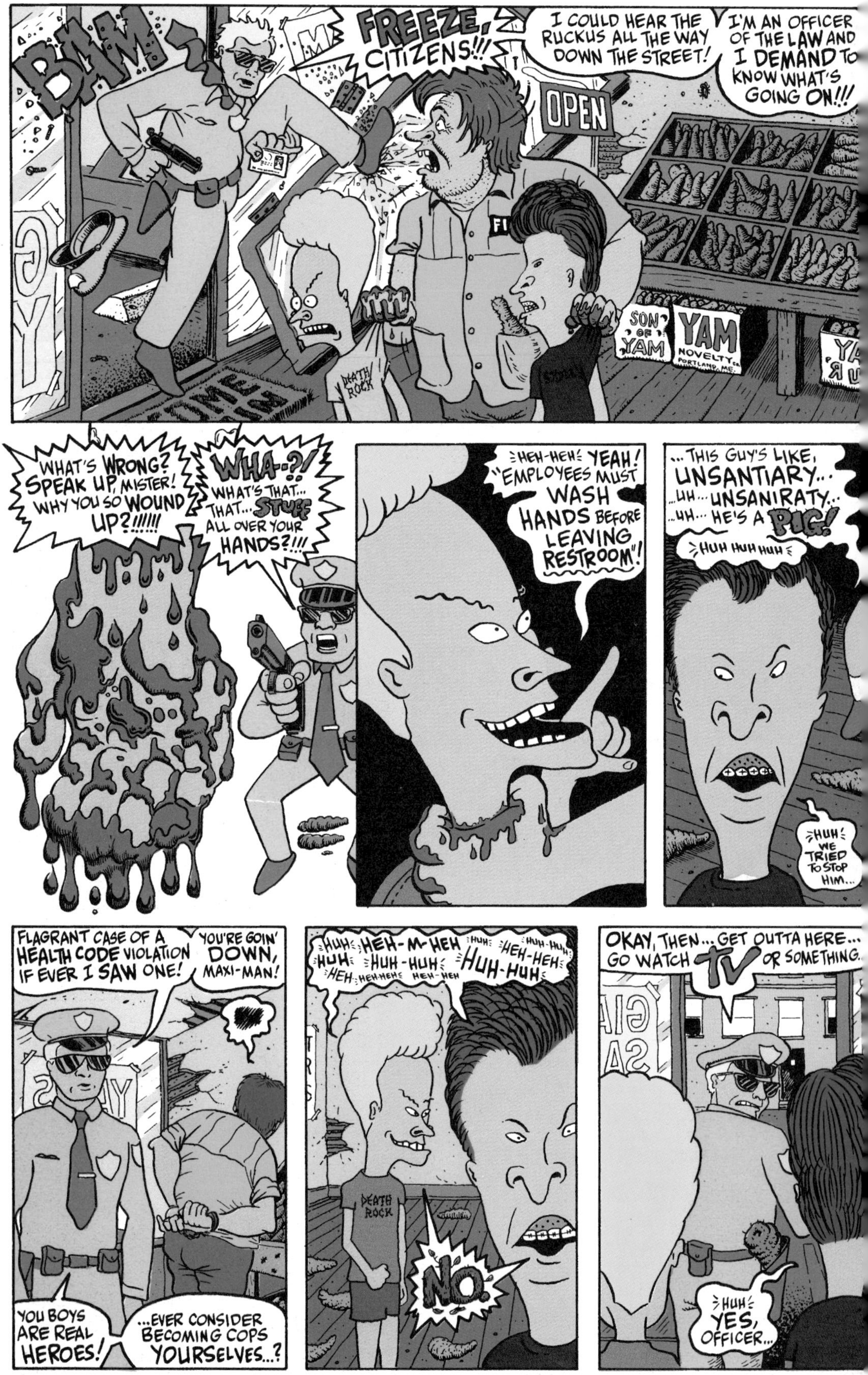
BAM
FREEZE, CITIZENS!!!
I COULD HEAR THE RUCKUS ALL THE WAY DOWN THE STREET!
I'M AN OFFICER OF THE LAW AND I DEMAND TO KNOW WHAT'S GOING ON!!!
OPEN
SON OF YAM
YAM NOVELTY CO. PORTLAND, ME.
DEATH ROCK
WHAT'S WRONG? SPEAK UP, MISTER! WHY YOU SO WOUND UP?!!!!!!
WHA-?! WHAT'S THAT... THAT... STUFF ALL OVER YOUR HANDS?!!!
HEH-HEH YEAH! "EMPLOYEES MUST WASH HANDS BEFORE LEAVING RESTROOM"!
...THIS GUY'S LIKE, UNSANTIARY... ...UH... UNSANIRATY... ...UH... HE'S A PIG!
HUH HUH HUH
HUH WE TRIED TO STOP HIM...
FLAGRANT CASE OF A HEALTH CODE VIOLATION IF EVER I SAW ONE!
YOU'RE GOIN' DOWN, MAXI-MAN!
YOU BOYS ARE REAL HEROES!
...EVER CONSIDER BECOMING COPS YOURSELVES...?
HUH HEH-M-HEH HUH HUH-HUH HEH-HEH HUH HUH-HUH HUH-HUH HEH HEH-HEH HEH-HEH
NO.
DEATH ROCK
OKAY, THEN... GET OUTTA HERE... GO WATCH TV OR SOMETHING.
HUH YES, OFFICER...

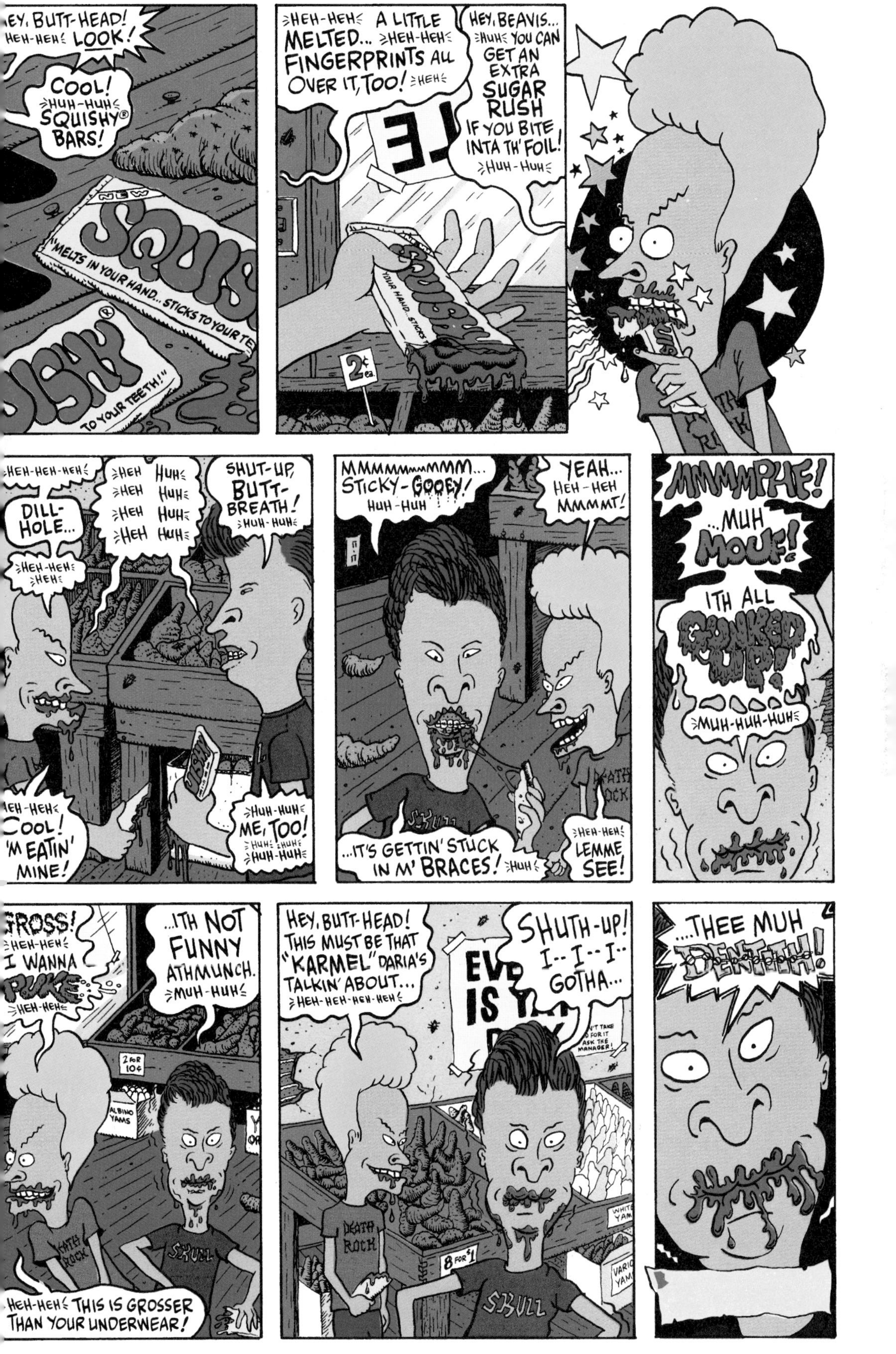

EY, BUTT-HEAD! HEH-HEH LOOK!
COOL! HUH-HUH SQUISHY® BARS!
NEW SQUISH
"MELTS IN YOUR HAND... STICKS TO YOUR TE
SQUISHY® TO YOUR TEETH!"
HEH-HEH A LITTLE MELTED... HEH-HEH FINGERPRINTS ALL OVER IT, TOO! HEH
HEY, BEAVIS... HUH YOU CAN GET AN EXTRA SUGAR RUSH IF YOU BITE INTA TH' FOIL! HUH-HUH
2¢ ea.
HEH-HEH-HEH
DILL-HOLE...
HEH-HEH HEH
HEH HUH HEH HUH HEH HUH HEH HUH
SHUT-UP, BUTT-BREATH! HUH-HUH
EH-HEH COOL! 'M EATIN' MINE!
HUH-HUH ME, TOO! HUH HUH HUH-HUH
MMMMMmmmMMM... STICKY-GOOEY! HUH-HUH
YEAH... HEH-HEH MMMMT!
...IT'S GETTIN' STUCK IN M' BRACES! HUH
HEH-HEH LEMME SEE!
MMMMPHE! ...MUH MOUF! ITH ALL GUNKED UP! MUH-HUH-HUH
GROSS! HEH-HEH I WANNA PUKE HEH-HEH
...ITH NOT FUNNY ATHMUNCH. MUH-HUH
2 FOR 10¢
ALBINO YAMS
HEH-HEH THIS IS GROSSER THAN YOUR UNDERWEAR!
HEY, BUTT-HEAD! THIS MUST BE THAT "KARMEL" DARIA'S TALKIN' ABOUT... HEH-HEH-HEH-HEH
SHUTH-UP! I-- I-- I-- GOTHA...
ASK THE MANAGER!
8 FOR $1
WHITE YAMS
...THEE MUH DENTATH!

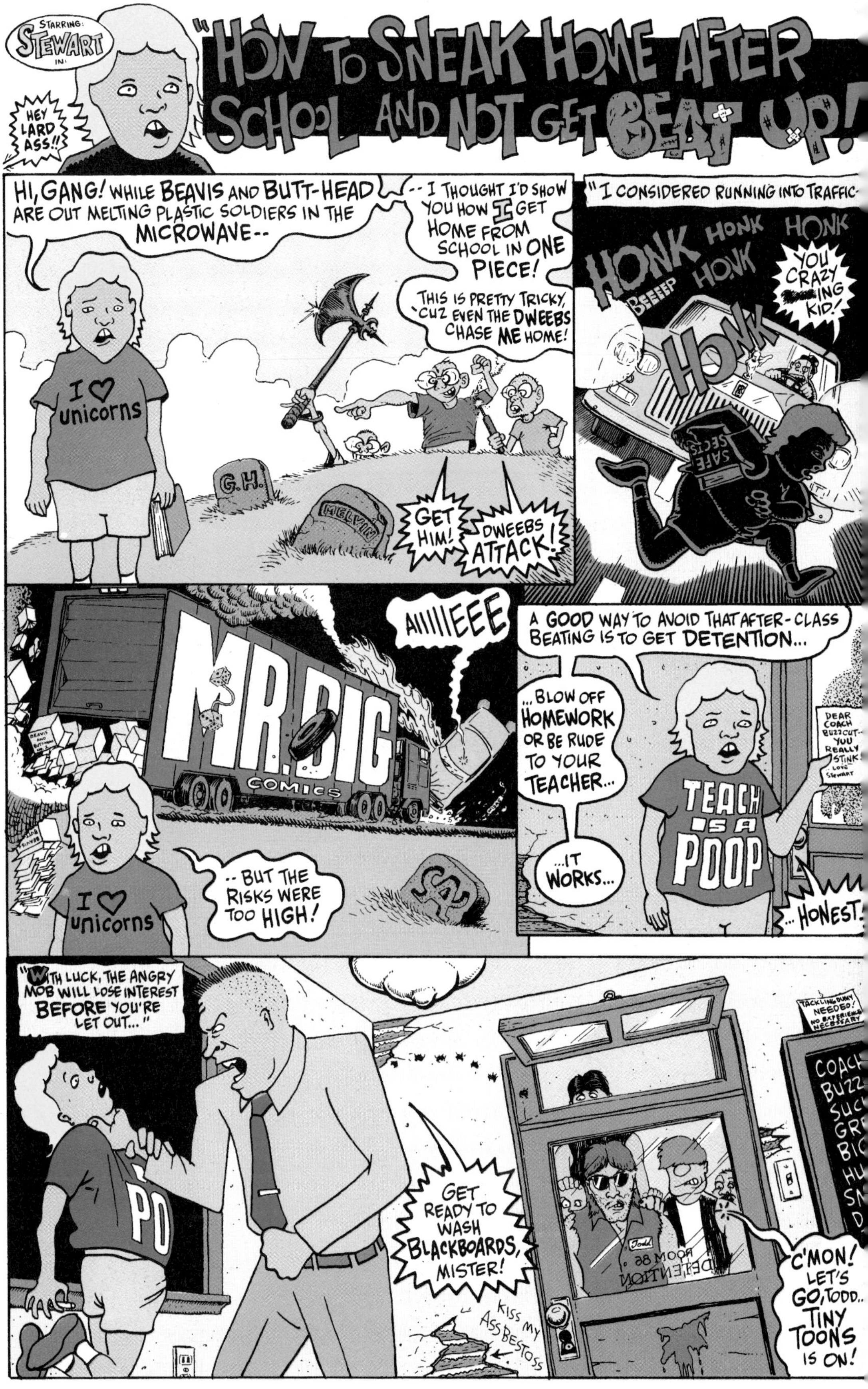
STARRING: STEWART IN:
HEY LARD ASS!!
"HOW TO SNEAK HOME AFTER SCHOOL AND NOT GET BEAT UP!"
HI, GANG! WHILE BEAVIS AND BUTT-HEAD ARE OUT MELTING PLASTIC SOLDIERS IN THE MICROWAVE--
--I THOUGHT I'D SHOW YOU HOW I GET HOME FROM SCHOOL IN ONE PIECE!
THIS IS PRETTY TRICKY, CUZ EVEN THE DWEEBS CHASE ME HOME!
I ♥ unicorns
G.H.
MELVIN
GET HIM!
DWEEBS ATTACK!
"I CONSIDERED RUNNING INTO TRAFFIC-
HONK HONK HONK HONK HONK HONK
BEEEEP
YOU CRAZY [redacted]ING KID!
SAFE SECTS
AIIIIIEEE
MR. BIG COMICS
-- BUT THE RISKS WERE TOO HIGH!
I ♥ unicorns
A GOOD WAY TO AVOID THAT AFTER-CLASS BEATING IS TO GET DETENTION...
... BLOW OFF HOMEWORK OR BE RUDE TO YOUR TEACHER...
...IT WORKS...
TEACH IS A POOP
DEAR COACH BUZZCUT- YOU REALLY STINK LOVE Stewart
... HONEST.
"WITH LUCK, THE ANGRY MOB WILL LOSE INTEREST BEFORE YOU'RE LET OUT..."
TACKLING DUMMY NEEDED! NO EXPERIENCE NECESSARY
COACH BUZZ SUC GR BIG HU SN D
PO
GET READY TO WASH BLACKBOARDS, MISTER!
ROOM 86 DETENTION
Todd
Kiss my AssBestoss
C'MON! LET'S GO, TODD... TINY TOONS IS ON!

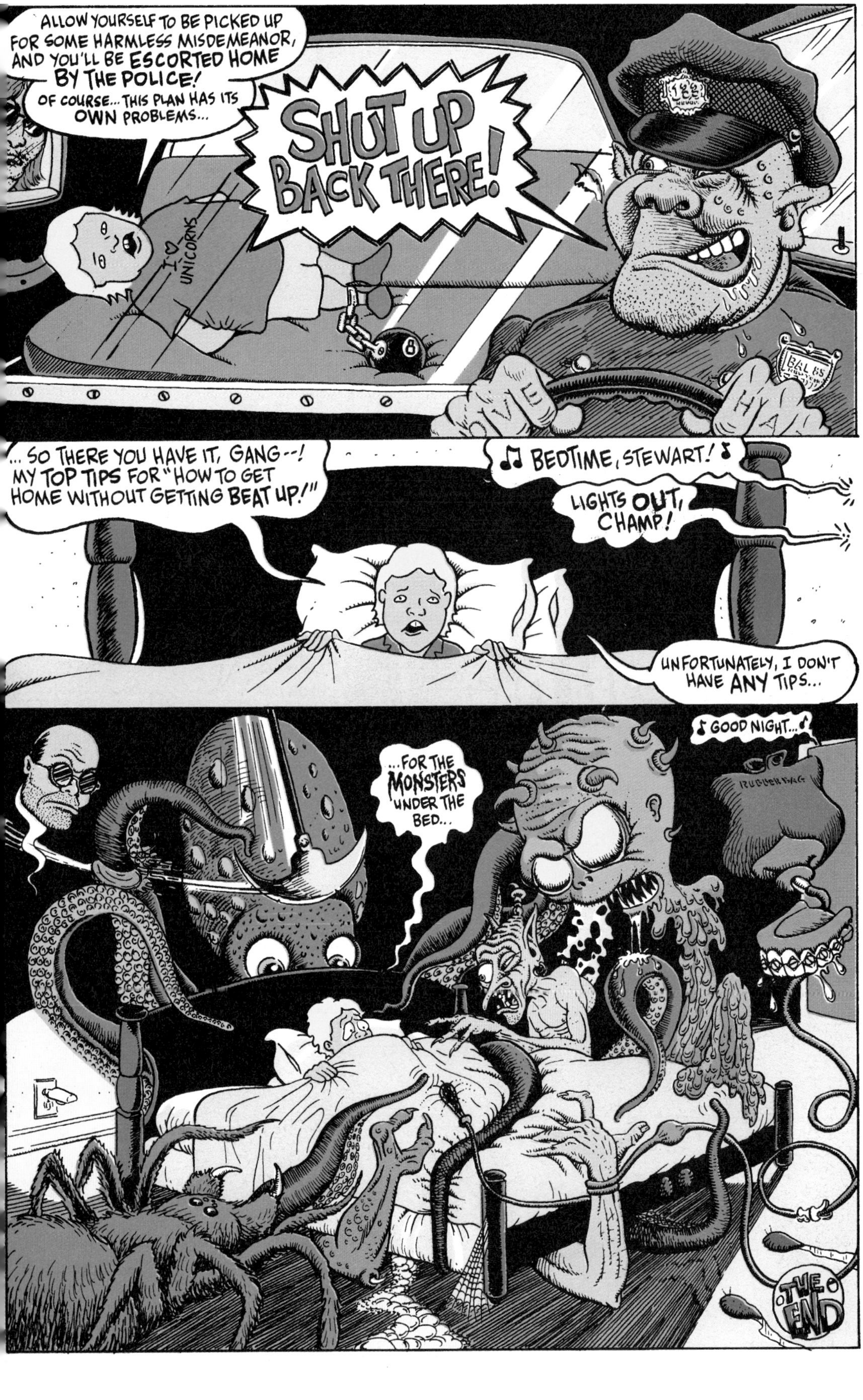
ALLOW YOURSELF TO BE PICKED UP FOR SOME HARMLESS MISDEMEANOR, AND YOU'LL BE ESCORTED HOME BY THE POLICE!
OF COURSE... THIS PLAN HAS ITS OWN PROBLEMS...
SHUT UP BACK THERE!
I ♡ UNICORNS
LOVE
HA
... SO THERE YOU HAVE IT, GANG--! MY TOP TIPS FOR "HOW TO GET HOME WITHOUT GETTING BEAT UP!"
♫ BEDTIME, STEWART! ♪
LIGHTS OUT, CHAMP!
UNFORTUNATELY, I DON'T HAVE ANY TIPS...
...FOR THE MONSTERS UNDER THE BED...
♪ GOOD NIGHT... ♪
RUBBER DAG
THE END

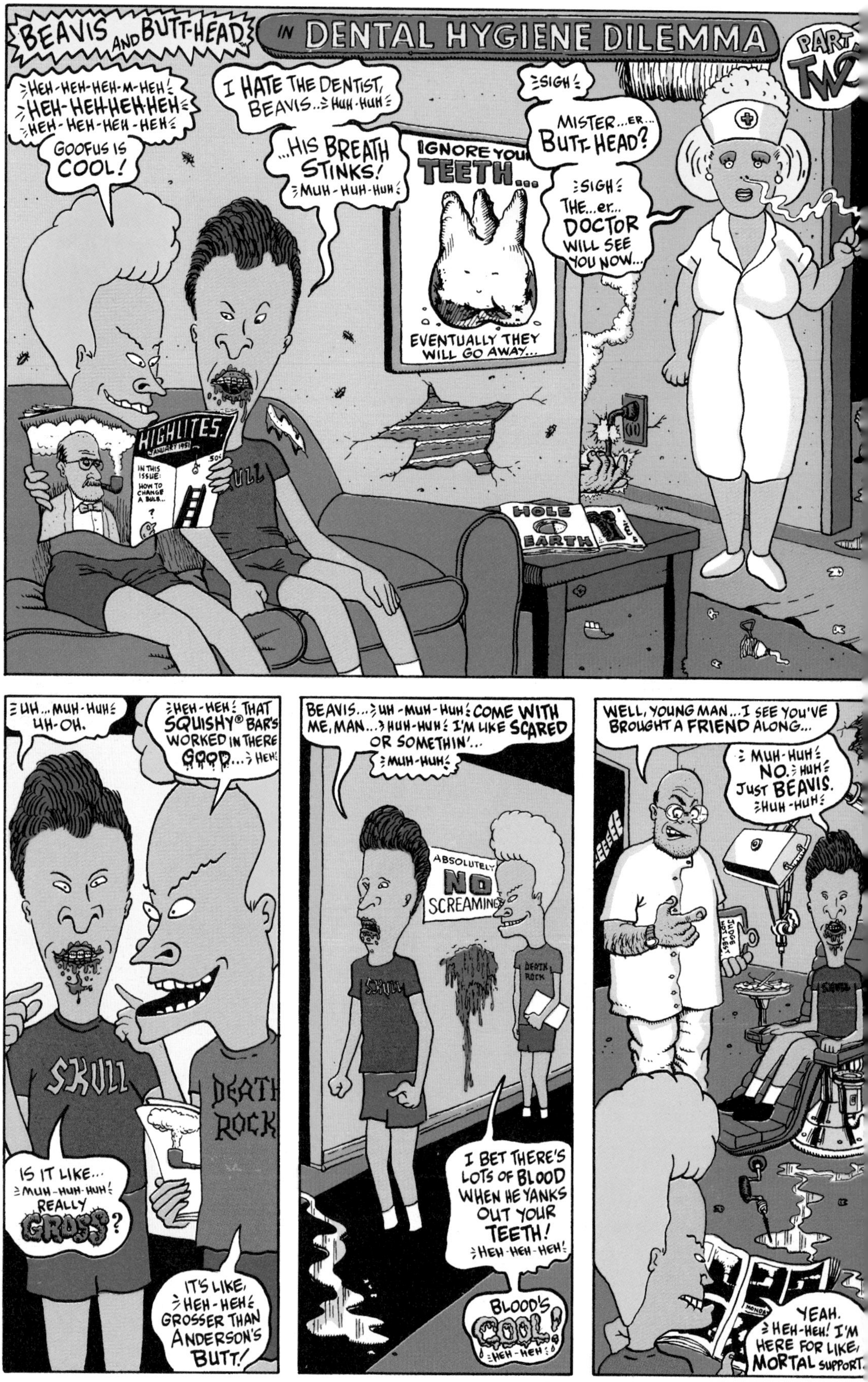
BEAVIS AND BUTT-HEAD
IN DENTAL HYGIENE DILEMMA
PART TWO
HEH-HEH-HEH-M-HEH! HEH-HEH-HEH-HEH HEH-HEH-HEH-HEH
GOOFUS IS COOL!
I HATE THE DENTIST, BEAVIS.. HUH-HUH
...HIS BREATH STINKS! MUH-HUH-HUH
IGNORE YOUR TEETH...
EVENTUALLY THEY WILL GO AWAY...
SIGH
MISTER...ER... BUTT-HEAD?
SIGH
THE...er... DOCTOR WILL SEE YOU NOW...
HIGHLITES.
JANUARY 1951
50¢
IN THIS ISSUE: HOW TO CHANGE A BULB...
SKULL
HOLE EARTH
UH...MUH-HUH UH-OH.
HEH-HEH THAT SQUISHY® BAR'S WORKED IN THERE GOOD... HEH!
IS IT LIKE... MUH-HUH-HUH! REALLY GROSS?
IT'S LIKE, HEH-HEH GROSSER THAN ANDERSON'S BUTT!
DEATH ROCK
BEAVIS... UH-MUH-HUH COME WITH ME, MAN... HUH-HUH I'M LIKE SCARED OR SOMETHIN'... MUH-HUH
ABSOLUTELY NO SCREAMING
I BET THERE'S LOTS OF BLOOD WHEN HE YANKS OUT YOUR TEETH! HEH-HEH-HEH!
BLOOD'S COOL! HEH-HEH
WELL, YOUNG MAN... I SEE YOU'VE BROUGHT A FRIEND ALONG...
MUH-HUH NO. HUH JUST BEAVIS. HUH-HUH
YEAH. HEH-HEH! I'M HERE FOR LIKE, MORTAL SUPPORT.

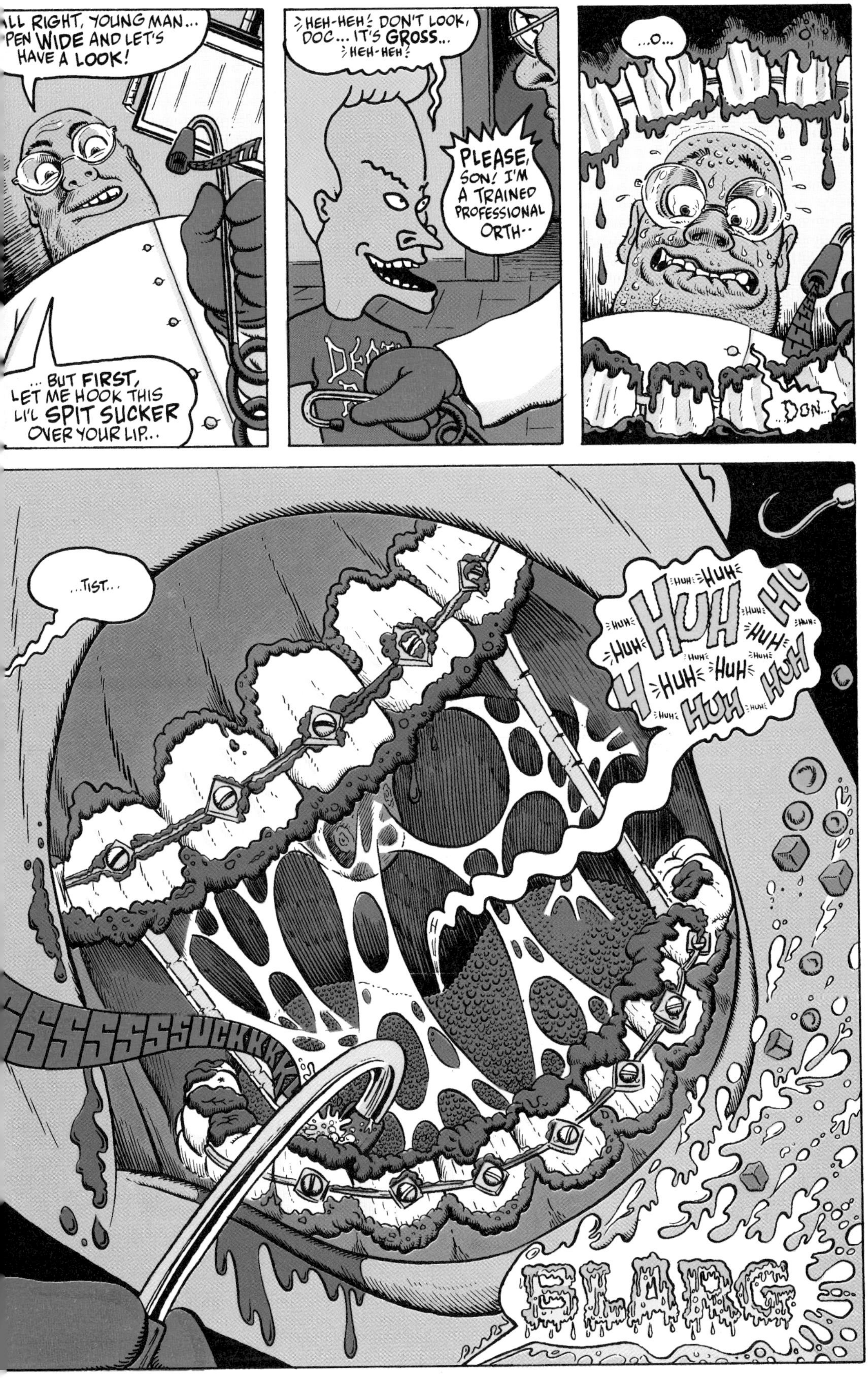
ALL RIGHT, YOUNG MAN... OPEN WIDE AND LET'S HAVE A LOOK!
... BUT FIRST, LET ME HOOK THIS LI'L SPIT SUCKER OVER YOUR LIP...
HEH-HEH DON'T LOOK, DOC... IT'S GROSS... HEH-HEH
PLEASE, SON! I'M A TRAINED PROFESSIONAL ORTH--
...O...
..DON...
...TIST...
HUH HUH HUH HUH HUH HUH HUH HUH HUH HUH HUH HUH HUH HUH
SSSSSSSSUCKKKK
BLARG

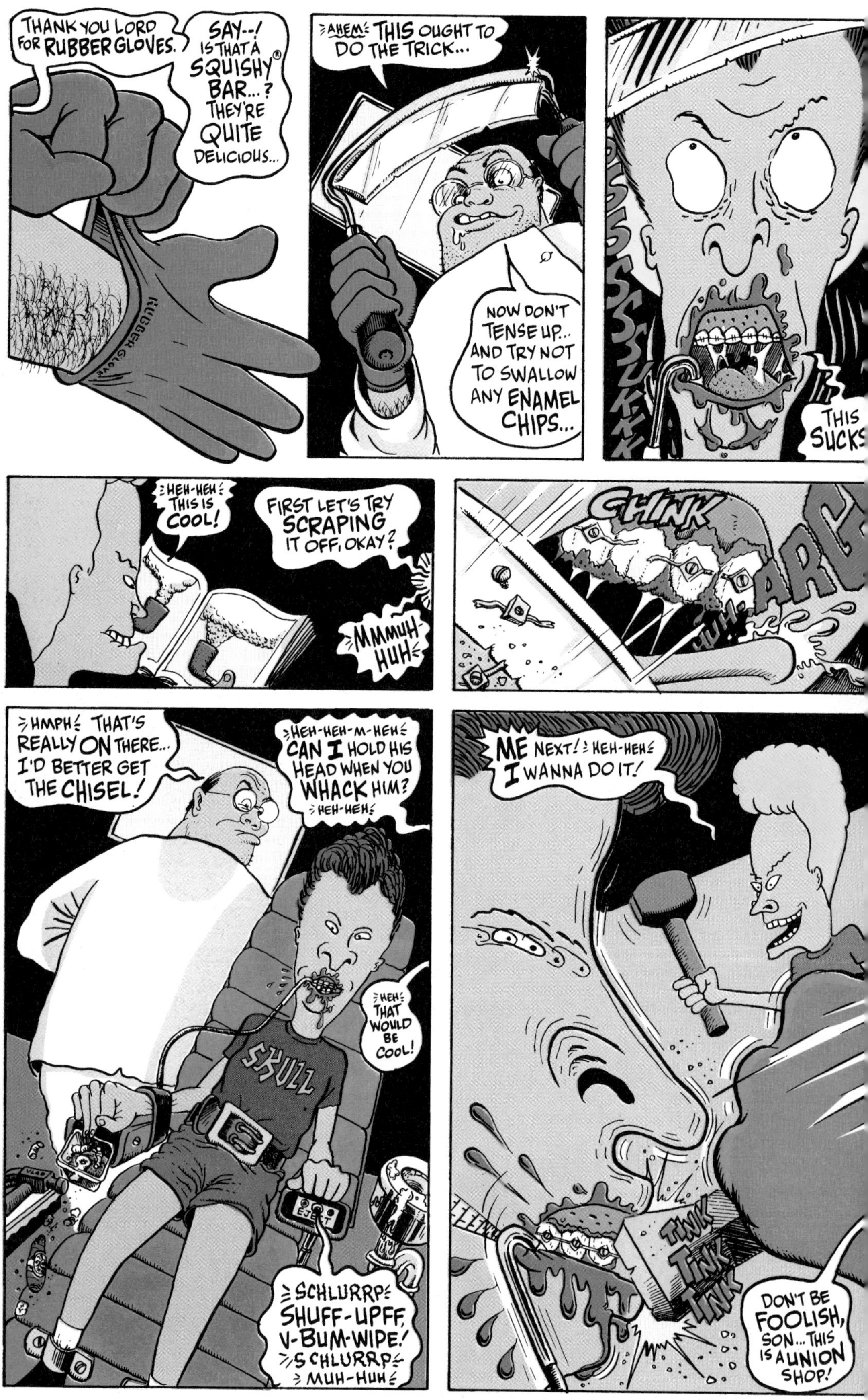
THANK YOU LORD FOR RUBBER GLOVES.
SAY--! IS THAT A SQUISHY® BAR...? THEY'RE QUITE DELICIOUS...
RUBBER GLOVE
AHEM THIS OUGHT TO DO THE TRICK...
NOW DON'T TENSE UP... AND TRY NOT TO SWALLOW ANY ENAMEL CHIPS...
SSSSSSUKKK
THIS SUCKS
HEH-HEH THIS IS COOL!
FIRST LET'S TRY SCRAPING IT OFF, OKAY?
MMMUH-HUH
CHINK
ARG
HMPH THAT'S REALLY ON THERE... I'D BETTER GET THE CHISEL!
HEH-HEH-M-HEH CAN I HOLD HIS HEAD WHEN YOU WHACK HIM? HEH-HEH
HEH THAT WOULD BE COOL!
SKULL
EJECT
SCHLURRP SHUFF-UPFF V-BUM-WIPE! SCHLURRP MUH-HUH
ME NEXT! HEH-HEH I WANNA DO IT!
TINK TINK TINK
DON'T BE FOOLISH, SON... THIS IS A UNION SHOP!

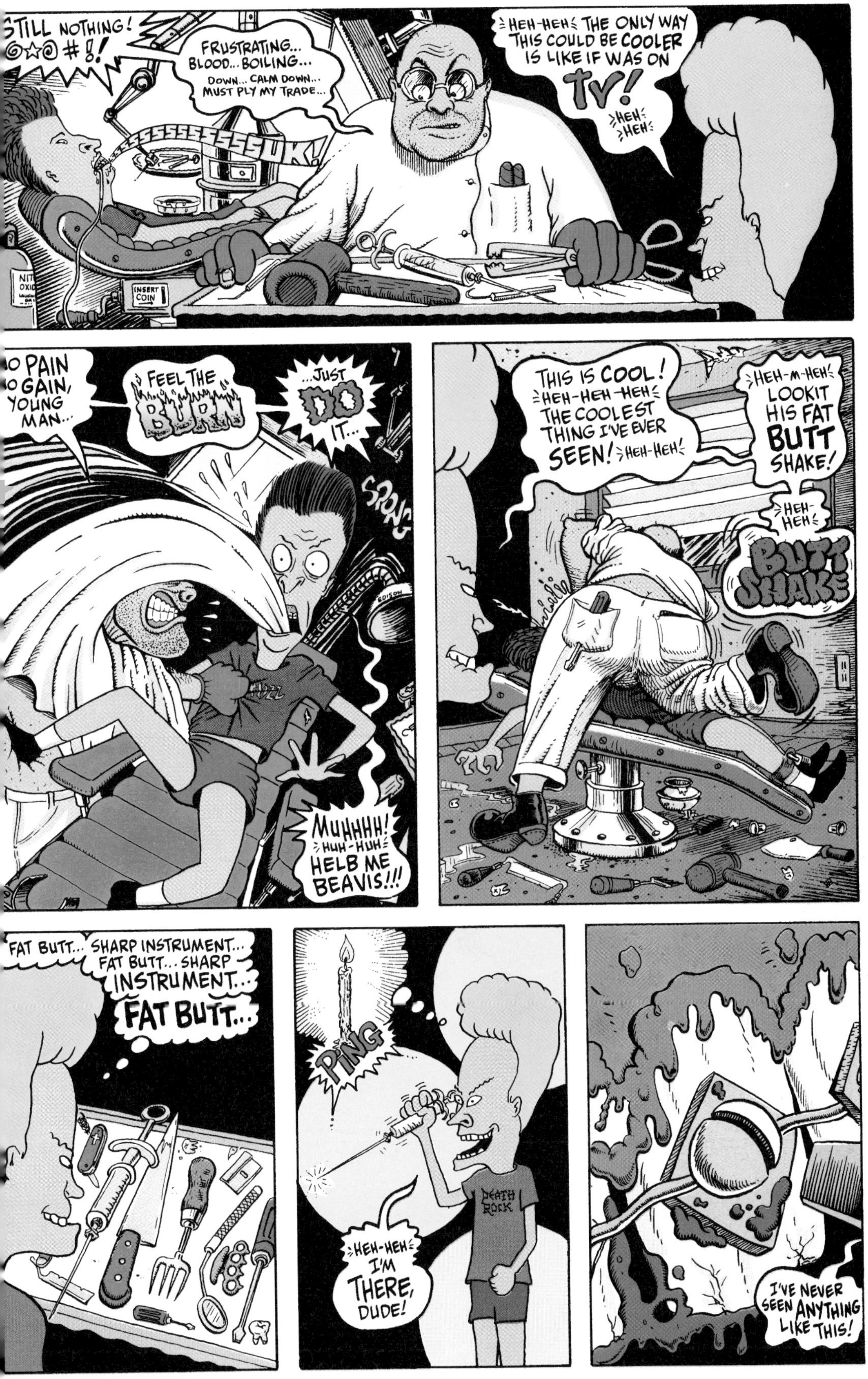

STILL NOTHING! @☆@#!!
FRUSTRATING... BLOOD... BOILING... DOWN... CALM DOWN... MUST PLY MY TRADE...
SSSSSSSSSSSSUK!
HEH-HEH THE ONLY WAY THIS COULD BE COOLER IS LIKE IF WAS ON TV! HEH HEH
NITROUS OXIDE
INSERT COIN
NO PAIN NO GAIN, YOUNG MAN...
FEEL THE BURN
...JUST DO IT...
SPRONG
EDISON
MUHHHH! HUH-HUH HELB ME BEAVIS!!!
THIS IS COOL! HEH-HEH-HEH THE COOLEST THING I'VE EVER SEEN! HEH-HEH!
HEH-M-HEH! LOOKIT HIS FAT BUTT SHAKE!
HEH-HEH
BUTT SHAKE
FAT BUTT... SHARP INSTRUMENT... FAT BUTT... SHARP INSTRUMENT... FAT BUTT...
PING
DEATH ROCK
HEH-HEH I'M THERE, DUDE!
I'VE NEVER SEEN ANYTHING LIKE THIS!

MMMPH!
AARG!!
MEANWHILE.......
HEH
HEH HEH
HEH
SOMETHING'S GONNA GIVE, KID... AND IT WON'T BE MY ARM!
HEH
YOW
NOVACAINE... RUSHING INTO MY BUTT... FLOODING IT... MY LEGS... WEAK FALLING... INTO... GAS TANKS... CRACKING THE... SEALS...
HEH-HEH I GOT HIM FOR YA, BUTT-HEAD!
HUH-HUH THANKS, DILL-WEED HUH-HUH
HEY! HEH I SMELL GAS!
HUH-HUH HE WHO SMELT IT, DEALT IT! HUH-HUH-HUH
DEATH ROCK
SKULL
NITROUS OXIDE
LAUGHING GAS

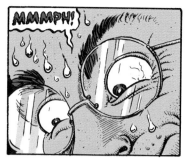

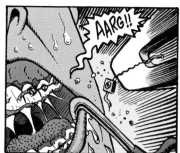

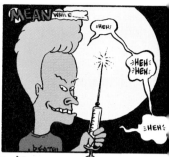

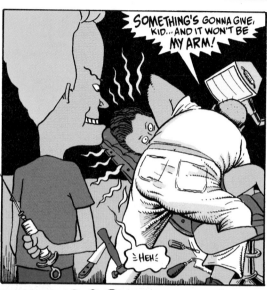

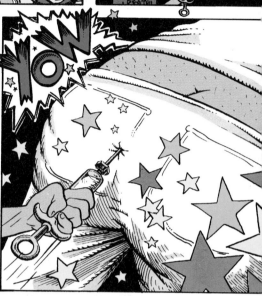

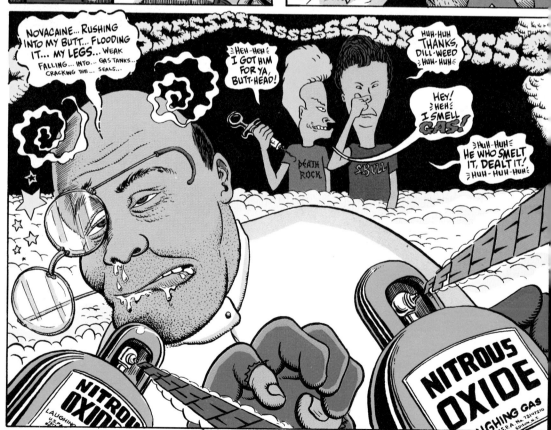

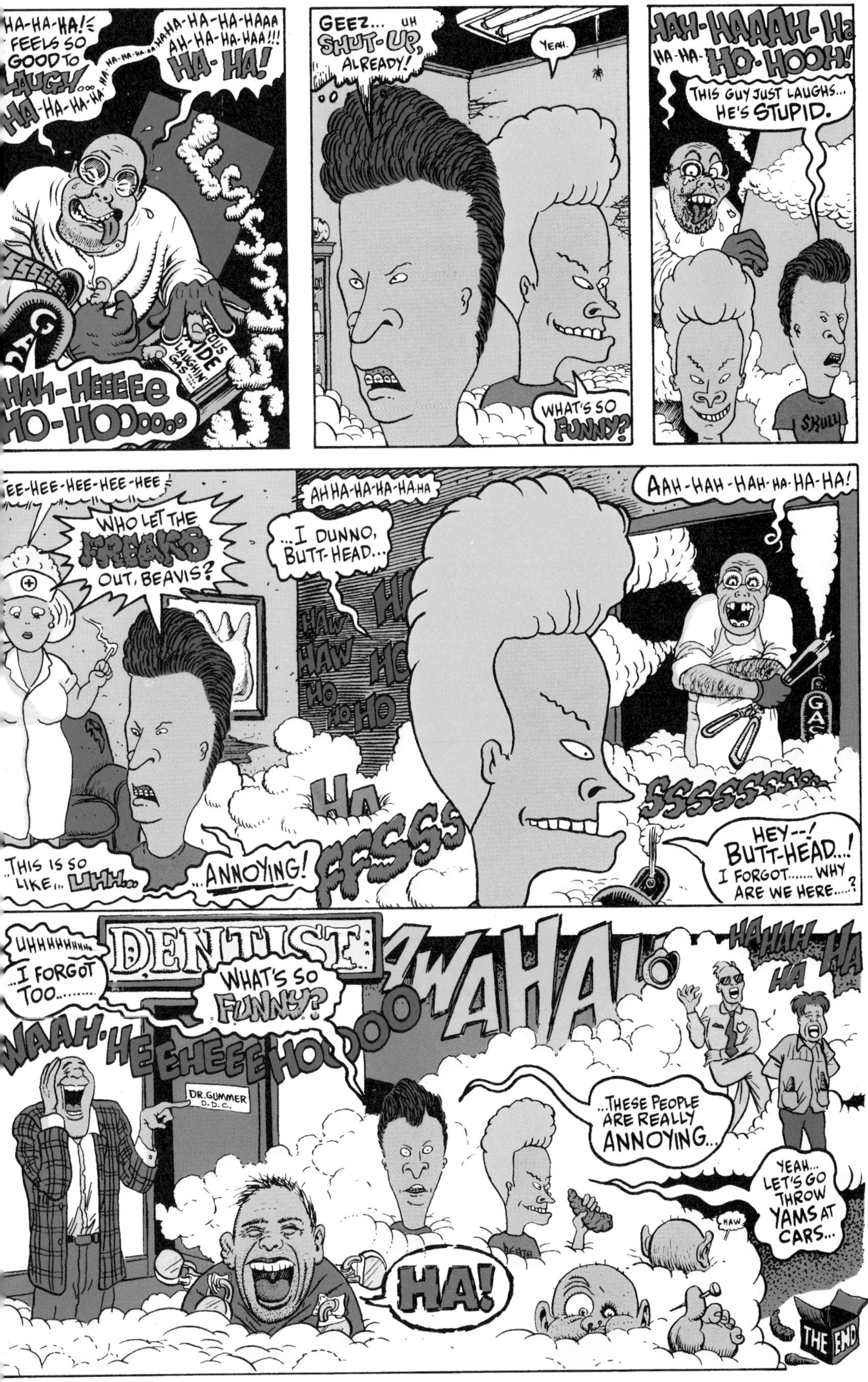
HA-HA-HA! FEELS SO GOOD TO LAUGH!... HA-HA-HA-HA-HA-HA-HA-HA-HA
HAHA-HA-HA-HAAA AH-HA-HA-HAA!!! HA-HA!
LAUGHIN GAS
HAH-HEEEEe HO-HOOoooo
GEEZ... UH SHUT-UP, ALREADY!
YEAH.
WHAT'S SO FUNNY?
HAH-HAAAH-HA HA-HA-HO-HOOH!
THIS GUY JUST LAUGHS... HE'S STUPID.
EE-HEE-HEE-HEE-HEE
WHO LET THE FREAKS OUT, BEAVIS?
AHHA-HA-HA-HA-HA
...I DUNNO, BUTT-HEAD...
AAH-HAH-HAH-HA-HA-HA!
HAW HAW HO HO HO
HA HO HO
HA
FFSSSS
SSSSSSSS
THIS IS SO LIKE... UHH...
...ANNOYING!
HEY--! BUTT-HEAD...! I FORGOT....... WHY ARE WE HERE.....?
UHHHHHHHH... ...I FORGOT TOO.........
DENTIST
WHAT'S SO FUNNY?
WAAH-HEEHEEE HOOOOO
AWAHA!
HAHAH HA HA
DR. GUMMER D.D.C.
...THESE PEOPLE ARE REALLY ANNOYING...
YEAH... LET'S GO THROW YAMS AT CARS...
HAW
HA!
THE END

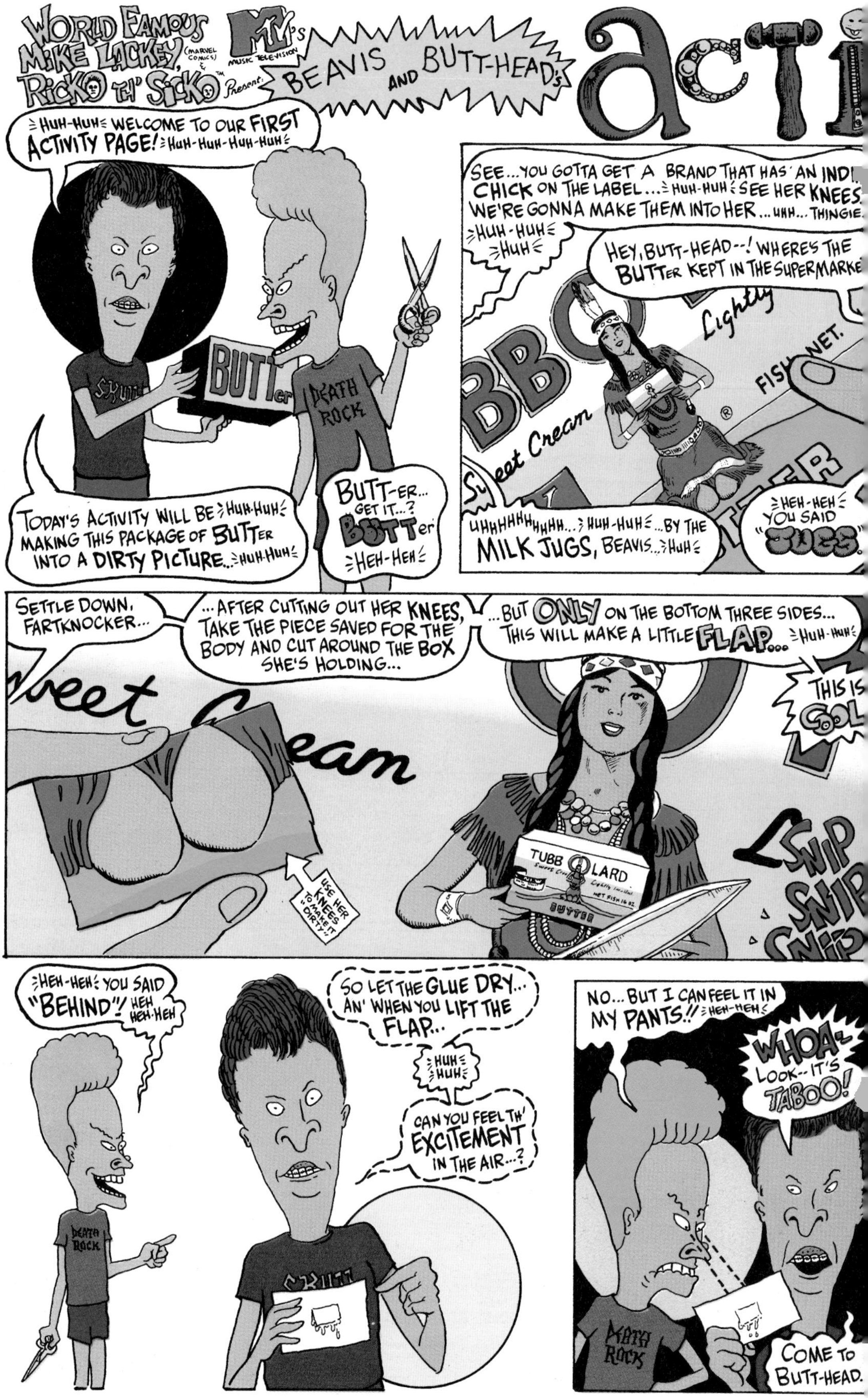

WORLD FAMOUS MIKE LACKEY, (MARVEL COMICS) & RICKO TH' SICKO™ Present: MTV's MUSIC TELEVISION BEAVIS AND BUTT-HEAD's ACTI
HUH-HUH WELCOME TO OUR FIRST ACTIVITY PAGE! HUH-HUH-HUH-HUH
BUTTer
SKULL
DEATH ROCK
TODAY'S ACTIVITY WILL BE HUH-HUH MAKING THIS PACKAGE OF BUTTER INTO A DIRTY PICTURE.. HUH-HUH
BUTT-ER... GET IT...? BUTTer HEH-HEH
SEE...YOU GOTTA GET A BRAND THAT HAS AN INDI CHICK ON THE LABEL... HUH-HUH SEE HER KNEES WE'RE GONNA MAKE THEM INTO HER... UHH... THINGIE
HUH-HUH HUH
HEY, BUTT-HEAD--! WHERE'S THE BUTTER KEPT IN THE SUPERMARKE
Lightly
FISH NET.
Sweet Cream
UHHHHHHHHHH... HUH-HUH ...BY THE MILK JUGS, BEAVIS... HUH
HEH-HEH YOU SAID "JUGS"
SETTLE DOWN, FARTKNOCKER...
...AFTER CUTTING OUT HER KNEES, TAKE THE PIECE SAVED FOR THE BODY AND CUT AROUND THE BOX SHE'S HOLDING...
...BUT ONLY ON THE BOTTOM THREE SIDES... THIS WILL MAKE A LITTLE FLAP... HUH-HUH
THIS IS COOL
Sweet Cream
USE HER KNEES TO MAKE IT "DIRTY"
TUBB LARD
BUTTER
SNIP SNIP SNIP
HEH-HEH YOU SAID "BEHIND"! HEH HEH-HEH
SO LET THE GLUE DRY... AN' WHEN YOU LIFT THE FLAP...
HUH HUH
CAN YOU FEEL TH' EXCITEMENT IN THE AIR...?
DEATH ROCK
SKULL
NO... BUT I CAN FEEL IT IN MY PANTS!! HEH-HEH
WHOA- LOOK--IT'S TABOO!
COME TO BUTT-HEAD.

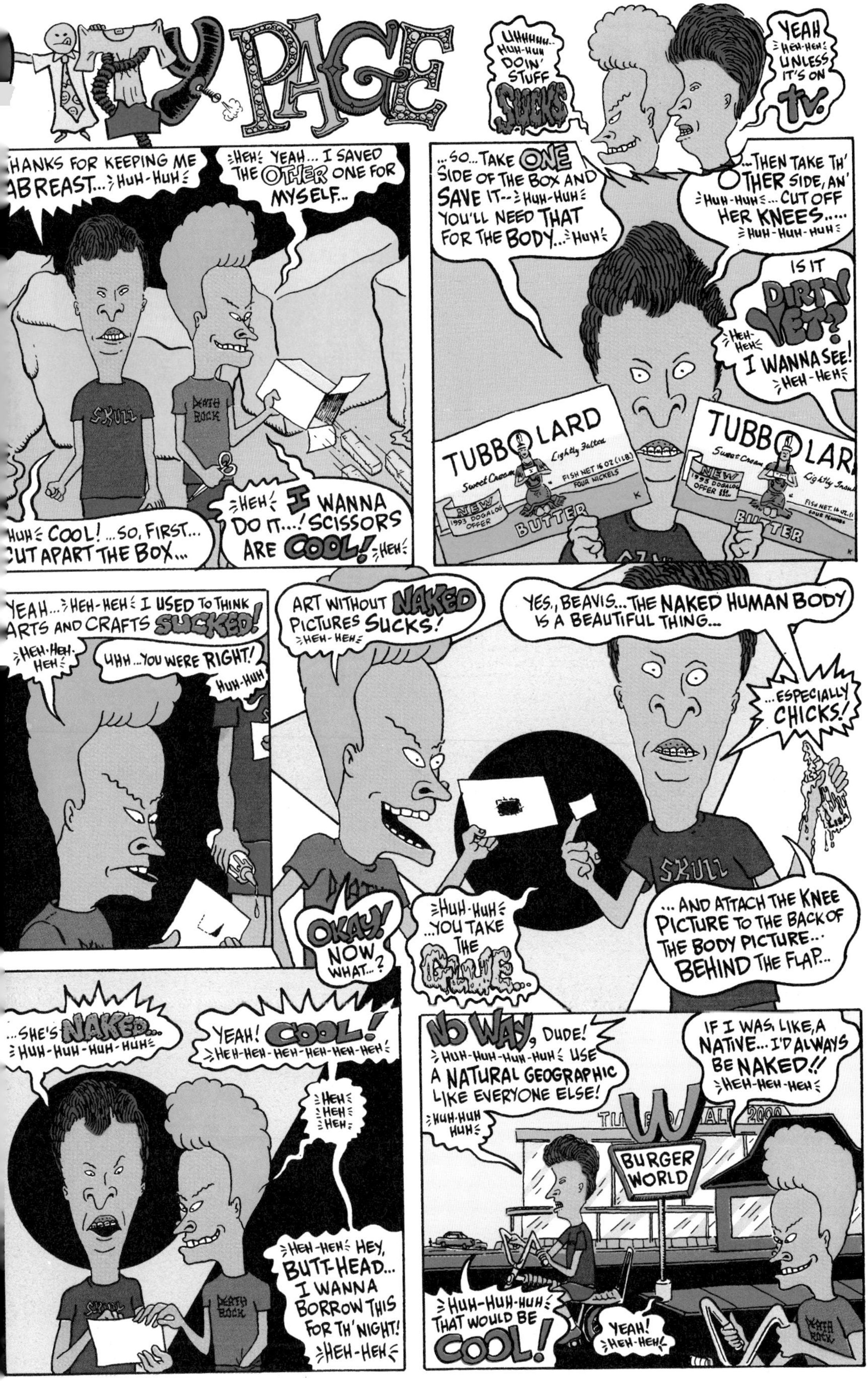

PAGE
UHHHHH.. HUH-HUH DOIN' STUFF SUCKS
YEAH HEH-HEH UNLESS IT'S ON TV.
HANKS FOR KEEPING ME ABREAST... HUH-HUH
HEH YEAH... I SAVED THE OTHER ONE FOR MYSELF..
HUH COOL! ...SO, FIRST... CUT APART THE BOX...
HEH I WANNA DO IT...! SCISSORS ARE COOL! HEH
...SO... TAKE ONE SIDE OF THE BOX AND SAVE IT-- HUH-HUH YOU'LL NEED THAT FOR THE BODY... HUH
...THEN TAKE TH' OTHER SIDE, AN' HUH-HUH ... CUT OFF HER KNEES..... HUH-HUH-HUH
IS IT DIRTY YET? HEH-HEH I WANNA SEE! HEH-HEH
TUBBOLARD Sweet Cream Lightly Salted NEW 1993 DOGALOG OFFER FISH NET 16 OZ (1LB) FOUR NICKELS BUTTER
YEAH... HEH-HEH I USED TO THINK ARTS AND CRAFTS SUCKED!
HEH-HEH-HEH
UHH... YOU WERE RIGHT! HUH-HUH
ART WITHOUT NAKED PICTURES SUCKS! HEH-HEH
YES, BEAVIS... THE NAKED HUMAN BODY IS A BEAUTIFUL THING...
...ESPECIALLY CHICKS!
OKAY! NOW WHAT...?
HUH-HUH ...YOU TAKE THE GLUE...
... AND ATTACH THE KNEE PICTURE TO THE BACK OF THE BODY PICTURE... BEHIND THE FLAP...
...SHE'S NAKED... HUH-HUH-HUH-HUH
YEAH! COOL! HEH-HEH-HEH-HEH-HEH-HEH
HEH HEH HEH
HEH-HEH HEY, BUTT-HEAD... I WANNA BORROW THIS FOR TH' NIGHT! HEH-HEH
NO WAY, DUDE! HUH-HUH-HUH-HUH USE A NATURAL GEOGRAPHIC LIKE EVERYONE ELSE!
HUH-HUH HUH
IF I WAS, LIKE, A NATIVE... I'D ALWAYS BE NAKED!! HEH-HEH-HEH
BURGER WORLD
HUH-HUH-HUH THAT WOULD BE COOL!
YEAH! HEH-HEH

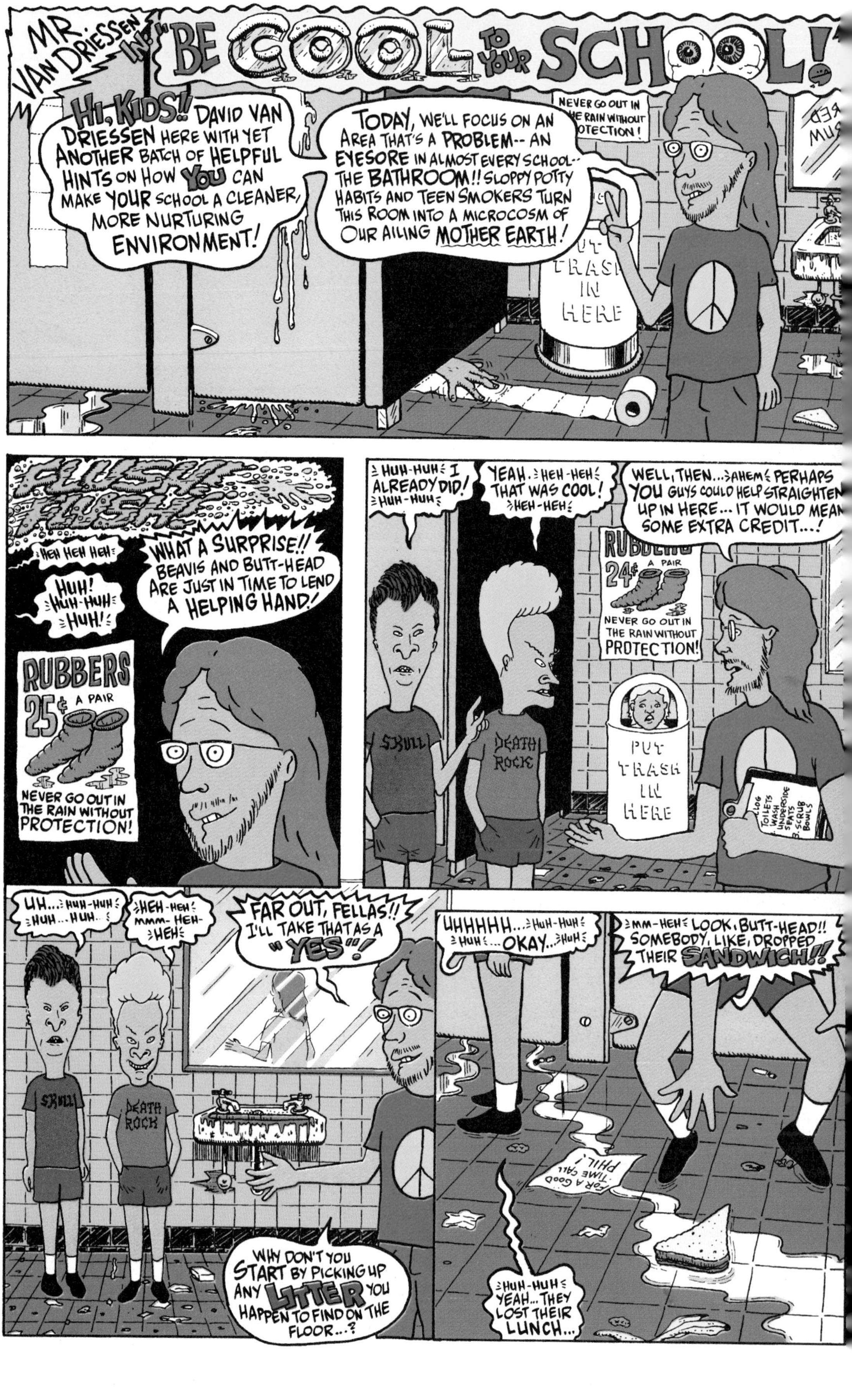
MR. VAN DRIESSEN IN: "BE COOL TO YOUR SCHOOL!"
NEVER GO OUT IN THE RAIN WITHOUT PROTECTION!
HI, KIDS!! DAVID VAN DRIESSEN HERE WITH YET ANOTHER BATCH OF HELPFUL HINTS ON HOW YOU CAN MAKE YOUR SCHOOL A CLEANER, MORE NURTURING ENVIRONMENT!
TODAY, WE'LL FOCUS ON AN AREA THAT'S A PROBLEM-- AN EYESORE IN ALMOST EVERY SCHOOL-- THE BATHROOM!! SLOPPY POTTY HABITS AND TEEN SMOKERS TURN THIS ROOM INTO A MICROCOSM OF OUR AILING MOTHER EARTH!
PUT TRASH IN HERE
HEH HEH HEH
HUH! HUH-HUH HUH!
WHAT A SURPRISE!! BEAVIS AND BUTT-HEAD ARE JUST IN TIME TO LEND A HELPING HAND!
RUBBERS 25¢ A PAIR
NEVER GO OUT IN THE RAIN WITHOUT PROTECTION!
HUH-HUH I ALREADY DID! HUH-HUH
YEAH. HEH-HEH THAT WAS COOL! HEH-HEH
WELL, THEN... AHEM PERHAPS YOU GUYS COULD HELP STRAIGHTEN UP IN HERE... IT WOULD MEAN SOME EXTRA CREDIT...!
24¢ A PAIR
NEVER GO OUT IN THE RAIN WITHOUT PROTECTION!
SKULL
DEATH ROCK
PUT TRASH IN HERE
UH... HUH-HUH HUH... HUH...
HEH-HEH MMM- HEH- HEH
FAR OUT, FELLAS!! I'LL TAKE THAT AS A "YES"!
WHY DON'T YOU START BY PICKING UP ANY LITTER YOU HAPPEN TO FIND ON THE FLOOR...?
UHHHHH... HUH-HUH HUH... OKAY... HUH
MM-HEH LOOK, BUTT-HEAD!! SOMEBODY, LIKE, DROPPED THEIR SANDWICH!!
FOR A GOOD TIME CALL PHIL!
HUH-HUH YEAH... THEY LOST THEIR LUNCH...

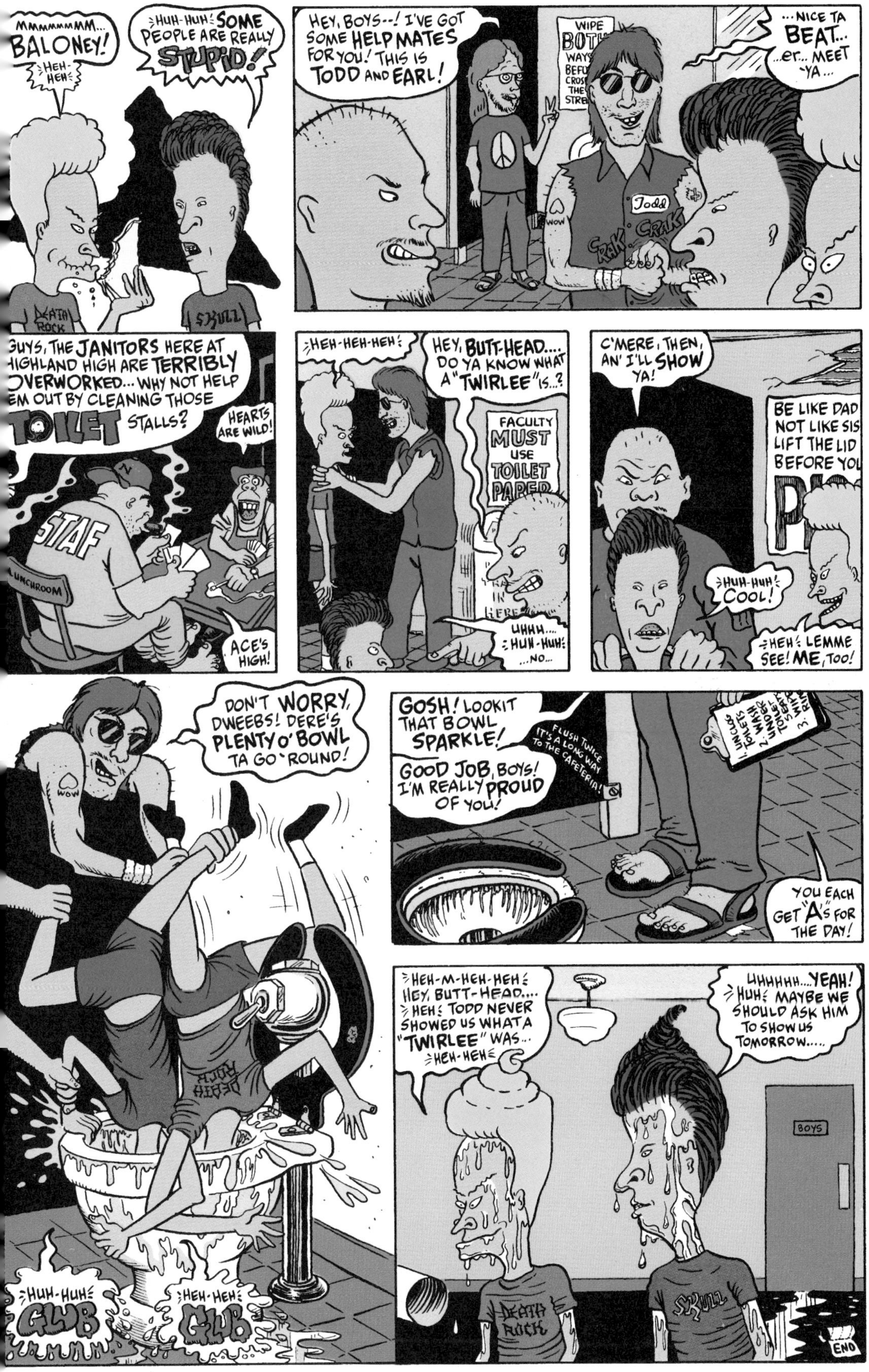

MMMMMMMM... BALONEY!
HEH-HEH
HUH-HUH SOME PEOPLE ARE REALLY STUPID!
DEATH ROCK
SKULL
HEY, BOYS--! I'VE GOT SOME HELP MATES FOR YOU! THIS IS TODD AND EARL!
WIPE BOTH WAYS BEFO CROS THE STRE
...NICE TA BEAT... er... MEET YA...
Todd
WOW
CRAK CRAK
GUYS, THE JANITORS HERE AT HIGHLAND HIGH ARE TERRIBLY OVERWORKED... WHY NOT HELP EM OUT BY CLEANING THOSE TOILET STALLS?
HEARTS ARE WILD!
STAF
LUNCHROOM
ACE'S HIGH!
HEH-HEH-HEH
HEY, BUTT-HEAD.... DO YA KNOW WHAT A "TWIRLEE" IS...?
FACULTY MUST USE TOILET PAPER
UHHH.... HUH-HUH ...NO...
C'MERE, THEN, AN' I'LL SHOW YA!
BE LIKE DAD NOT LIKE SIS LIFT THE LID BEFORE YOU
HUH-HUH COOL!
HEH LEMME SEE! ME, TOO!
DON'T WORRY, DWEEBS! DERE'S PLENTY O' BOWL TA GO 'ROUND!
WOW
DEATH ROCK
HUH-HUH GLUB
HEH-HEH GLUB
GOSH! LOOKIT THAT BOWL SPARKLE!
GOOD JOB, BOYS! I'M REALLY PROUD OF YOU!
FLUSH TWICE IT'S A LONG WAY TO THE CAFETERIA!
1. UNCLOG TOILETS 2. WASH UNDER TOILET SEATS 3. WIPE RIM
YOU EACH GET "A"s FOR THE DAY!
HEH-M-HEH-HEH HEY, BUTT-HEAD.... HEH TODD NEVER SHOWED US WHAT A "TWIRLEE" WAS...
HEH-HEH
UHHHHH....YEAH! HUH MAYBE WE SHOULD ASK HIM TO SHOW US TOMORROW.....
BOYS
DEATH ROCK
SKULL
END

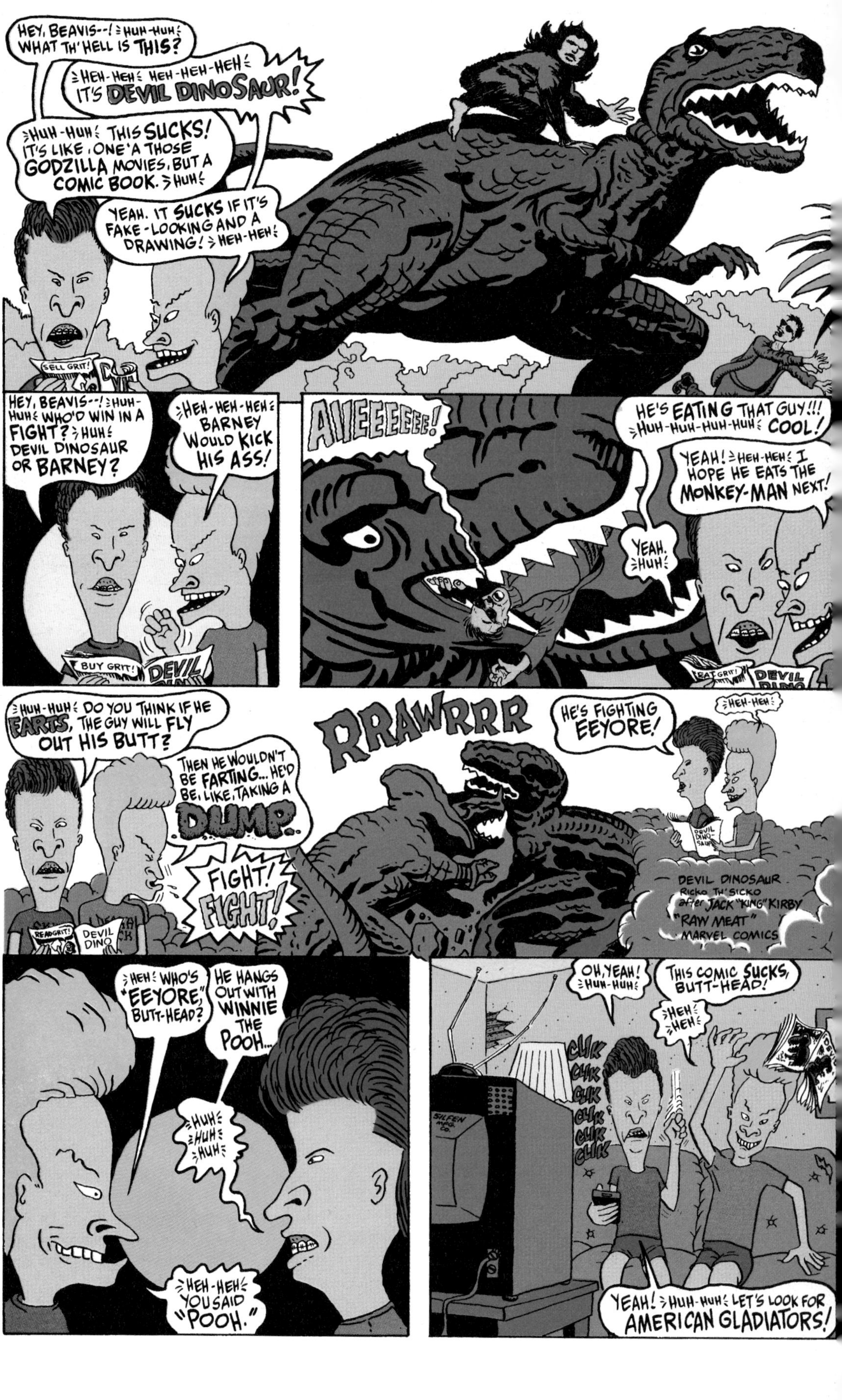
HEY, BEAVIS--! HUH-HUH WHAT TH' HELL IS THIS?
HEH-HEH HEH-HEH-HEH IT'S DEVIL DINOSAUR!
HUH-HUH THIS SUCKS! IT'S LIKE, ONE'A THOSE GODZILLA MOVIES, BUT A COMIC BOOK. HUH
YEAH. IT SUCKS IF IT'S FAKE-LOOKING AND A DRAWING! HEH-HEH
SELL GRIT!
HEY, BEAVIS--! HUH-HUH WHO'D WIN IN A FIGHT? HUH DEVIL DINOSAUR OR BARNEY?
HEH-HEH-HEH BARNEY WOULD KICK HIS ASS!
BUY GRIT!
DEVIL
AIEEEEEEE!
HE'S EATING THAT GUY!!! HUH-HUH-HUH-HUH COOL!
YEAH! HEH-HEH I HOPE HE EATS THE MONKEY-MAN NEXT!
YEAH. HUH
EAT GRIT!
DEVIL DINO
HUH-HUH DO YOU THINK IF HE FARTS, THE GUY WILL FLY OUT HIS BUTT?
THEN HE WOULDN'T BE FARTING... HE'D BE, LIKE, TAKING A DUMP.
RRAWRRR
HE'S FIGHTING EEYORE!
HEH-HEH
FIGHT! FIGHT!
READ GRIT!
DEVIL DINO
DEVIL DINOSAUR
DEVIL DINOSAUR Ricko Th' Sicko after JACK "KING" KIRBY "RAW MEAT" MARVEL COMICS
HEH WHO'S "EEYORE," BUTT-HEAD?
HE HANGS OUT WITH WINNIE THE POOH...
HUH HUH HUH
HEH-HEH YOU SAID "POOH."
OH, YEAH! HUH-HUH
THIS COMIC SUCKS, BUTT-HEAD!
HEH HEH
CLIK CLIK CLIK CLIK CLIK CLIK
SILFEN MFG. CO.
YEAH! HUH-HUH LET'S LOOK FOR AMERICAN GLADIATORS!

HUH-HUH THIS IS COOL, BEAVIS! IT'S, LIKE, A BONUS ACTIVITY PAGE.!!!
YEAH! COOL! HEH-HEH HEY, WAIT--! IT'S GOT WORDS... WORDS SUCK!! HEH
SETTLE DOWN, BEAVIS... IT'S STILL COOL!
NAME YOUR OWN, LIKE, SUPER HERO
R. PARKER

JUST MIX AN' MATCH A WORD FROM EACH COLUMN-THINGIE... AN', UH... LIKE, PUT IT TOGETHER TA FORM A NEW SUPER HERO!

	POWER	COOL MIDDLE NAME	SEX	CHARACTER
	FLYING	BLOOD	MAN	----------
	POWER	NIGHT	BOY	----------
	HAIRY	FIST	GOD	----------
	BIG-BUTT	GORILLA	KNOCKER	----------
	DOCTOR	FUR	IDIOT	----------
	STINKY	DEAD	JERK	----------
	PROFESSOR	DARK	BUTT	----------
	MISTER	BLACK	WOMAN	----------
	BROTHER	GHOST	GEEK	----------
	GIANT	HELL	BABY	----------
	RADIOACTIVE	MOON	WOLF	----------
	GREASY	X	DUDE	----------
	GREEN	FART	GUY	----------
4.	FANTASTIC	"THE WONDER"	GIRL	----------
	SUPER	BUTT	DOG	----------
6.	SILVER	CYBER	LADY	----------
	MUTANT	TURD	CHILD	----------
	EVIL	ATOMIC	KID	----------
	FAT	SKULL	RABBIT	----------
0.	MISTRESS	NACHO	DUCK	----------
1.	NINJA	SNOT	ALIEN	----------
2.	ULTRA	SCARY	CHICK	----------
3.	CAPTAIN	TUBA	KNIGHT	----------
4.	SWAMP	FIRE	MONKEY	----------
5.	AMAZING	SWAMP	TEEN	----------

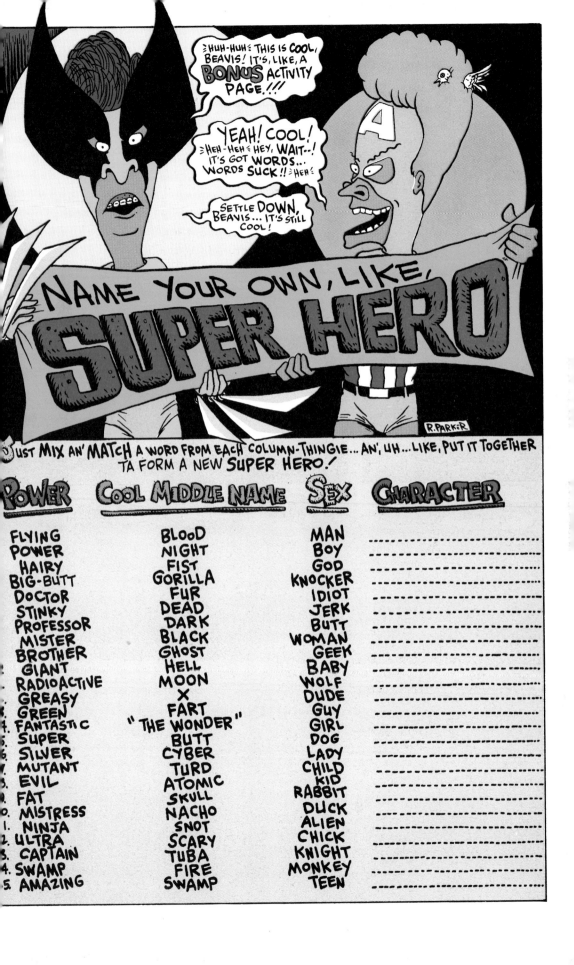

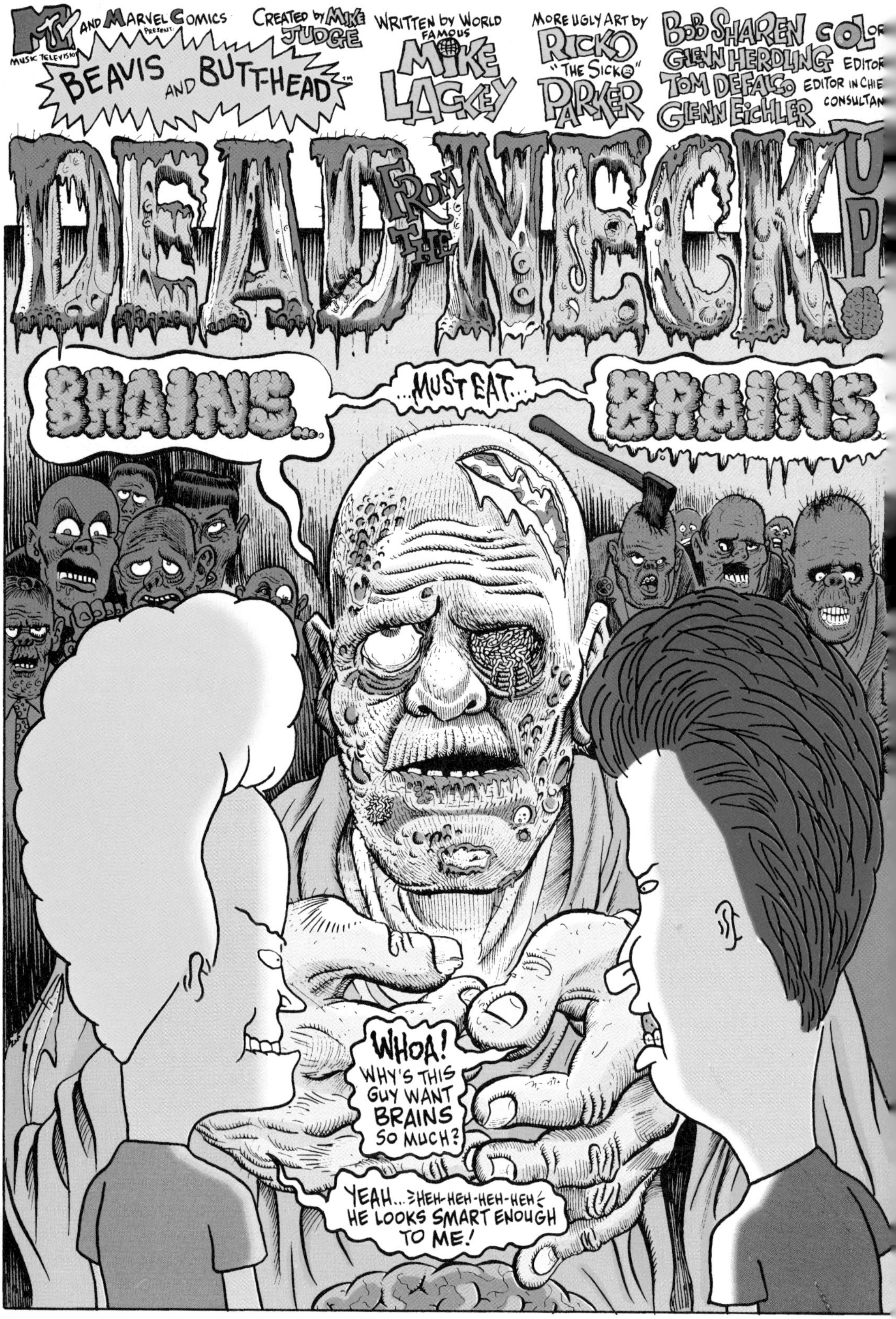
MTV MUSIC TELEVISION AND MARVEL COMICS PRESENT:
BEAVIS AND BUTT-HEAD™
CREATED BY MIKE JUDGE
WRITTEN BY WORLD FAMOUS MIKE LACKEY
MORE UGLY ART BY RICKO "THE SICKO" PARKER
BOB SHAREN COLOR
GLENN HERDLING EDITOR
TOM DEFALCO EDITOR IN CHIEF
GLENN EICHLER CONSULTANT
DEAD FROM THE NECK UP
BRAINS... ...MUST EAT... BRAINS
WHOA! WHY'S THIS GUY WANT BRAINS SO MUCH?
YEAH... HEH-HEH-HEH-HEH HE LOOKS SMART ENOUGH TO ME!

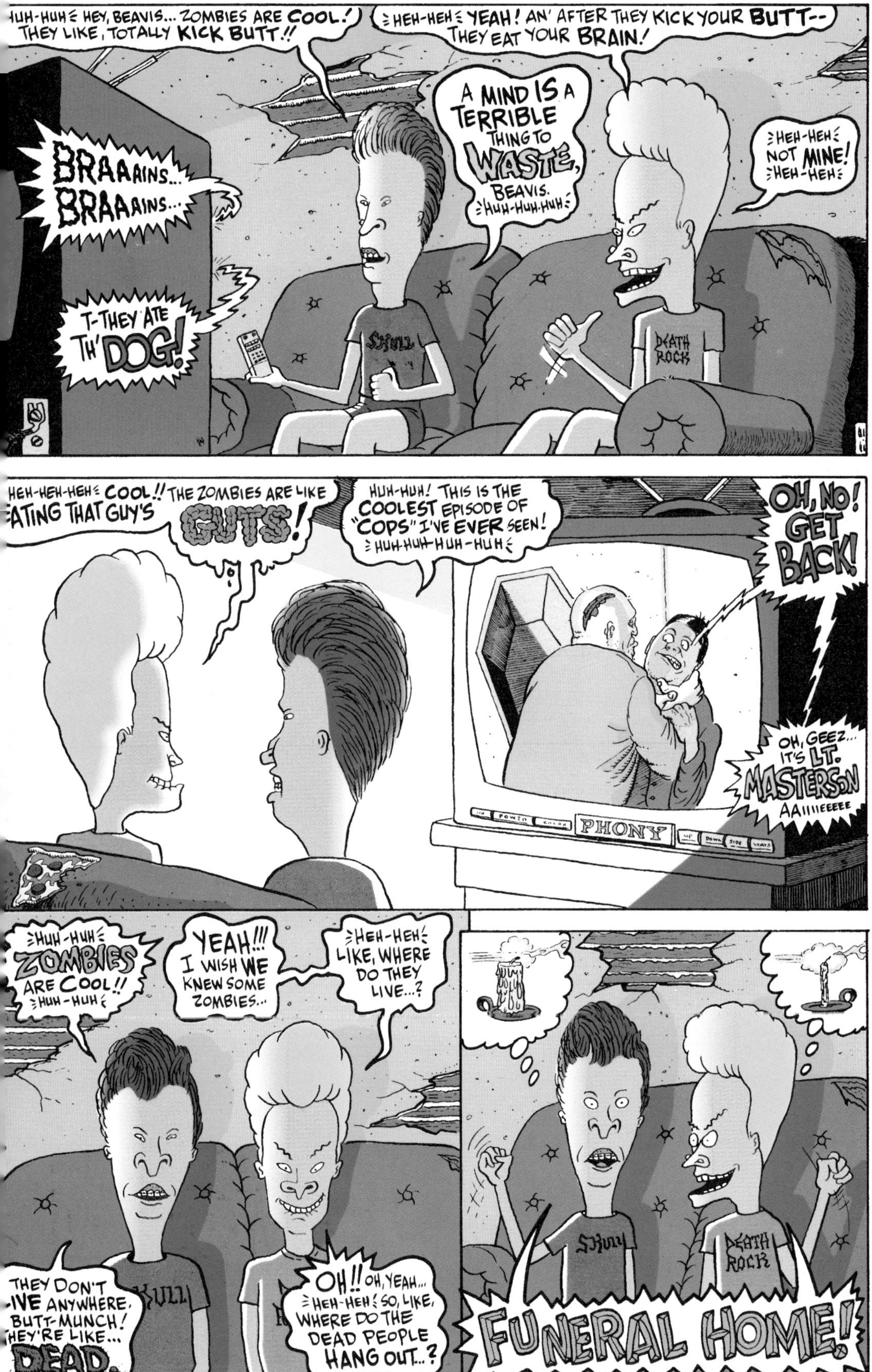
UH-HUH HEY, BEAVIS... ZOMBIES ARE COOL! THEY LIKE, TOTALLY KICK BUTT!!
HEH-HEH YEAH! AN' AFTER THEY KICK YOUR BUTT-- THEY EAT YOUR BRAIN!
BRAAAINS... BRAAAINS...
A MIND IS A TERRIBLE THING TO WASTE, BEAVIS. HUH-HUH-HUH
HEH-HEH NOT MINE! HEH-HEH
T-THEY ATE TH' DOG!
SKULL
DEATH ROCK
EH-HEH-HEH COOL!! THE ZOMBIES ARE LIKE ATING THAT GUY'S GUTS!
HUH-HUH! THIS IS THE COOLEST EPISODE OF "COPS" I'VE EVER SEEN! HUH-HUH-HUH-HUH
OH, NO! GET BACK!
OH, GEEZ... IT'S LT. MASTERSON AAIIIEEEEE
PHONY
HUH-HUH ZOMBIES ARE COOL!! HUH-HUH
YEAH!!! I WISH WE KNEW SOME ZOMBIES...
HEH-HEH LIKE, WHERE DO THEY LIVE...?
THEY DON'T IVE ANYWHERE, BUTT-MUNCH! HEY'RE LIKE... DEAD.
OH!! OH, YEAH... HEH-HEH SO, LIKE, WHERE DO THE DEAD PEOPLE HANG OUT...?
FUNERAL HOME!

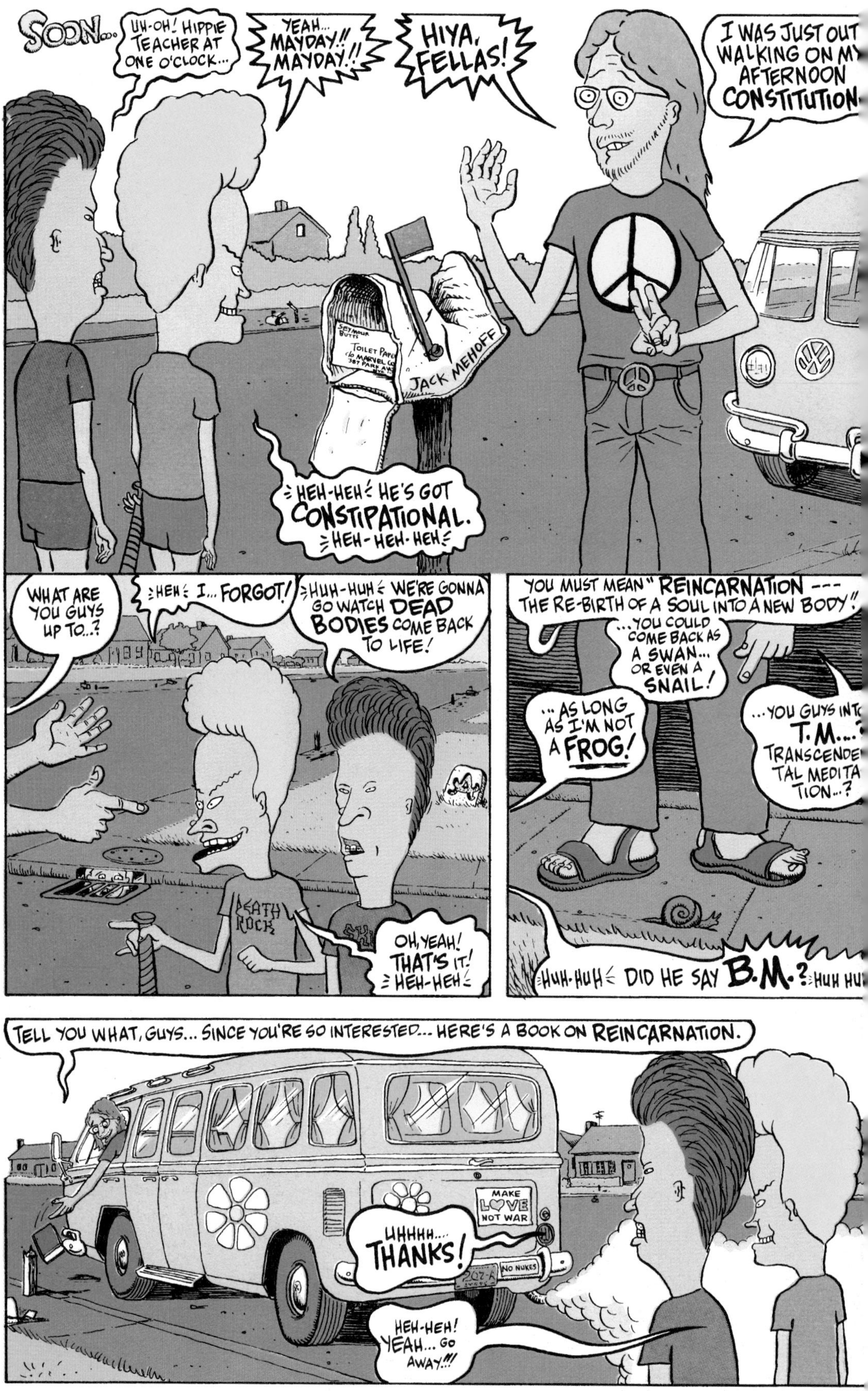
SOON...
UH-OH! HIPPIE TEACHER AT ONE O'CLOCK...
YEAH... MAYDAY!! MAYDAY!!
HIYA, FELLAS!
I WAS JUST OUT WALKING ON MY AFTERNOON CONSTITUTION
JACK MEHOFF
HEH-HEH! HE'S GOT CONSTIPATIONAL. HEH-HEH-HEH
WHAT ARE YOU GUYS UP TO..?
HEH! I... FORGOT!
HUH-HUH! WE'RE GONNA GO WATCH DEAD BODIES COME BACK TO LIFE!
DEATH ROCK
OH, YEAH! THAT'S IT! HEH-HEH
YOU MUST MEAN "REINCARNATION --- THE RE-BIRTH OF A SOUL INTO A NEW BODY"!
...YOU COULD COME BACK AS A SWAN... OR EVEN A SNAIL!
...AS LONG AS I'M NOT A FROG!
...YOU GUYS INTO T.M...? TRANSCENDENTAL MEDITATION...?
HUH-HUH! DID HE SAY B.M.? HUH HUH
TELL YOU WHAT, GUYS... SINCE YOU'RE SO INTERESTED... HERE'S A BOOK ON REINCARNATION.
MAKE LOVE NOT WAR
NO NUKES
UHHHH.... THANKS!
HEH-HEH! YEAH... GO AWAY!!!

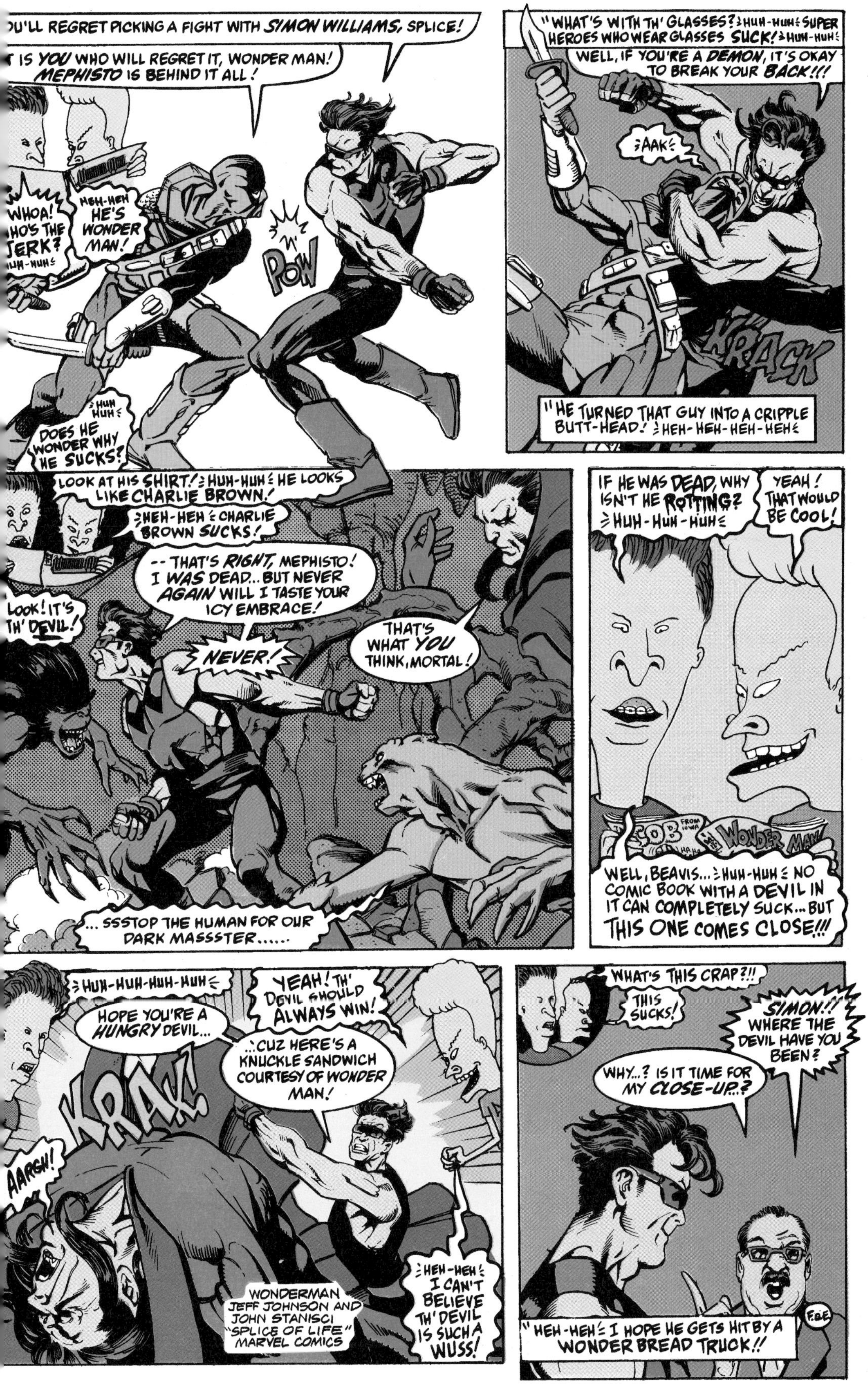

OU'LL REGRET PICKING A FIGHT WITH SIMON WILLIAMS, SPLICE!
T IS YOU WHO WILL REGRET IT, WONDER MAN! MEPHISTO IS BEHIND IT ALL!
WHOA! HO'S THE JERK? HUH-HUH
HEH-HEH HE'S WONDER MAN!
POW
HUH HUH DOES HE WONDER WHY HE SUCKS?
"WHAT'S WITH TH' GLASSES? HUH-HUH SUPER HEROES WHO WEAR GLASSES SUCK! HUH-HUH
WELL, IF YOU'RE A DEMON, IT'S OKAY TO BREAK YOUR BACK!!!
AAK
KRACK
"HE TURNED THAT GUY INTO A CRIPPLE BUTT-HEAD! HEH-HEH-HEH-HEH
LOOK AT HIS SHIRT! HUH-HUH HE LOOKS LIKE CHARLIE BROWN!
HEH-HEH CHARLIE BROWN SUCKS!
-- THAT'S RIGHT, MEPHISTO! I WAS DEAD... BUT NEVER AGAIN WILL I TASTE YOUR ICY EMBRACE!
LOOK! IT'S TH' DEVIL!
NEVER!
THAT'S WHAT YOU THINK, MORTAL!
... SSSTOP THE HUMAN FOR OUR DARK MASSSTER......
IF HE WAS DEAD, WHY ISN'T HE ROTTING? HUH-HUH-HUH
YEAH! THAT WOULD BE COOL!
WELL, BEAVIS... HUH-HUH NO COMIC BOOK WITH A DEVIL IN IT CAN COMPLETELY SUCK... BUT THIS ONE COMES CLOSE!!!
HUH-HUH-HUH-HUH
HOPE YOU'RE A HUNGRY DEVIL...
YEAH! TH' DEVIL SHOULD ALWAYS WIN!
...CUZ HERE'S A KNUCKLE SANDWICH COURTESY OF WONDER MAN!
KRAK!
AARGH!
HEH-HEH I CAN'T BELIEVE TH' DEVIL IS SUCH A WUSS!
WONDERMAN JEFF JOHNSON AND JOHN STANISCI "SPLICE OF LIFE" MARVEL COMICS
WHAT'S THIS CRAP?!!
THIS SUCKS!
SIMON!! WHERE THE DEVIL HAVE YOU BEEN?
WHY...? IS IT TIME FOR MY CLOSE-UP...?
"HEH-HEH I HOPE HE GETS HIT BY A WONDER BREAD TRUCK!!

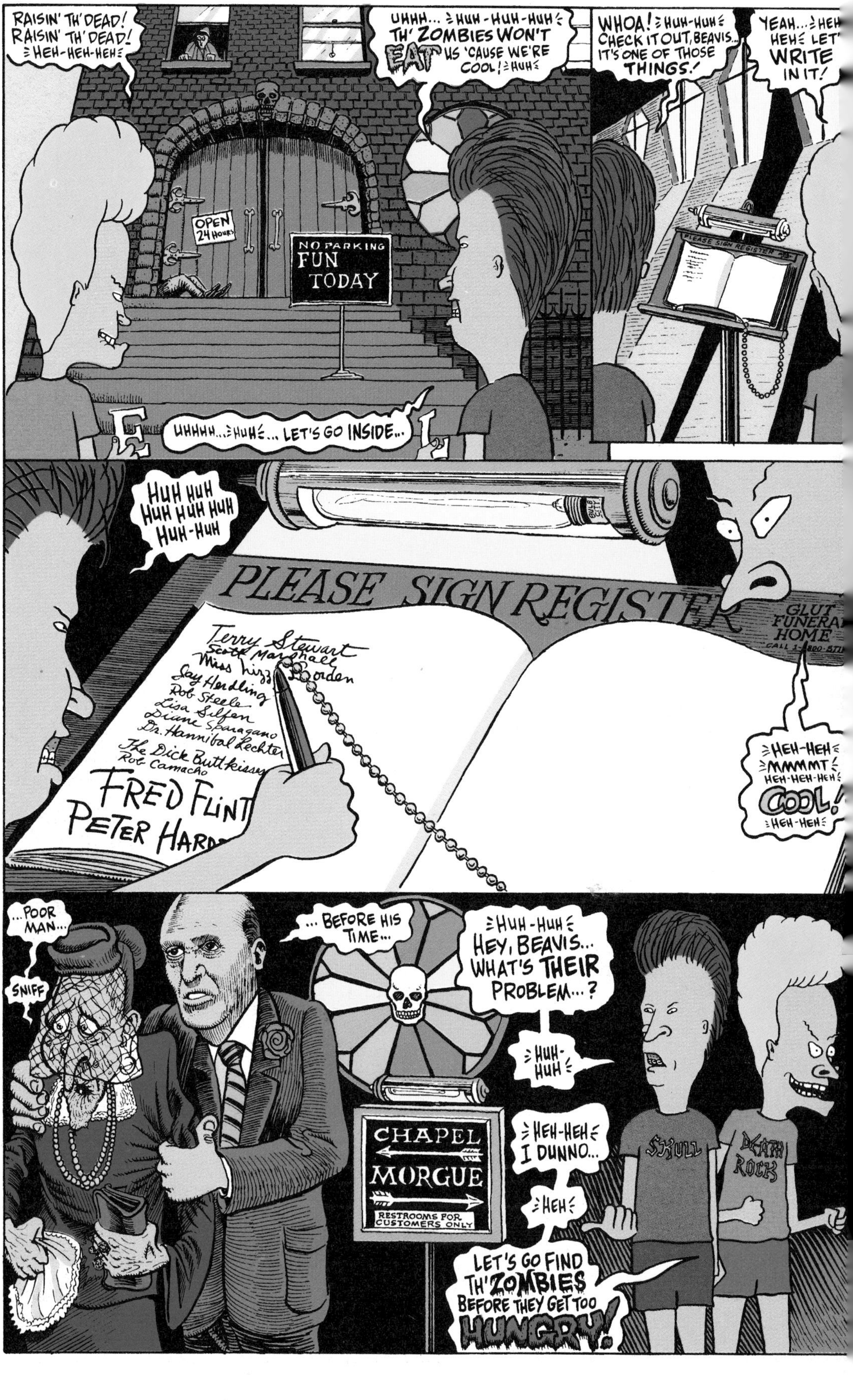

RAISIN' TH' DEAD! RAISIN' TH' DEAD! HEH-HEH-HEH
UHHH... HUH-HUH-HUH TH' ZOMBIES WON'T EAT US 'CAUSE WE'RE COOL! HUH
OPEN 24 HOURS
NO PARKING FUN TODAY
UHHHH... HUH... LET'S GO INSIDE...
WHOA! HUH-HUH CHECK IT OUT, BEAVIS... IT'S ONE OF THOSE THINGS!
YEAH... HEH HEH LET' WRITE IN IT!
HUH HUH HUH HUH HUH HUH-HUH
PLEASE SIGN REGISTER
GLUT FUNERA HOME
Terry Stewart
Scott Marshall
Say Hendling
Rob Steele
Lisa Silfen
Diane Sparagano
Dr. Hannibal Lechter
The Dick Buttkisser
Rob Camacho
FRED FLINT
PETER HARD
HEH-HEH MMMMT! HEH-HEH-HEH COOL! HEH-HEH
...POOR MAN...
SNIFF
...BEFORE HIS TIME...
HUH-HUH HEY, BEAVIS... WHAT'S THEIR PROBLEM...?
HUH-HUH
CHAPEL
MORGUE
RESTROOMS FOR CUSTOMERS ONLY
HEH-HEH I DUNNO...
HEH
SKULL
DEATH ROCK
LET'S GO FIND TH' ZOMBIES BEFORE THEY GET TOO HUNGRY!

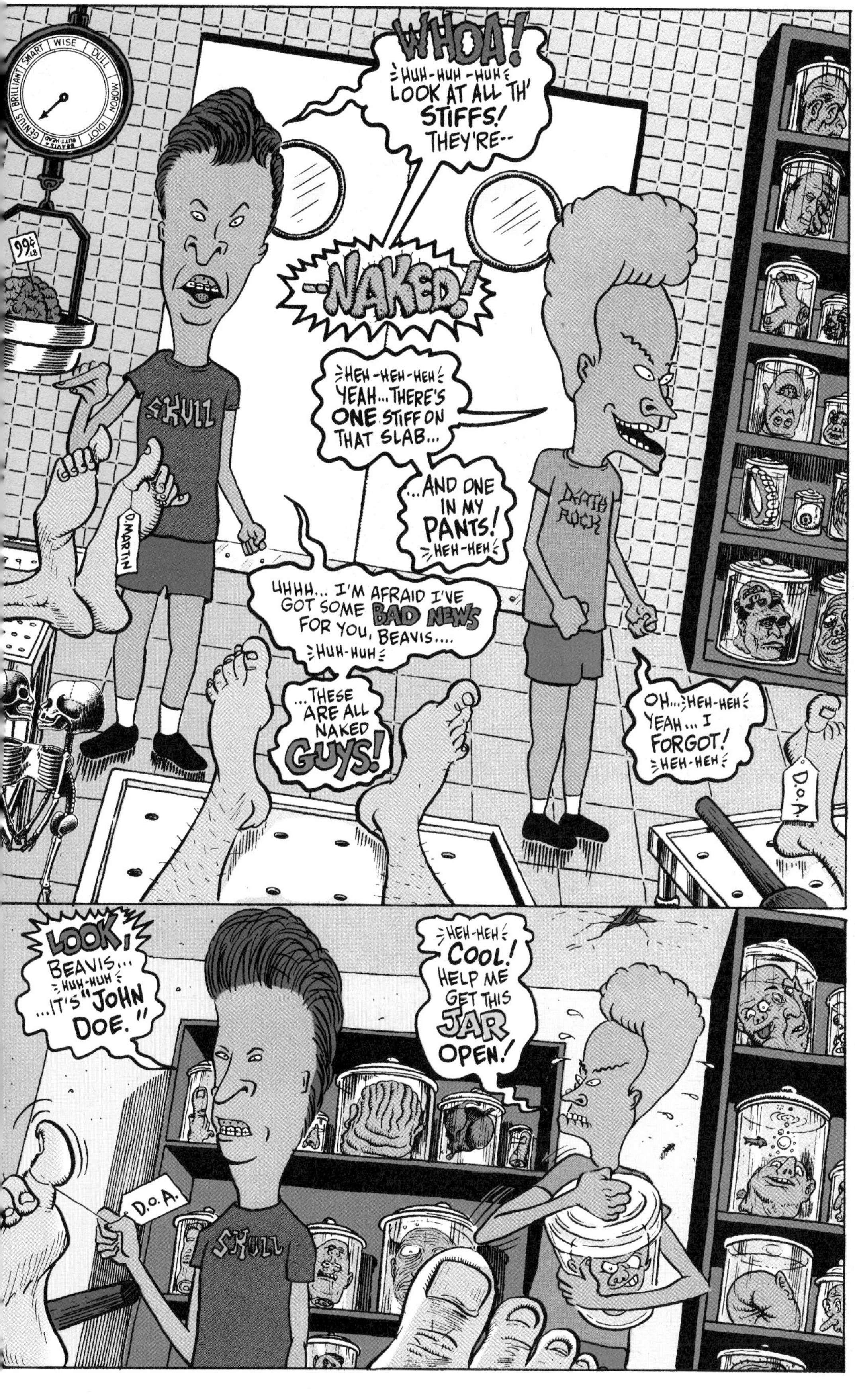
GENIUS BRILLIANT SMART WISE DULL MORON IDIOT
BEAVIS & BUTT-HEAD
99¢ LB
WHOA!
HUH-HUH-HUH LOOK AT ALL TH' STIFFS! THEY'RE--
--NAKED!
HEH-HEH-HEH YEAH... THERE'S ONE STIFF ON THAT SLAB...
...AND ONE IN MY PANTS! HEH-HEH
SKULL
DEATH ROCK
D.MARTIN
UHHH... I'M AFRAID I'VE GOT SOME BAD NEWS FOR YOU, BEAVIS.... HUH-HUH
...THESE ARE ALL NAKED GUYS!
OH... HEH-HEH YEAH... I FORGOT! HEH-HEH
D.O.A.
LOOK, BEAVIS... HUH-HUH ...IT'S "JOHN DOE."
HEH-HEH COOL! HELP ME GET THIS JAR OPEN!
D.O.A.
SKULL

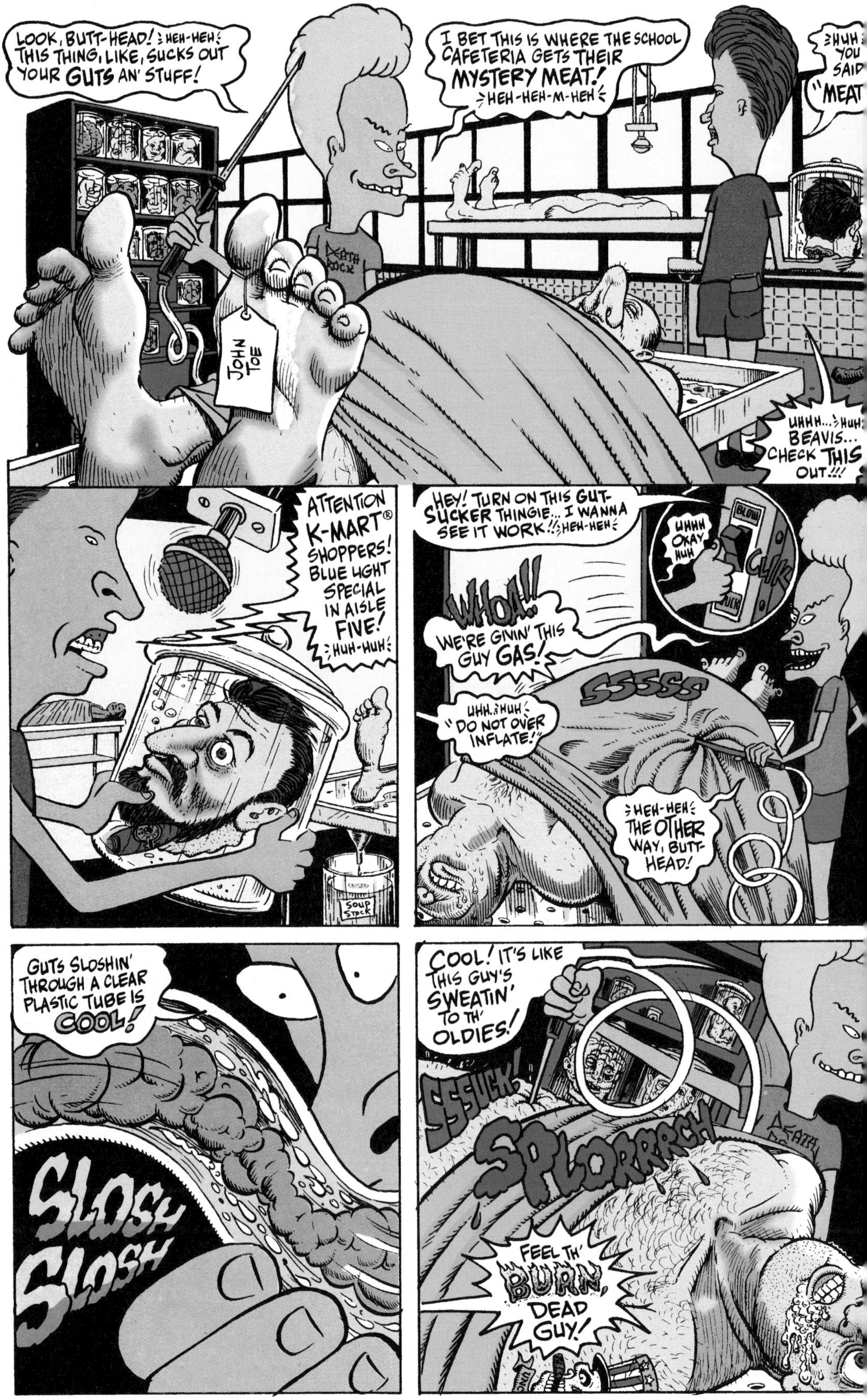
LOOK, BUTT-HEAD! HEH-HEH THIS THING, LIKE, SUCKS OUT YOUR GUTS AN' STUFF!
I BET THIS IS WHERE THE SCHOOL CAFETERIA GETS THEIR MYSTERY MEAT! HEH-HEH-M-HEH
HUH YOU SAID "MEAT
JOHN DOE
UHHH... HUH BEAVIS... CHECK THIS OUT!!!
ATTENTION K-MART® SHOPPERS! BLUE LIGHT SPECIAL IN AISLE FIVE! HUH-HUH
SOUP STOCK
HEY! TURN ON THIS GUT-SUCKER THINGIE... I WANNA SEE IT WORK!! HEH-HEH
UHHH OKAY HUH
BLOW
CLIK
WHOA!!
WE'RE GIVIN' THIS GUY GAS!
SSSSS
UHH. HUH DO NOT OVER INFLATE!
HEH-HEH THE OTHER WAY, BUTT-HEAD!
GUTS SLOSHIN' THROUGH A CLEAR PLASTIC TUBE IS COOL!
SLOSH SLOSH
COOL! IT'S LIKE THIS GUY'S SWEATIN' TO TH' OLDIES!
SSSUCK!
SPLORRRCH
FEEL TH' BURN, DEAD GUY!

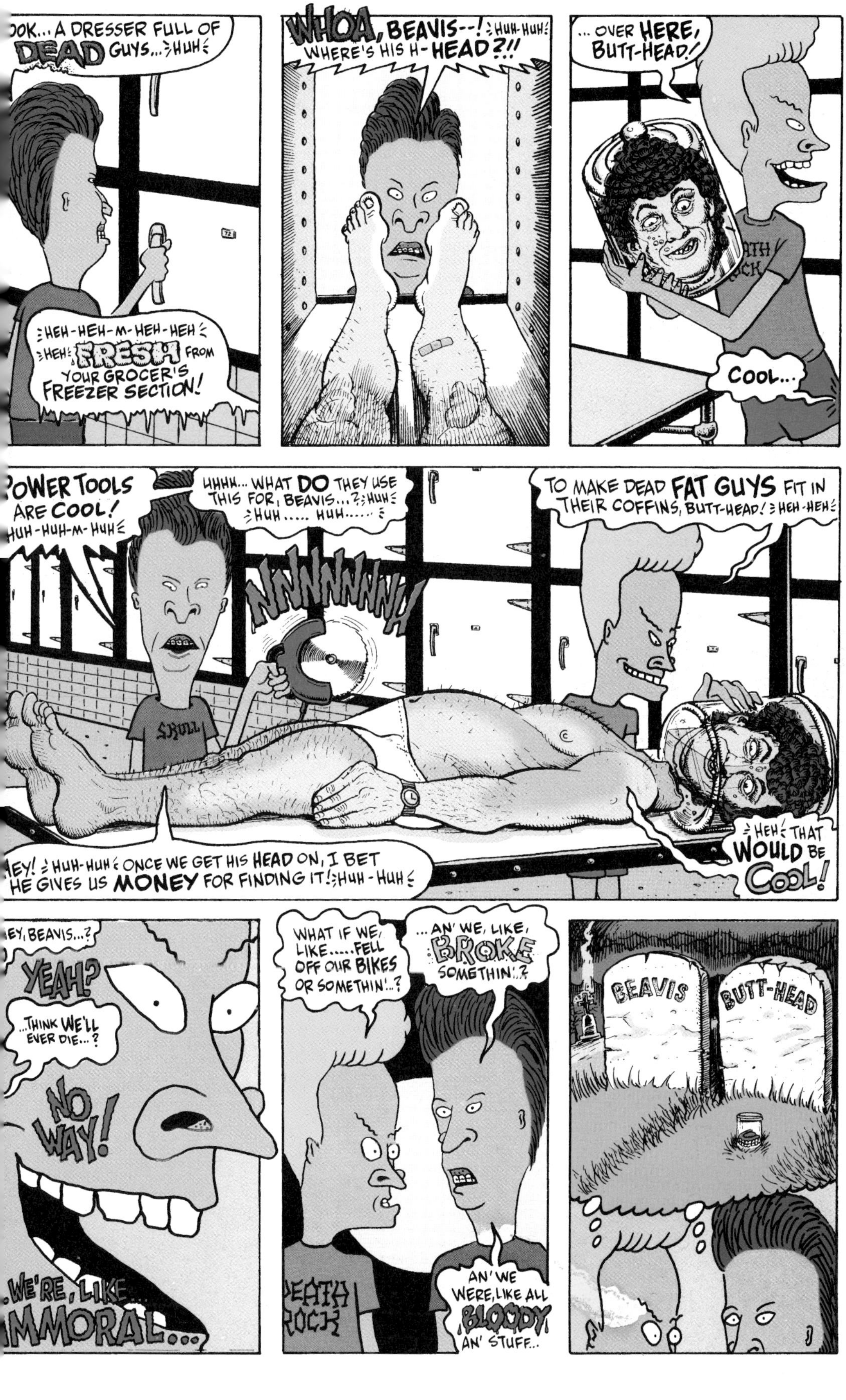
OOK... A DRESSER FULL OF DEAD GUYS... HUH
HEH-HEH-M-HEH-HEH HEH FRESH FROM YOUR GROCER'S FREEZER SECTION!
WHOA, BEAVIS--! HUH-HUH WHERE'S HIS H-HEAD?!!
... OVER HERE, BUTT-HEAD!
COOL...
POWER TOOLS ARE COOL! HUH-HUH-M-HUH
UHHH... WHAT DO THEY USE THIS FOR, BEAVIS...? HUH HUH..... HUH.....
NNNNNNNH
TO MAKE DEAD FAT GUYS FIT IN THEIR COFFINS, BUTT-HEAD! HEH-HEH
EY! HUH-HUH ONCE WE GET HIS HEAD ON, I BET HE GIVES US MONEY FOR FINDING IT! HUH-HUH
HEH THAT WOULD BE COOL!
EY, BEAVIS...?
YEAH?
...THINK WE'LL EVER DIE...?
NO WAY!
.WE'RE, LIKE... MMORAL...
WHAT IF WE, LIKE.....FELL OFF OUR BIKES OR SOMETHIN'...?
... AN' WE, LIKE, BROKE SOMETHIN'...?
AN' WE WERE, LIKE ALL BLOODY AN' STUFF...
BEAVIS
BUTT-HEAD

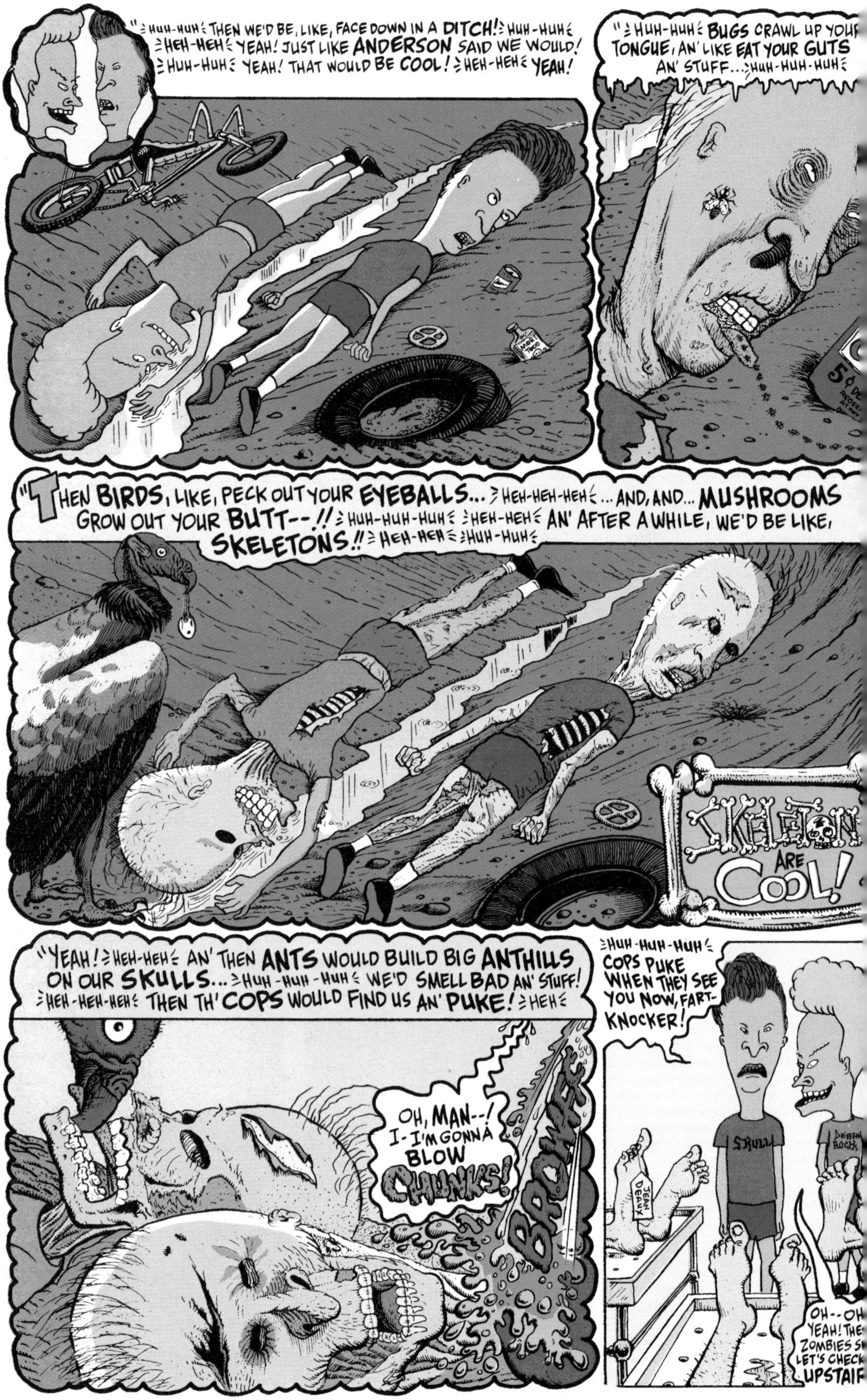
"≥HUH-HUH≤ THEN WE'D BE, LIKE, FACE DOWN IN A DITCH!≥HUH-HUH≤
≥HEH-HEH≤ YEAH! JUST LIKE ANDERSON SAID WE WOULD!
≥HUH-HUH≤ YEAH! THAT WOULD BE COOL! ≥HEH-HEH≤ YEAH!
"≥HUH-HUH≤ BUGS CRAWL UP YOUR
TONGUE, AN' LIKE EAT YOUR GUTS
AN' STUFF...≥HUH-HUH-HUH≤
"THEN BIRDS, LIKE, PECK OUT YOUR EYEBALLS... ≥HEH-HEH-HEH≤ ...AND, AND... MUSHROOMS
GROW OUT YOUR BUTT--!! ≥HUH-HUH-HUH≤ ≥HEH-HEH≤ AN' AFTER A WHILE, WE'D BE LIKE,
SKELETONS!! ≥HEH-HEH≤ ≥HUH-HUH≤
SKELETONS ARE COOL!
"YEAH! ≥HEH-HEH≤ AN' THEN ANTS WOULD BUILD BIG ANTHILLS
ON OUR SKULLS... ≥HUH-HUH-HUH≤ WE'D SMELL BAD AN' STUFF!
≥HEH-HEH-HEH≤ THEN TH' COPS WOULD FIND US AN' PUKE! ≥HEH≤
OH, MAN--! I-I'M GONNA BLOW CHUNKS!
BROWAR!
≥HUH-HUH-HUH≤
COPS PUKE WHEN THEY SEE YOU NOW, FART-KNOCKER!
SKULL
DEATH ROCK
JEAN DEAUX
OH--OH
YEAH! THE
ZOMBIES S
LET'S CHECK
UPSTAIR

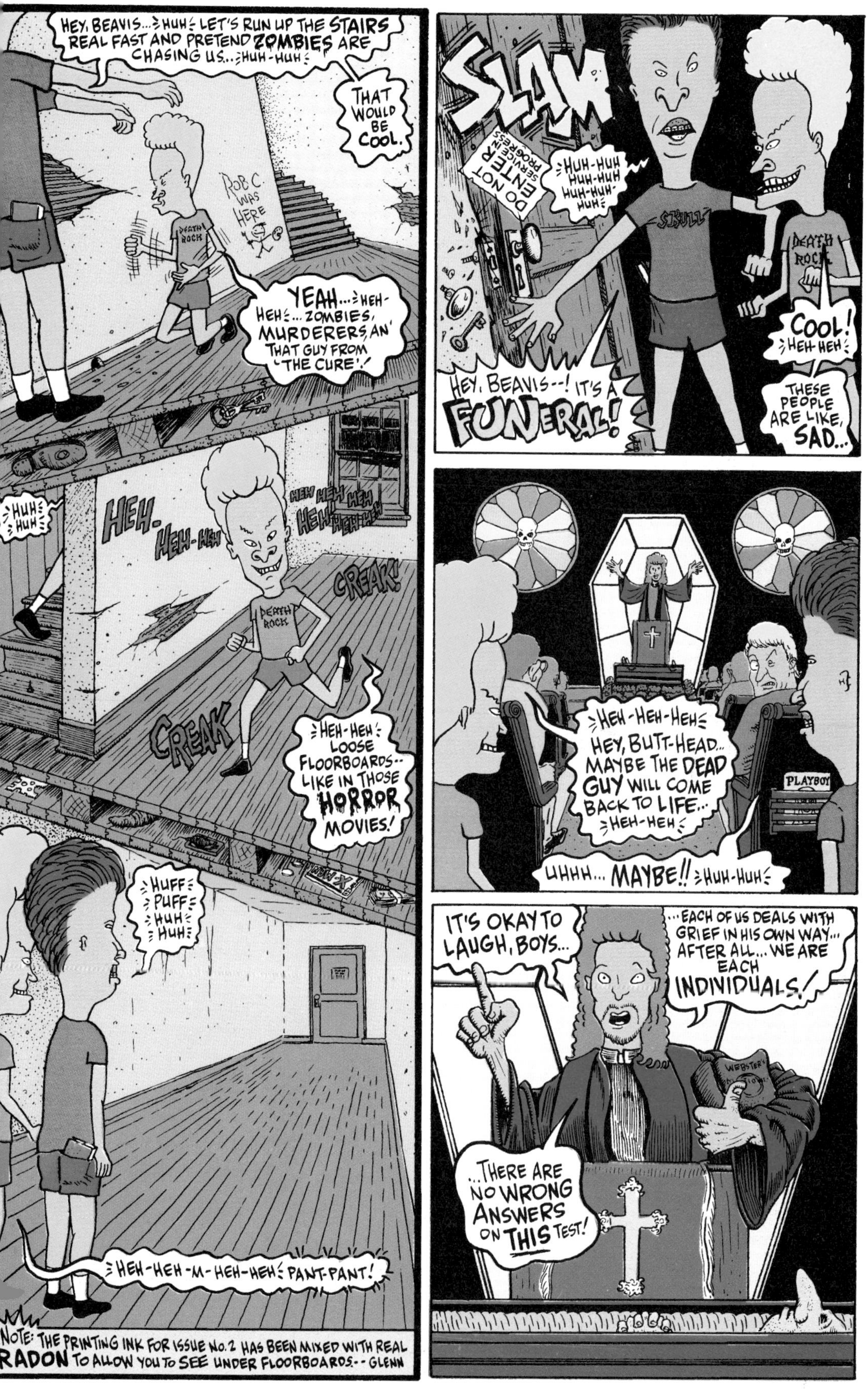
HEY, BEAVIS... HUH LET'S RUN UP THE STAIRS REAL FAST AND PRETEND ZOMBIES ARE CHASING US... HUH-HUH
THAT WOULD BE COOL.
ROB C. WAS HERE
DEATH ROCK
YEAH... HEH-HEH... ZOMBIES, MURDERERS, AN' THAT GUY FROM 'THE CURE'!
HUH HUH
HEH-HEH-HEH
HEH HEH HEH HEH HEH HEH
CREAK!
CREAK
HEH-HEH LOOSE FLOORBOARDS-- LIKE IN THOSE HORROR MOVIES!
HUFF PUFF HUH HUH
HEH-HEH-M-HEH-HEH PANT-PANT!
NOTE: THE PRINTING INK FOR ISSUE NO. 2 HAS BEEN MIXED WITH REAL RADON TO ALLOW YOU TO SEE UNDER FLOORBOARDS. -- GLENN
SLAM
DO NOT ENTER SERVICE IN PROGRESS
HUH-HUH HUH-HUH HUH-HUH-HUH
SKULL
HEY, BEAVIS--! IT'S A FUNERAL!
COOL! HEH-HEH
THESE PEOPLE ARE LIKE, SAD...
HEH-HEH-HEH HEY, BUTT-HEAD... MAYBE THE DEAD GUY WILL COME BACK TO LIFE... HEH-HEH
PLAYBOY
UHHH... MAYBE!! HUH-HUH
IT'S OKAY TO LAUGH, BOYS...
...EACH OF US DEALS WITH GRIEF IN HIS OWN WAY... AFTER ALL... WE ARE EACH INDIVIDUALS!
WEBSTER'S
...THERE ARE NO WRONG ANSWERS ON THIS TEST!

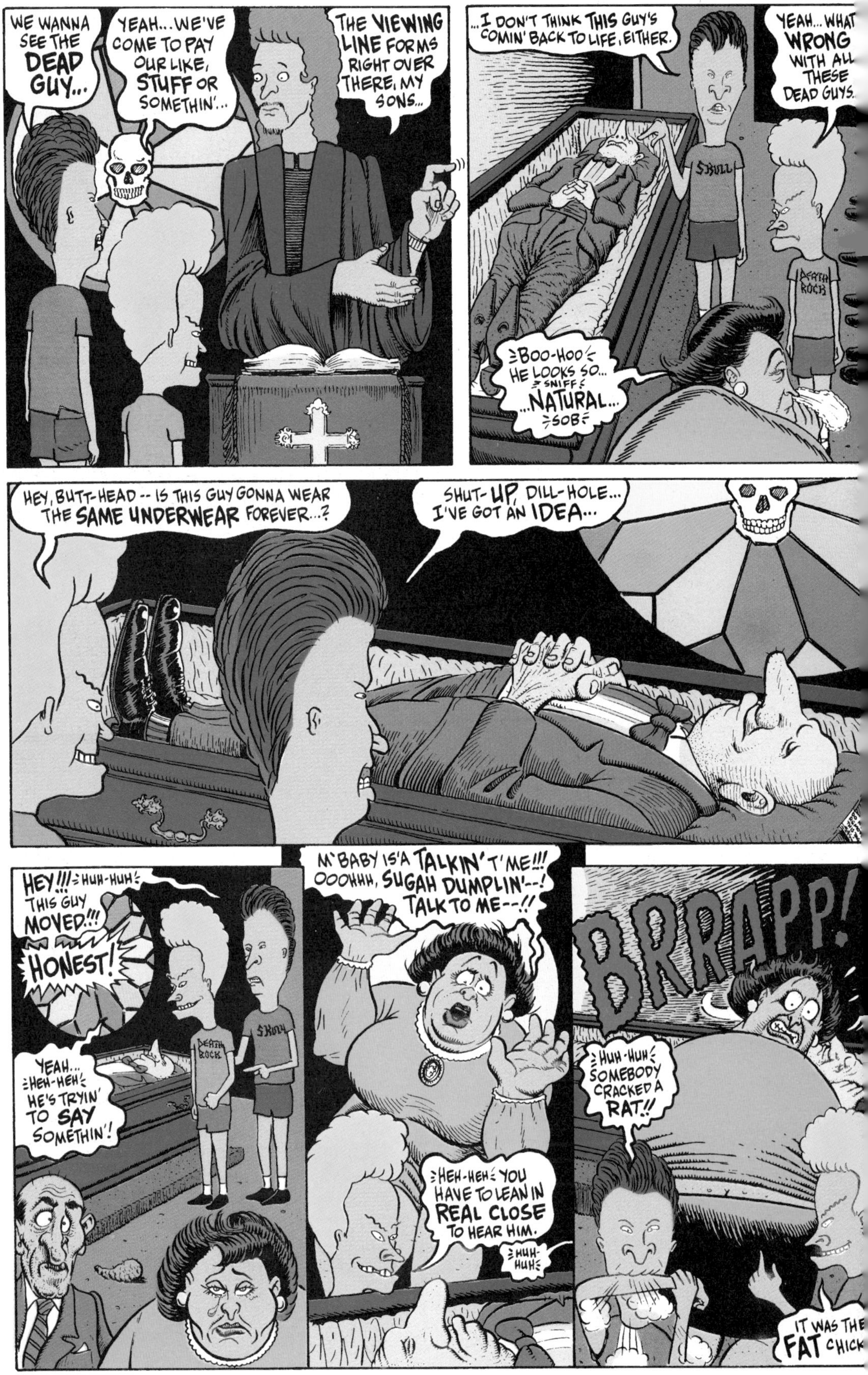
WE WANNA SEE THE DEAD GUY...
YEAH... WE'VE COME TO PAY OUR LIKE, STUFF OR SOMETHIN'...
THE VIEWING LINE FORMS RIGHT OVER THERE, MY SONS...
...I DON'T THINK THIS GUY'S COMIN' BACK TO LIFE, EITHER.
YEAH... WHAT WRONG WITH ALL THESE DEAD GUYS...
SKULL
DEATH ROCK
BOO-HOO HE LOOKS SO... SNIFF ...NATURAL... SOB
HEY, BUTT-HEAD -- IS THIS GUY GONNA WEAR THE SAME UNDERWEAR FOREVER...?
SHUT-UP, DILL-HOLE... I'VE GOT AN IDEA...
HEY!!! HUH-HUH THIS GUY MOVED!!! HONEST!
YEAH... HEH-HEH HE'S TRYIN' TO SAY SOMETHIN'!
DEATH ROCK
SKULL
M'BABY IS'A TALKIN' T'ME!!! OOOHHH, SUGAH DUMPLIN'--! TALK TO ME--!!
HEH-HEH YOU HAVE TO LEAN IN REAL CLOSE TO HEAR HIM.
HUH-HUH
BRRAPP!
HUH-HUH SOMEBODY CRACKED A RAT!!
IT WAS THE FAT CHICK

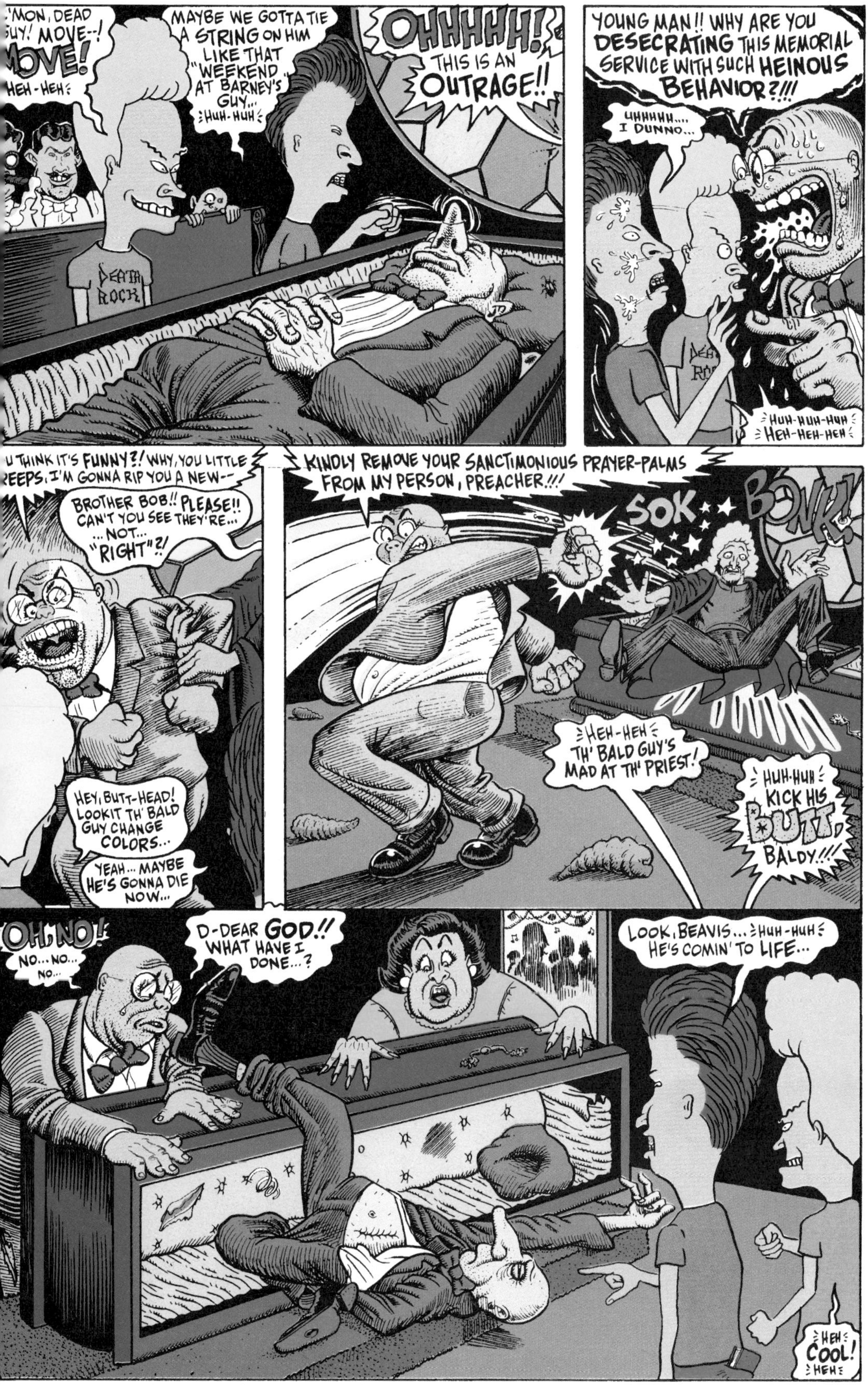
'MON, DEAD GUY! MOVE--! MOVE! HEH-HEH
MAYBE WE GOTTA TIE A STRING ON HIM LIKE THAT "WEEKEND AT BARNEY'S" GUY... HUH-HUH
OHHHHH! THIS IS AN OUTRAGE!!
DEATH ROCK
YOUNG MAN!! WHY ARE YOU DESECRATING THIS MEMORIAL SERVICE WITH SUCH HEINOUS BEHAVIOR?!!!
UHHHHH.... I DUNNO...
HUH-HUH-HUH HEH-HEH-HEH
U THINK IT'S FUNNY?! WHY, YOU LITTLE REEPS. I'M GONNA RIP YOU A NEW--
BROTHER BOB!! PLEASE!! CAN'T YOU SEE THEY'RE... ...NOT... "RIGHT"?!
HEY, BUTT-HEAD! LOOKIT TH' BALD GUY CHANGE COLORS...
YEAH... MAYBE HE'S GONNA DIE NOW...
KINDLY REMOVE YOUR SANCTIMONIOUS PRAYER-PALMS FROM MY PERSON, PREACHER!!!
SOK
BONK!
HEH-HEH TH' BALD GUY'S MAD AT TH' PRIEST!
HUH-HUH KICK HIS BUTT, BALDY!!!
OH, NO! NO... NO... NO...
D-DEAR GOD!! WHAT HAVE I DONE...?
LOOK, BEAVIS... HUH-HUH HE'S COMIN' TO LIFE...
HEH COOL! HEH

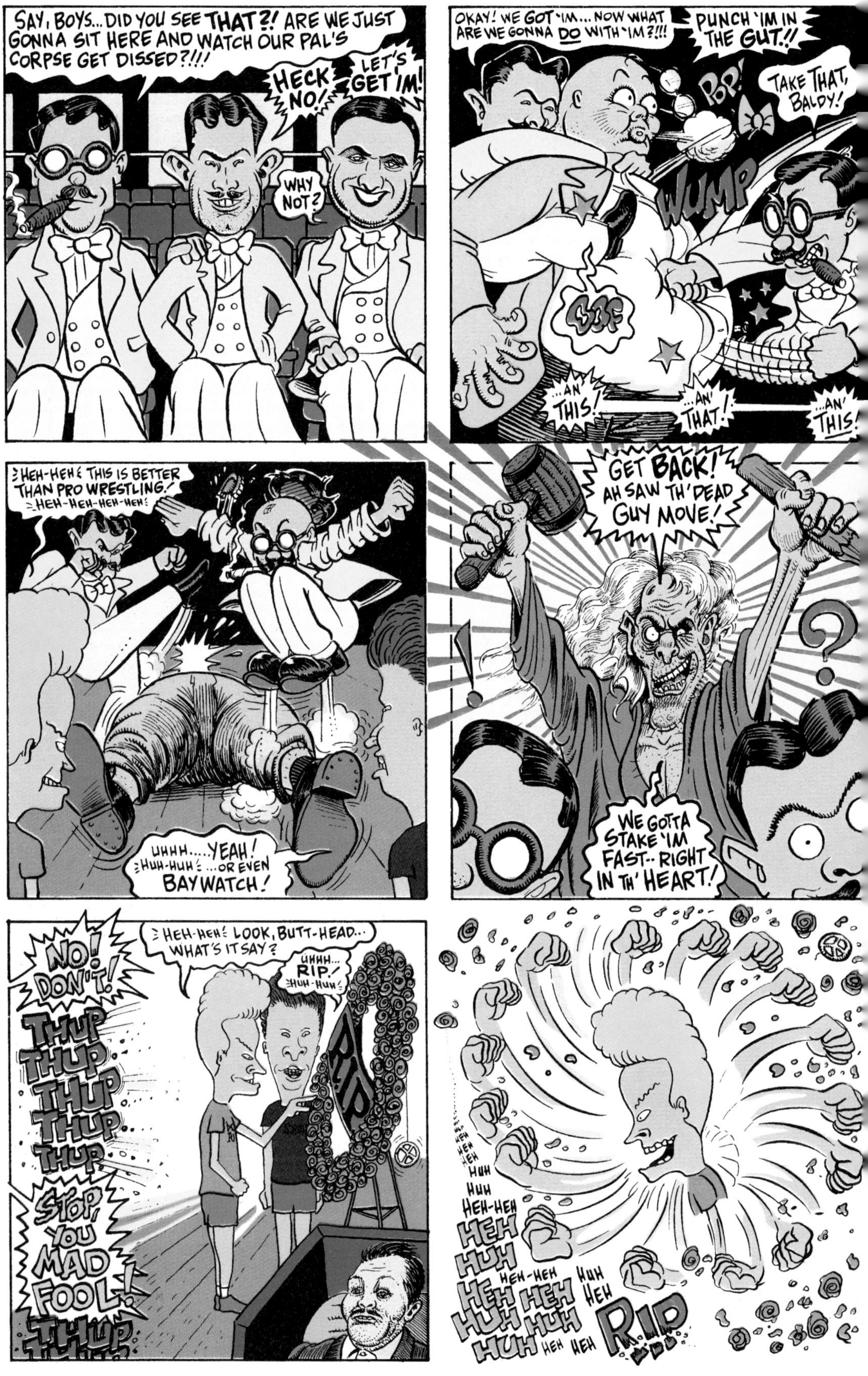
SAY, BOYS... DID YOU SEE THAT?! ARE WE JUST GONNA SIT HERE AND WATCH OUR PAL'S CORPSE GET DISSED?!!!
HECK NO!
LET'S GET 'IM!
WHY NOT?
OKAY! WE GOT 'IM... NOW WHAT ARE WE GONNA DO WITH 'IM?!!!
PUNCH 'IM IN THE GUT!!
POP!
TAKE THAT, BALDY!
WUMP
OOF
...AN' THIS!
...AN' THAT!
...AN' THIS!
HEH-HEH THIS IS BETTER THAN PRO WRESTLING! HEH-HEH-HEH-HEH
UHHH.....YEAH! HUH-HUH ...OR EVEN BAYWATCH!
GET BACK! AH SAW TH' DEAD GUY MOVE!
WE GOTTA STAKE 'IM FAST.. RIGHT IN TH' HEART!
NO! DON'T!
THUP THUP THUP THUP THUP
STOP, YOU MAD FOOL!
THUP
HEH-HEH LOOK, BUTT-HEAD... WHAT'S IT SAY?
UHHH... RIP! HUH-HUH
RIP
HEH HEH HEH HUH HUH HEH-HEH HEH HUH HEH HUH HUH
HEH-HEH HEH HUH HUH HEH HEH HEH
HUH HEH
RIP

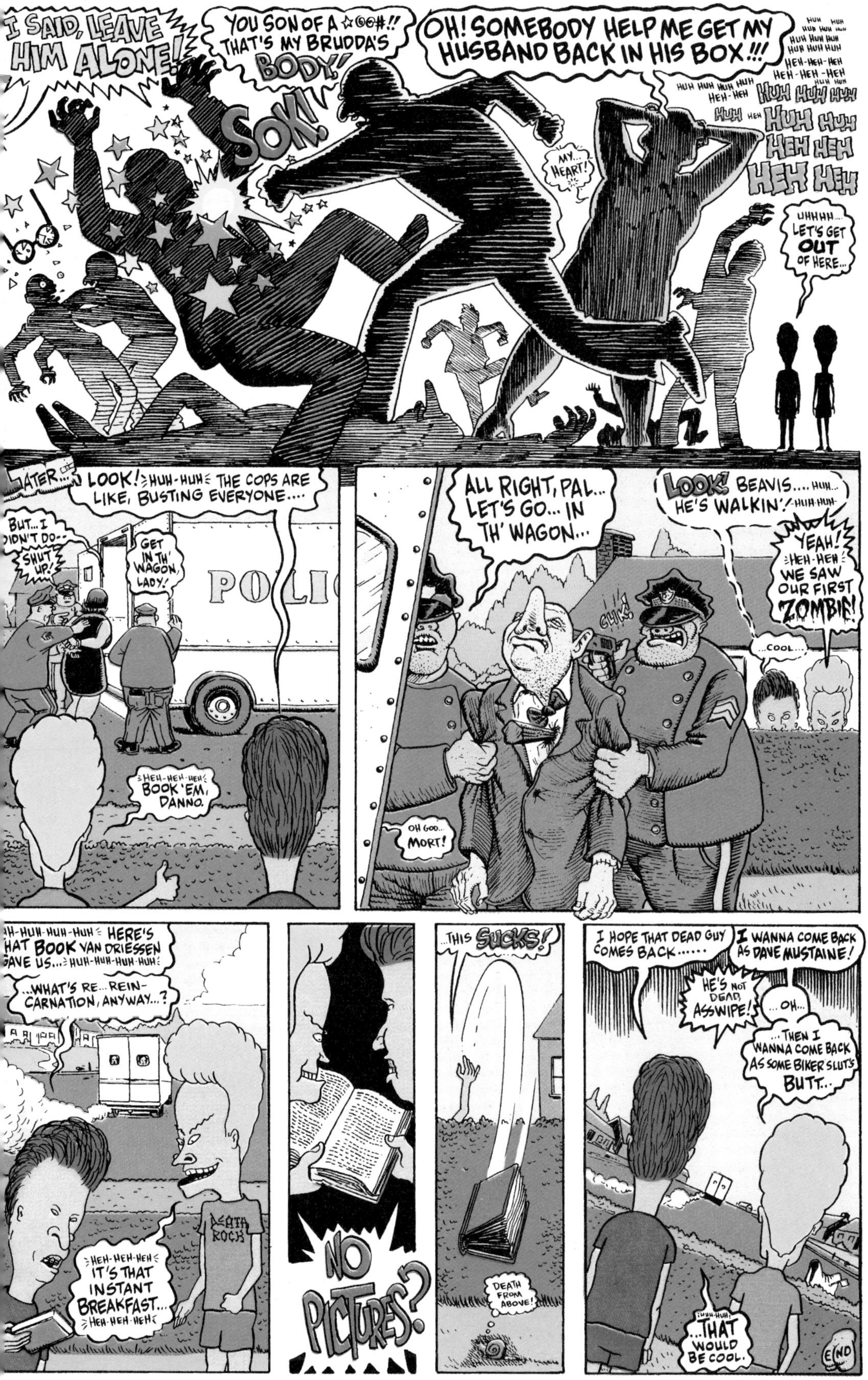
I SAID, LEAVE HIM ALONE!
YOU SON OF A ☆@@#!! THAT'S MY BRUDDA'S BODY!
SOK!
OH! SOMEBODY HELP ME GET MY HUSBAND BACK IN HIS BOX!!!
MY... HEART!
HUH HUH HUH HUH HUH HUH HUH HUH HUH HUH HUH HEH-HEH-HEH HEH-HEH-HEH
HUH HUH HUH HUH HEH-HEH HUH HUH HUH
HUH HEH HUH HUH HEH HEH HEH HEH
UHHHH... LET'S GET OUT OF HERE...
LATER...
LOOK! HUH-HUH THE COPS ARE LIKE, BUSTING EVERYONE....
BUT... I DIDN'T DO...
SHUT UP!
GET IN TH' WAGON, LADY!
POLIC
HEH-HEH-HEH BOOK 'EM, DANNO.
ALL RIGHT, PAL... LET'S GO... IN TH' WAGON...
CLIK!
OH GOD... MORT!
LOOK! BEAVIS.... HUH... HE'S WALKIN'! HUH-HUH
YEAH! HEH-HEH WE SAW OUR FIRST ZOMBIE!
...COOL....
HUH-HUH-HUH-HUH HERE'S THAT BOOK VAN DRIESSEN GAVE US... HUH-HUH-HUH-HUH
...WHAT'S RE... REIN-CARNATION, ANYWAY...?
DEATH ROCK
HEH-HEH-HEH IT'S THAT INSTANT BREAKFAST... HEH-HEH-HEH
NO PICTURES?
...THIS SUCKS!
DEATH FROM ABOVE!
I HOPE THAT DEAD GUY COMES BACK......
I WANNA COME BACK AS DAVE MUSTAINE!
HE'S NOT DEAD, ASSWIPE!
...OH...
...THEN I WANNA COME BACK AS SOME BIKER SLUT'S BUTT...
HUH-HUH ...THAT WOULD BE COOL.
END

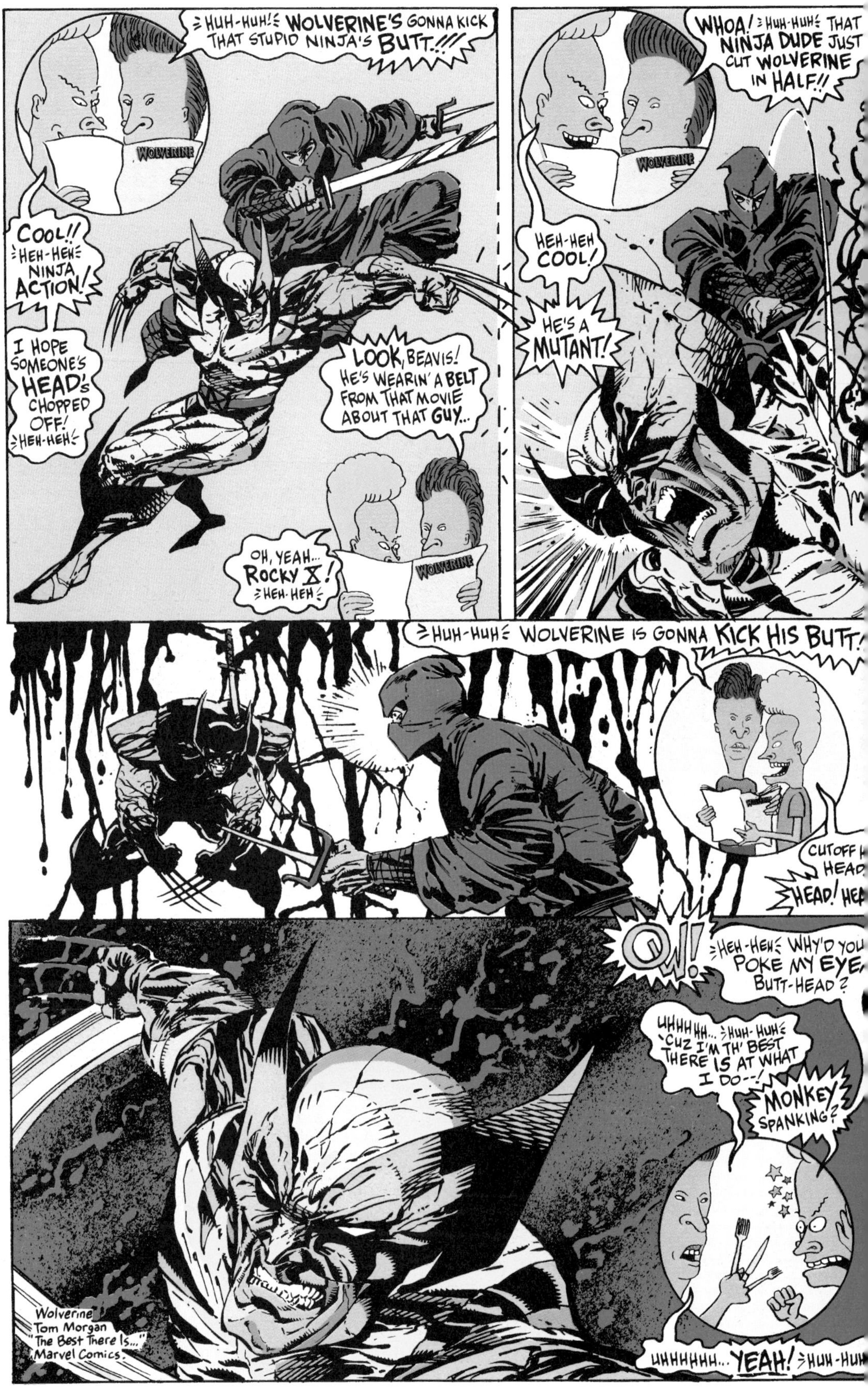

HUH-HUH! WOLVERINE'S GONNA KICK THAT STUPID NINJA'S BUTT!!!
COOL!! HEH-HEH NINJA ACTION!
I HOPE SOMEONE'S HEAD'S CHOPPED OFF! HEH-HEH
LOOK, BEAVIS! HE'S WEARIN' A BELT FROM THAT MOVIE ABOUT THAT GUY...
OH, YEAH... ROCKY X! HEH-HEH
WOLVERINE
WHOA! HUH-HUH THAT NINJA DUDE JUST CUT WOLVERINE IN HALF!!
HEH-HEH COOL!
HE'S A MUTANT!
HUH-HUH WOLVERINE IS GONNA KICK HIS BUTT
CUTOFF H HEAD HEAD! HE
OW!
HEH-HEH WHY'D YOU POKE MY EYE, BUTT-HEAD?
UHHHHH... HUH-HUH 'CUZ I'M TH' BEST THERE IS AT WHAT I DO--!
MONKEY SPANKING?
UHHHHHH... YEAH! HUH-HUH
Wolverine Tom Morgan "The Best There Is..." Marvel Comics.

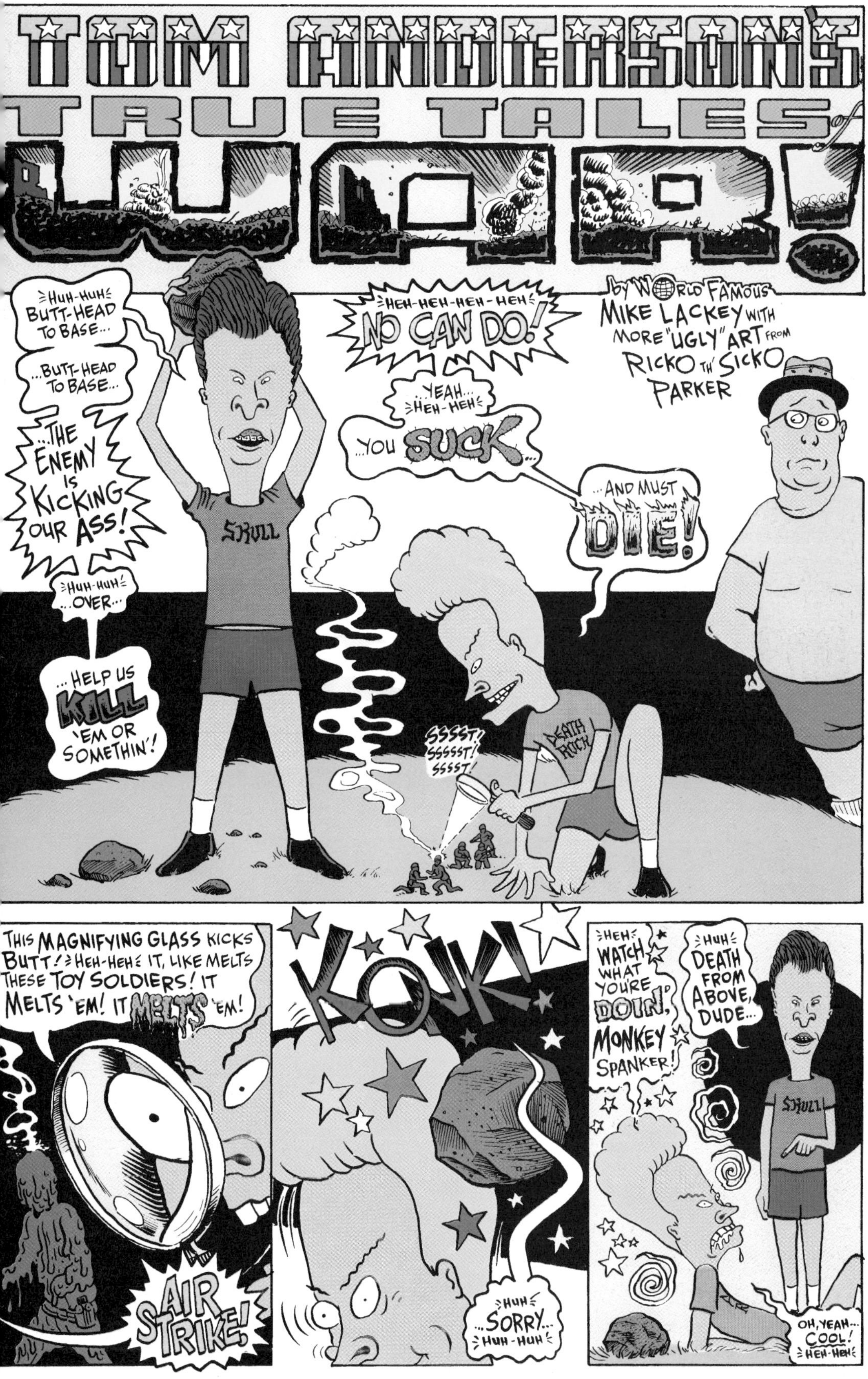
TOM ANDERSON'S TRUE TALES of WAR!
by WORLD FAMOUS MIKE LACKEY WITH MORE "UGLY" ART FROM RICKO TH' SICKO PARKER
HUH-HUH BUTT-HEAD TO BASE...
...BUTT-HEAD TO BASE...
...THE ENEMY IS KICKING OUR ASS!
HUH-HUH ...OVER...
...HELP US KILL 'EM OR SOMETHIN'!
HEH-HEH-HEH-HEH NO CAN DO!
...YEAH... HEH-HEH
...YOU SUCK...
...AND MUST DIE!
SKULL
DEATH ROCK
SSSST! SSSSST! SSSST!
THIS MAGNIFYING GLASS KICKS BUTT! HEH-HEH IT, LIKE MELTS THESE TOY SOLDIERS! IT MELTS 'EM! IT MELTS 'EM!
AIR STRIKE!
KONK!
HUH ...SORRY... HUH-HUH
HEH WATCH WHAT YOU'RE DOIN', MONKEY SPANKER!
HUH DEATH FROM ABOVE, DUDE...
SKULL
OH, YEAH... COOL! HEH-HEH

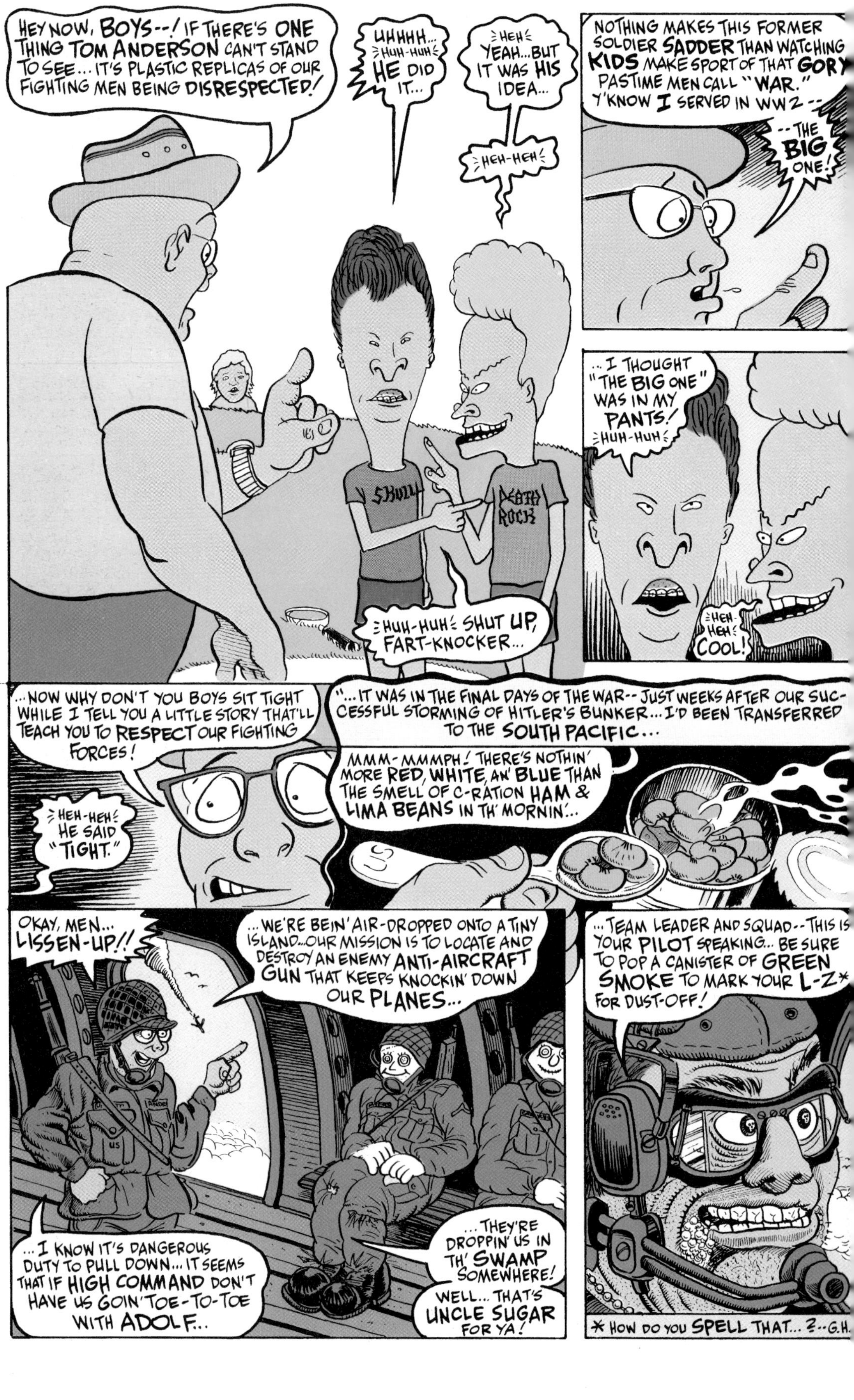
HEY NOW, BOYS--! IF THERE'S ONE THING TOM ANDERSON CAN'T STAND TO SEE... IT'S PLASTIC REPLICAS OF OUR FIGHTING MEN BEING DISRESPECTED!
UHHHH... HUH-HUH HE DID IT...
HEH YEAH... BUT IT WAS HIS IDEA...
HEH-HEH
HUH-HUH SHUT UP, FART-KNOCKER...
SKULL
DEATH ROCK
NOTHING MAKES THIS FORMER SOLDIER SADDER THAN WATCHING KIDS MAKE SPORT OF THAT GORY PASTIME MEN CALL "WAR." Y'KNOW I SERVED IN WW2--
--THE BIG ONE!
...I THOUGHT "THE BIG ONE" WAS IN MY PANTS! HUH-HUH
HEH-HEH COOL!
...NOW WHY DON'T YOU BOYS SIT TIGHT WHILE I TELL YOU A LITTLE STORY THAT'LL TEACH YOU TO RESPECT OUR FIGHTING FORCES!
HEH-HEH HE SAID "TIGHT."
"...IT WAS IN THE FINAL DAYS OF THE WAR-- JUST WEEKS AFTER OUR SUCCESSFUL STORMING OF HITLER'S BUNKER... I'D BEEN TRANSFERRED TO THE SOUTH PACIFIC...
MMM-MMMPH! THERE'S NOTHIN' MORE RED, WHITE, AN' BLUE THAN THE SMELL OF C-RATION HAM & LIMA BEANS IN TH' MORNIN'...
OKAY, MEN... LISSEN-UP!!
...WE'RE BEIN' AIR-DROPPED ONTO A TINY ISLAND...OUR MISSION IS TO LOCATE AND DESTROY AN ENEMY ANTI-AIRCRAFT GUN THAT KEEPS KNOCKIN' DOWN OUR PLANES...
...I KNOW IT'S DANGEROUS DUTY TO PULL DOWN... IT SEEMS THAT IF HIGH COMMAND DON'T HAVE US GOIN' TOE-TO-TOE WITH ADOLF...
...THEY'RE DROPPIN' US IN TH' SWAMP SOMEWHERE!
WELL... THAT'S UNCLE SUGAR FOR YA!
...TEAM LEADER AND SQUAD-- THIS IS YOUR PILOT SPEAKING... BE SURE TO POP A CANISTER OF GREEN SMOKE TO MARK YOUR L-Z* FOR DUST-OFF!
* HOW DO YOU SPELL THAT...?--G.H.

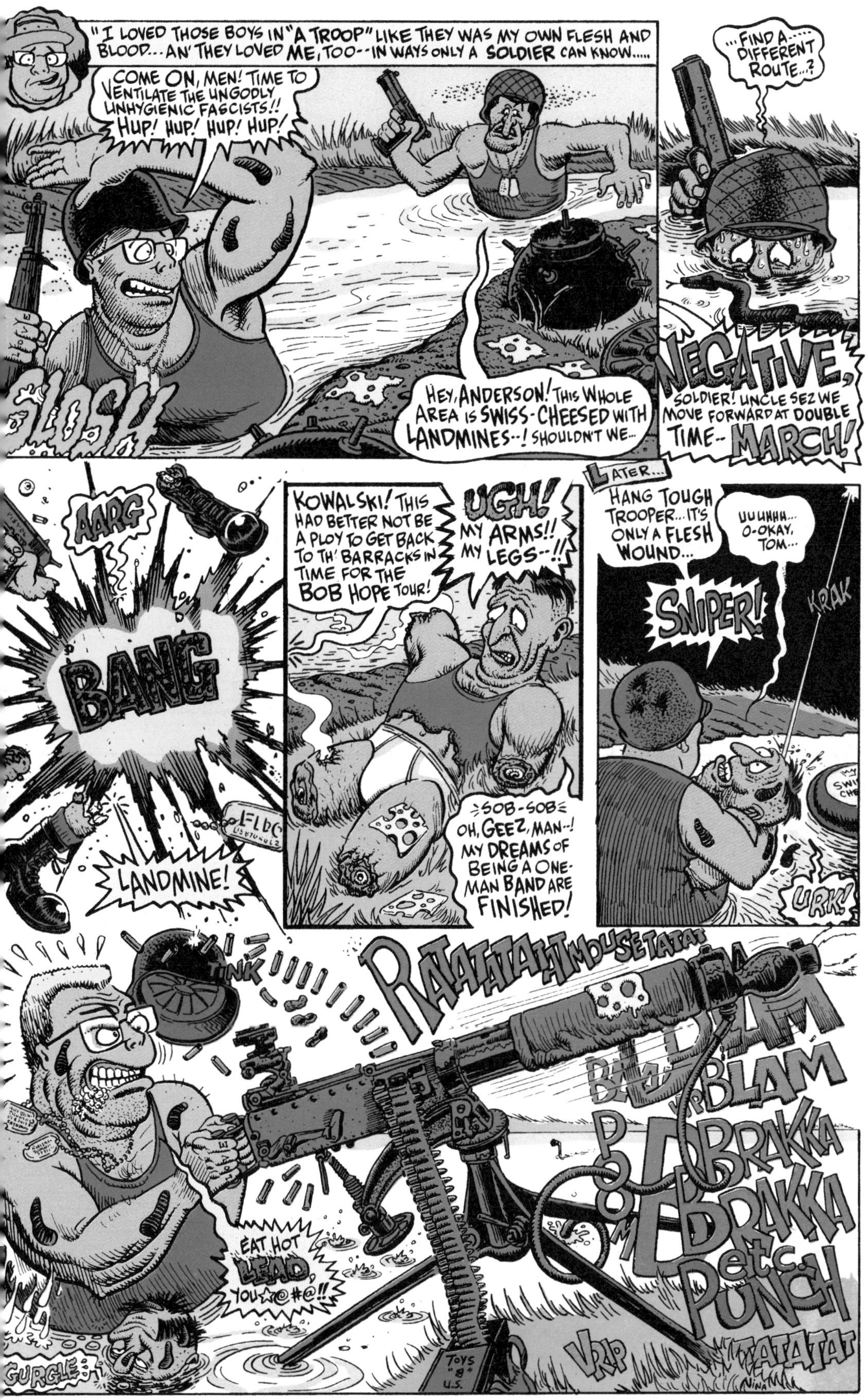

"I LOVED THOSE BOYS IN "A TROOP" LIKE THEY WAS MY OWN FLESH AND BLOOD... AN' THEY LOVED ME, TOO--IN WAYS ONLY A SOLDIER CAN KNOW.....
COME ON, MEN! TIME TO VENTILATE THE UNGODLY UNHYGIENIC FASCISTS!! HUP! HUP! HUP! HUP!
SLOSH
HEY, ANDERSON! THIS WHOLE AREA IS SWISS-CHEESED WITH LANDMINES--! SHOULDN'T WE...
...FIND A DIFFERENT ROUTE...?
NEGATIVE, SOLDIER! UNCLE SEZ WE MOVE FORWARD AT DOUBLE TIME-- MARCH!
AARG
BANG
LANDMINE!
KOWALSKI! THIS HAD BETTER NOT BE A PLOY TO GET BACK TO TH' BARRACKS IN TIME FOR THE BOB HOPE TOUR!
UGH! MY ARMS!! MY LEGS--!!
-SOB-SOB-
OH, GEEZ, MAN--! MY DREAMS OF BEING A ONE-MAN BAND ARE FINISHED!
LATER...
HANG TOUGH TROOPER... IT'S ONLY A FLESH WOUND...
UUUHHH... O-OKAY, TOM...
SNIPER!
KRAK
URK!
TINK
RATATATATATMOUSETATAT
BLAM
BLAM
BRAKKA
BRAKKA
BOOM
etc.
PUNCH
EAT HOT LEAD, YOU☆@#@!!
GURGLE
VRIP
TATATAT

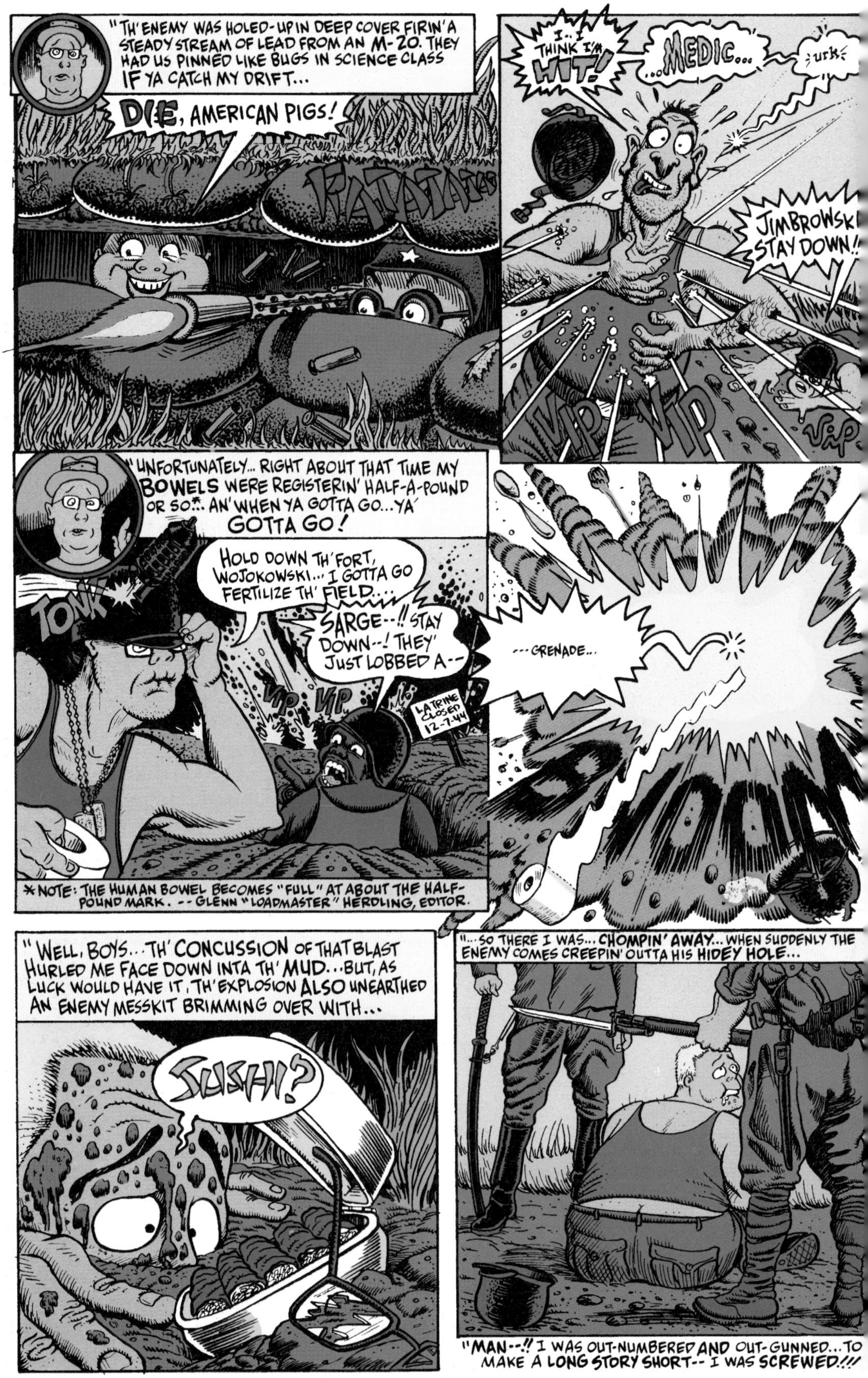
"TH' ENEMY WAS HOLED-UP IN DEEP COVER FIRIN' A STEADY STREAM OF LEAD FROM AN M-20. THEY HAD US PINNED LIKE BUGS IN SCIENCE CLASS IF YA CATCH MY DRIFT...
DIE, AMERICAN PIGS!
I.. I THINK I'M HIT!
...MEDIC...
urk
JIMBROWSKI STAY DOWN!
VIP VIP
VIP
"UNFORTUNATELY... RIGHT ABOUT THAT TIME MY BOWELS WERE REGISTERIN' HALF-A-POUND OR SO*... AN' WHEN YA GOTTA GO... YA' GOTTA GO!
TONK
HOLD DOWN TH' FORT, WOJOKOWSKI... I GOTTA GO FERTILIZE TH' FIELD...
SARGE--!! STAY DOWN--! THEY' JUST LOBBED A--
VIP VIP
LATRINE CLOSED 12-7-44
---GRENADE...
*NOTE: THE HUMAN BOWEL BECOMES "FULL" AT ABOUT THE HALF-POUND MARK. --GLENN "LOADMASTER" HERDLING, EDITOR.
"WELL, BOYS... TH' CONCUSSION OF THAT BLAST HURLED ME FACE DOWN INTA TH' MUD... BUT, AS LUCK WOULD HAVE IT, TH' EXPLOSION ALSO UNEARTHED AN ENEMY MESSKIT BRIMMING OVER WITH...
SUSHI?
"...SO THERE I WAS... CHOMPIN' AWAY... WHEN SUDDENLY THE ENEMY COMES CREEPIN' OUTTA HIS HIDEY HOLE...
"MAN--!! I WAS OUT-NUMBERED AND OUT-GUNNED... TO MAKE A LONG STORY SHORT-- I WAS SCREWED!!!

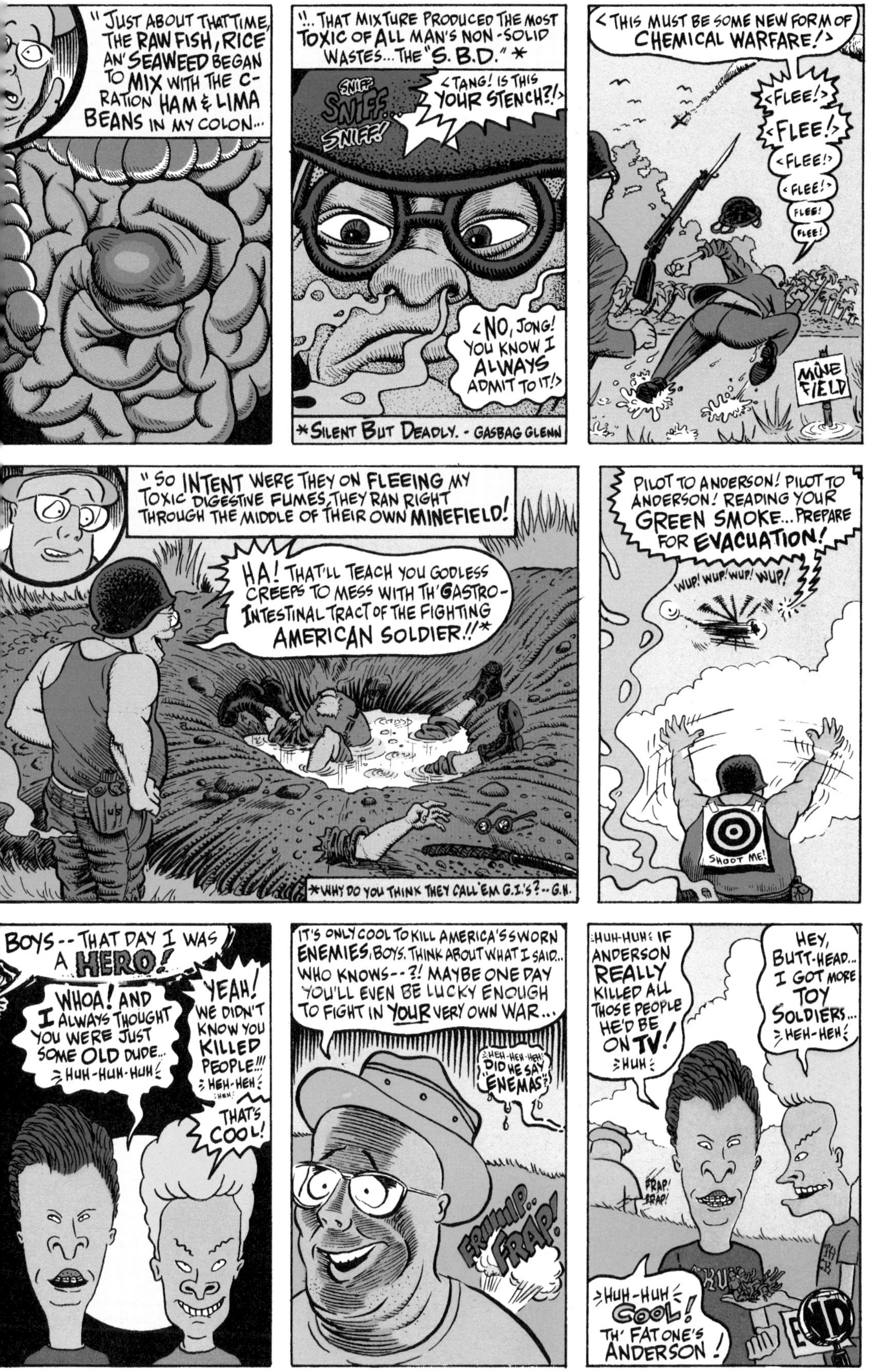
"JUST ABOUT THAT TIME, THE RAW FISH, RICE AN' SEAWEED BEGAN TO MIX WITH THE C-RATION HAM & LIMA BEANS IN MY COLON...
"... THAT MIXTURE PRODUCED THE MOST TOXIC OF ALL MAN'S NON-SOLID WASTES... THE "S.B.D." *
SNIFF SNIFF... SNIFF!
<TANG! IS THIS YOUR STENCH?!>
<NO, JONG! YOU KNOW I ALWAYS ADMIT TO IT!>
* SILENT BUT DEADLY. - GASBAG GLENN
<THIS MUST BE SOME NEW FORM OF CHEMICAL WARFARE!>
<FLEE!> <FLEE!> <FLEE!> <FLEE!> FLEE! FLEE!
MINE FIELD
"SO INTENT WERE THEY ON FLEEING MY TOXIC DIGESTIVE FUMES, THEY RAN RIGHT THROUGH THE MIDDLE OF THEIR OWN MINEFIELD!
HA! THAT'LL TEACH YOU GODLESS CREEPS TO MESS WITH TH' GASTRO-INTESTINAL TRACT OF THE FIGHTING AMERICAN SOLDIER!!*
US
*WHY DO YOU THINK THEY CALL 'EM G.I.'S? -- G.H.
PILOT TO ANDERSON! PILOT TO ANDERSON! READING YOUR GREEN SMOKE... PREPARE FOR EVACUATION!
WUP! WUP! WUP! WUP!
SHOOT ME!
BOYS -- THAT DAY I WAS A HERO!
WHOA! AND I ALWAYS THOUGHT YOU WERE JUST SOME OLD DUDE... HUH-HUH-HUH
YEAH! WE DIDN'T KNOW YOU KILLED PEOPLE!!! HEH-HEH HEH
THAT'S COOL!
IT'S ONLY COOL TO KILL AMERICA'S SWORN ENEMIES, BOYS. THINK ABOUT WHAT I SAID... WHO KNOWS--?! MAYBE ONE DAY YOU'LL EVEN BE LUCKY ENOUGH TO FIGHT IN YOUR VERY OWN WAR...
HEH-HEH-HEH DID HE SAY "ENEMAS"?
FRUMP... FRAP!
HUH-HUH IF ANDERSON REALLY KILLED ALL THOSE PEOPLE HE'D BE ON TV! HUH
HEY, BUTT-HEAD... I GOT MORE TOY SOLDIERS... HEH-HEH
FRAP! FRAP!
HUH-HUH COOL! TH' FAT ONE'S ANDERSON!
END

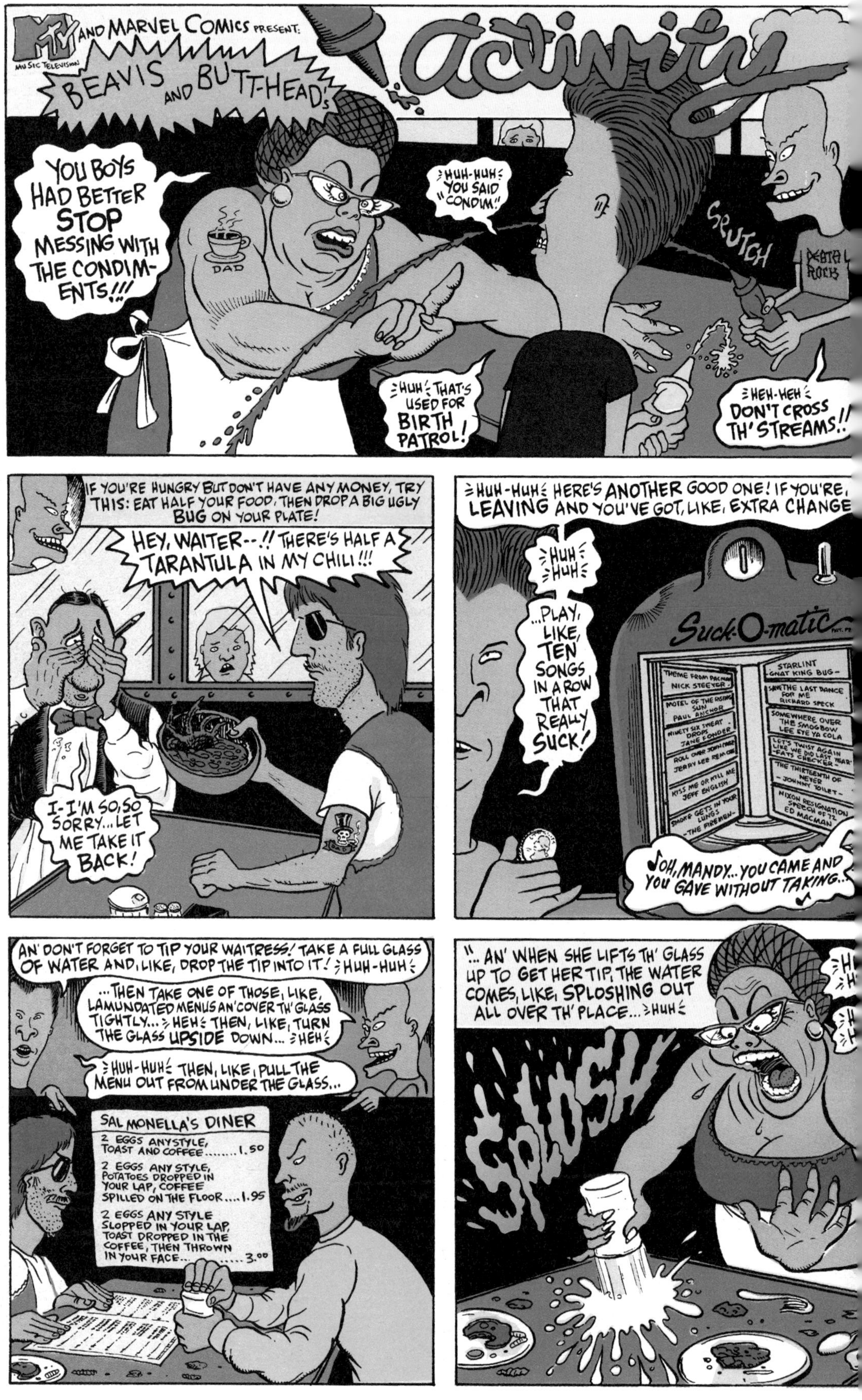
MTV MUSIC TELEVISION AND MARVEL COMICS PRESENT:
BEAVIS AND BUTT-HEAD'S
activity
YOU BOYS HAD BETTER STOP MESSING WITH THE CONDIMENTS!!!
DAD
HUH-HUH YOU SAID "CONDIM."
SQUTCH
DEATH ROCK
HUH THAT'S USED FOR BIRTH PATROL!
HEH-HEH DON'T CROSS TH' STREAMS!!
IF YOU'RE HUNGRY BUT DON'T HAVE ANY MONEY, TRY THIS: EAT HALF YOUR FOOD, THEN DROP A BIG UGLY BUG ON YOUR PLATE!
HEY, WAITER--!! THERE'S HALF A TARANTULA IN MY CHILI!!!
I-I'M SO, SO SORRY... LET ME TAKE IT BACK!
HUH-HUH HERE'S ANOTHER GOOD ONE! IF YOU'RE LEAVING AND YOU'VE GOT, LIKE, EXTRA CHANGE
HUH HUH
...PLAY, LIKE, TEN SONGS IN A ROW THAT REALLY SUCK!
Suck-O-matic
THEME FROM PACMAN NICK STEEVER
MOTEL OF THE RISING SUN PAUL ANCHOR
NINETY SIX SWEAT DROPS JANE FONDER
ROLL OVER JOHN CAGE JERRY LEE REM CAS
KISS ME OR KILL ME JEFF ENGLISH
SMOKE GETS IN YOUR LUNGS -THE FIREMEN-
STARLINT -GNAT KING BUG-
SAVE THE LAST DANCE FOR ME RICHARD SPECK
SOMEWHERE OVER THE SMOGBOW LEE EYE YA COLA
LET'S TWIST AGAIN LIKE WE DID LAST YEAR -FATS CHECKER-
THE THIRTEENTH OF NEVER -JOHNNY TOILET-
NIXON RESIGNATION SPEECH OF 72 ED MACMAN
OH, MANDY... YOU CAME AND YOU GAVE WITHOUT TAKING...
AN' DON'T FORGET TO TIP YOUR WAITRESS! TAKE A FULL GLASS OF WATER AND, LIKE, DROP THE TIP INTO IT! HUH-HUH
...THEN TAKE ONE OF THOSE, LIKE, LAMUNDATED MENUS AN' COVER TH' GLASS TIGHTLY... HEH THEN, LIKE, TURN THE GLASS UPSIDE DOWN... HEH
HUH-HUH THEN, LIKE, PULL THE MENU OUT FROM UNDER THE GLASS...
SAL MONELLA'S DINER
2 EGGS ANYSTYLE, TOAST AND COFFEE........1.50
2 EGGS ANY STYLE, POTATOES DROPPED IN YOUR LAP, COFFEE SPILLED ON THE FLOOR.....1.95
2 EGGS ANY STYLE SLOPPED IN YOUR LAP, TOAST DROPPED IN THE COFFEE, THEN THROWN IN YOUR FACE.........3.00
"... AN' WHEN SHE LIFTS TH' GLASS UP TO GET HER TIP, THE WATER COMES, LIKE, SPLOSHING OUT ALL OVER TH' PLACE... HUH
SPLOSH

"iPages"... DINER PRANKS

BY WORLD FAMOUS MIKE LACKEY AN' HIS PESKY PAL Rick☺ TH' Sick☹

GOIN' TO DINERS TO DO PRANKS IS COOL!! ⋛HEH⋚

UHHHHH...RIGHT!! MY FAVORITE IS "LOOSENING THE CAP ON THE SALT SHAKER!" ⋛HUH-HUH-HUH⋚

WHAT TH' DING DONG?!

UH...YOU MIGHT WANT TO GO A LITTLE LIGHTER ON THE SALT, SIR...

YEAH!! IT'S BAD FOR YOUR HYPER-TENNIS! ⋛HEH-M-HEH⋚

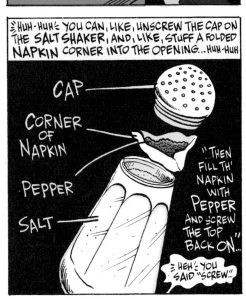

⋛HUH-HUH⋚ YOU CAN, LIKE, UNSCREW THE CAP ON THE SALT SHAKER, AND, LIKE, STUFF A FOLDED NAPKIN CORNER INTO THE OPENING...HUH-HUH

CAP

CORNER OF NAPKIN

PEPPER

SALT

"THEN FILL TH' NAPKIN WITH PEPPER AND SCREW THE TOP BACK ON..."

⋛HEH⋚ YOU SAID "SCREW"!!

⋛HUH-HUH⋚ THEN PEPPER COMES OUT OF TH' SALT SHAKER! ⋛HUH-HUH⋚ IT DRIVES 'EM NUTS!!

⋛HEH⋚ YOU SAID "NUTS"!!

BAM

FOR TH' LOVE O' DUCK!

⋛HUH-HUH-HUH⋚ SUCK-KERS!! ⋛HUH-HUH-HUH⋚

DINER PRANKS KICK BUTT!

YEAH! ⋛HEH⋚ PEOPLE WHO WORK IN DINERS ARE STU--

HEY, BOYS...

HEH HEH

⋛HEH-HEH⋚ HEY, BUTT-HEAD.....Y' KNOW TH' MOST IMPORTANT TIP OF ALL...?

NO...WHAT?

⋛HEH-HEH⋚ DON'T GET CAUGHT!

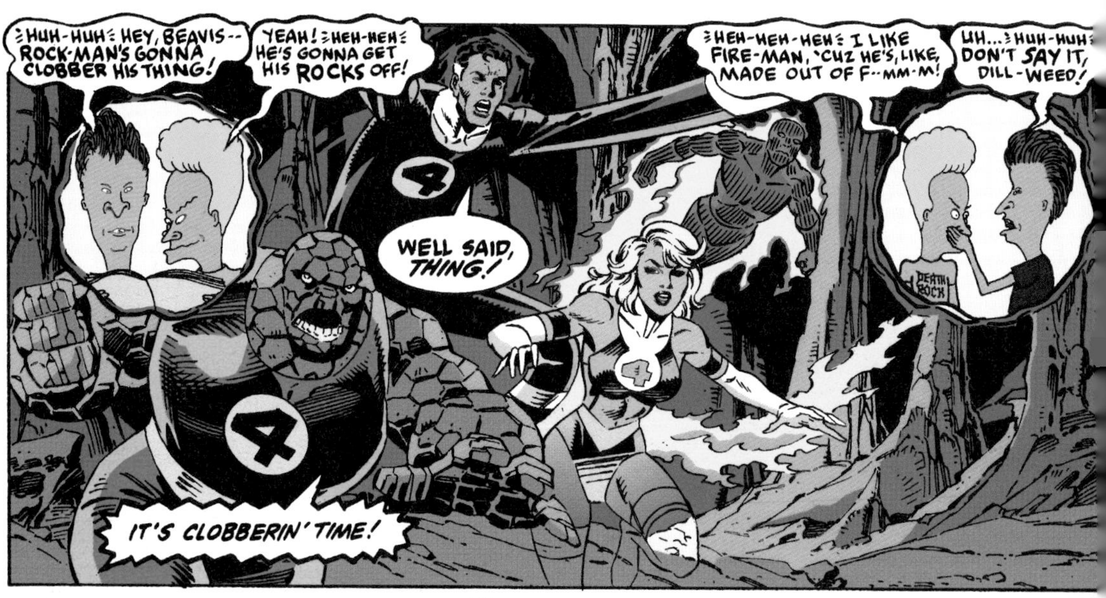

HUH-HUH HEY, BEAVIS-- ROCK-MAN'S GONNA CLOBBER HIS THING!
YEAH! HEH-HEH HE'S GONNA GET HIS ROCKS OFF!
HEH-HEH-HEH I LIKE FIRE-MAN, 'CUZ HE'S, LIKE, MADE OUT OF F--MM-M!
UH... HUH-HUH DON'T SAY IT, DILL-WEED!
DEATH ROCK
WELL SAID, THING!
IT'S CLOBBERIN' TIME!

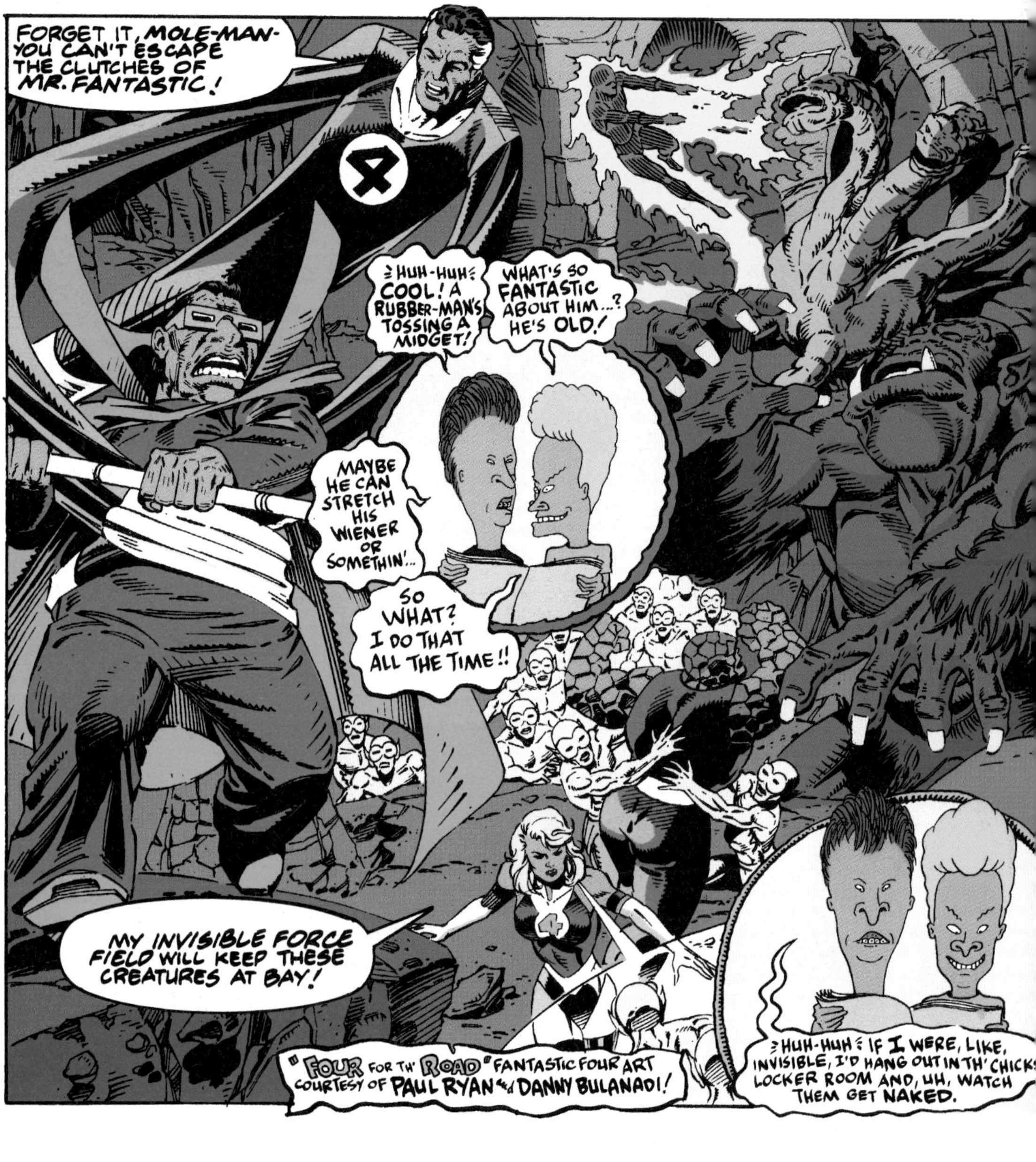

FORGET IT, MOLE-MAN-- YOU CAN'T ESCAPE THE CLUTCHES OF MR. FANTASTIC!
HUH-HUH COOL! A RUBBER-MAN'S TOSSING A MIDGET!
WHAT'S SO FANTASTIC ABOUT HIM...? HE'S OLD!
MAYBE HE CAN STRETCH HIS WIENER OR SOMETHIN'...
SO WHAT? I DO THAT ALL THE TIME!!
MY INVISIBLE FORCE FIELD WILL KEEP THESE CREATURES AT BAY!
"FOUR FOR TH' ROAD" FANTASTIC FOUR ART COURTESY OF PAUL RYAN and DANNY BULANADI!
HUH-HUH IF I WERE, LIKE, INVISIBLE, I'D HANG OUT IN TH' CHICKS' LOCKER ROOM AND, UH, WATCH THEM GET NAKED.

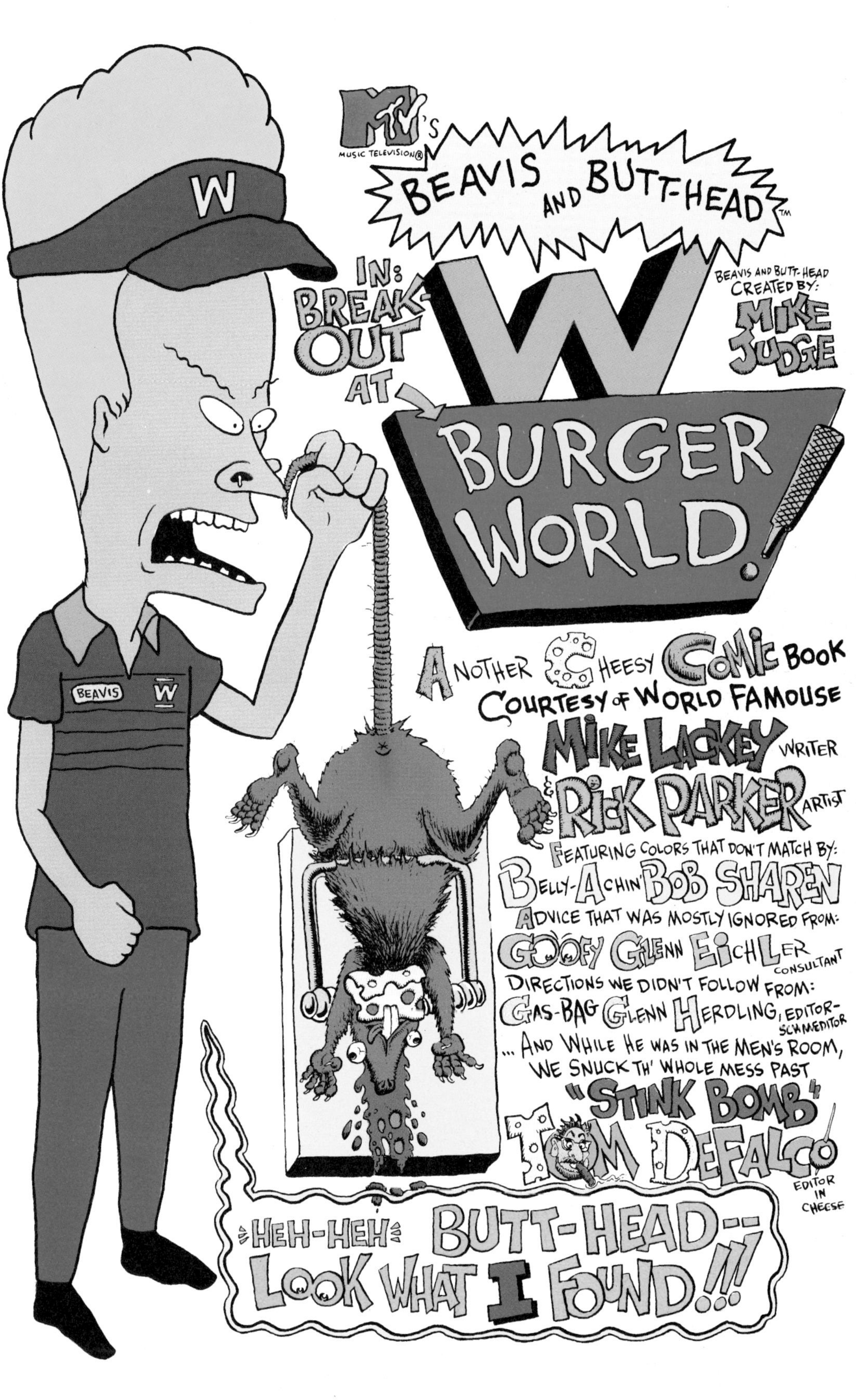

MTV'S
MUSIC TELEVISION®
BEAVIS AND BUTT-HEAD™
IN: BREAK-OUT AT
W
BURGER WORLD!
BEAVIS AND BUTT-HEAD CREATED BY: MIKE JUDGE
BEAVIS
W
ANOTHER CHEESY COMIC BOOK COURTESY OF WORLD FAMOUSE
MIKE LACKEY WRITER
& RICK PARKER ARTIST
FEATURING COLORS THAT DON'T MATCH BY:
BELLY-ACHIN' BOB SHAREN
ADVICE THAT WAS MOSTLY IGNORED FROM:
GOOFY GLENN EICHLER CONSULTANT
DIRECTIONS WE DIDN'T FOLLOW FROM:
GAS-BAG GLENN HERDLING, EDITOR-SCHMEDITOR
... AND WHILE HE WAS IN THE MEN'S ROOM, WE SNUCK TH' WHOLE MESS PAST
"STINK BOMB" TOM DEFALCO
EDITOR IN CHEESE
HEH-HEH BUTT-HEAD-- LOOK WHAT I FOUND!!!

ARTWORK BY ROWDY ROB CAMACHO

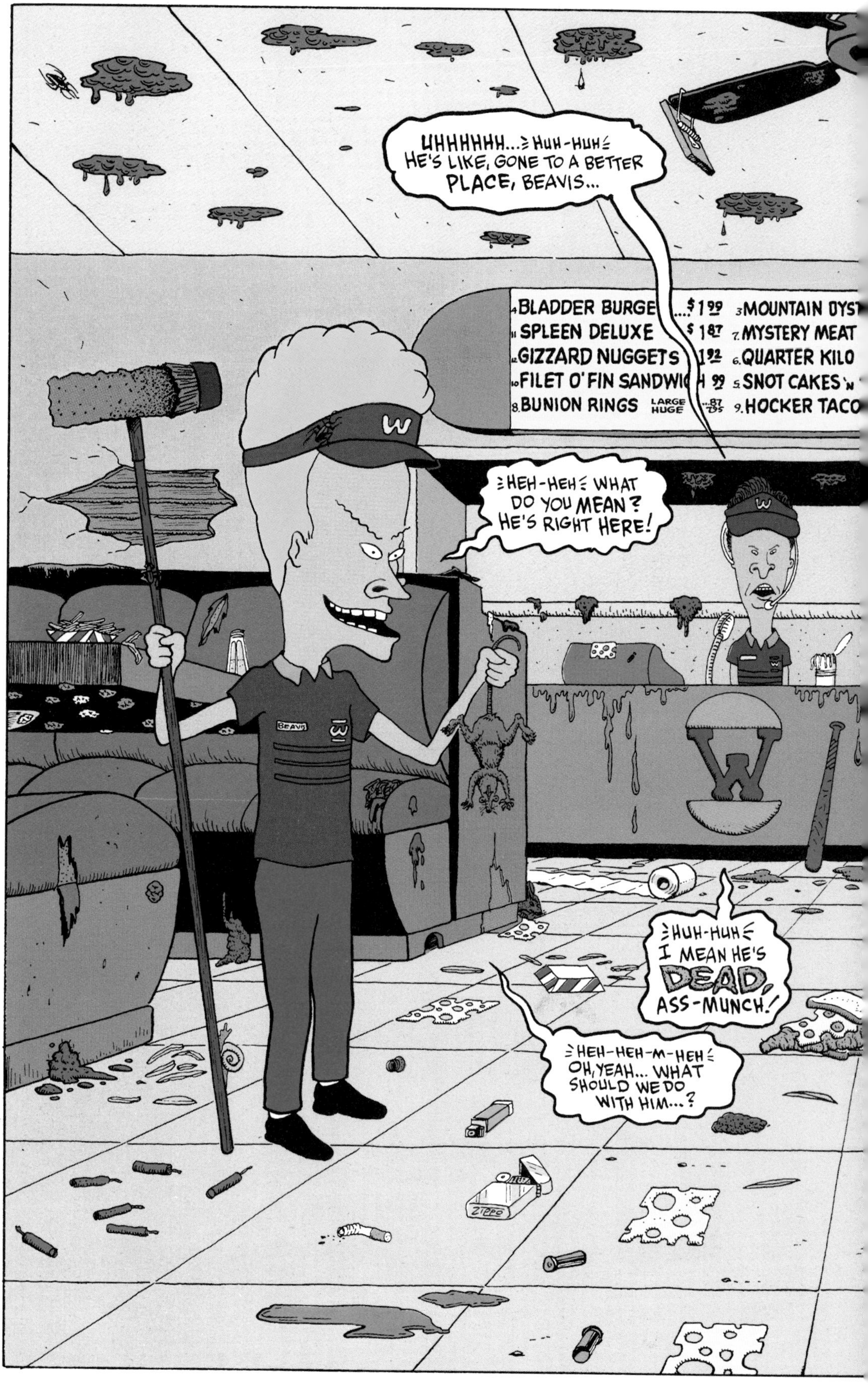
UHHHHHH... HUH-HUH HE'S LIKE, GONE TO A BETTER PLACE, BEAVIS...
HEH-HEH WHAT DO YOU MEAN? HE'S RIGHT HERE!
HUH-HUH I MEAN HE'S DEAD, ASS-MUNCH!
HEH-HEH-M-HEH OH, YEAH... WHAT SHOULD WE DO WITH HIM...?
BLADDER BURGE ...$1.99
SPLEEN DELUXE $1.87
GIZZARD NUGGETS 1.92
FILET O'FIN SANDWIC 99
BUNION RINGS LARGE HUGE
MOUNTAIN OYST
MYSTERY MEAT
QUARTER KILO
SNOT CAKES 'N
HOCKER TACO
BEAVIS
ZIPPO

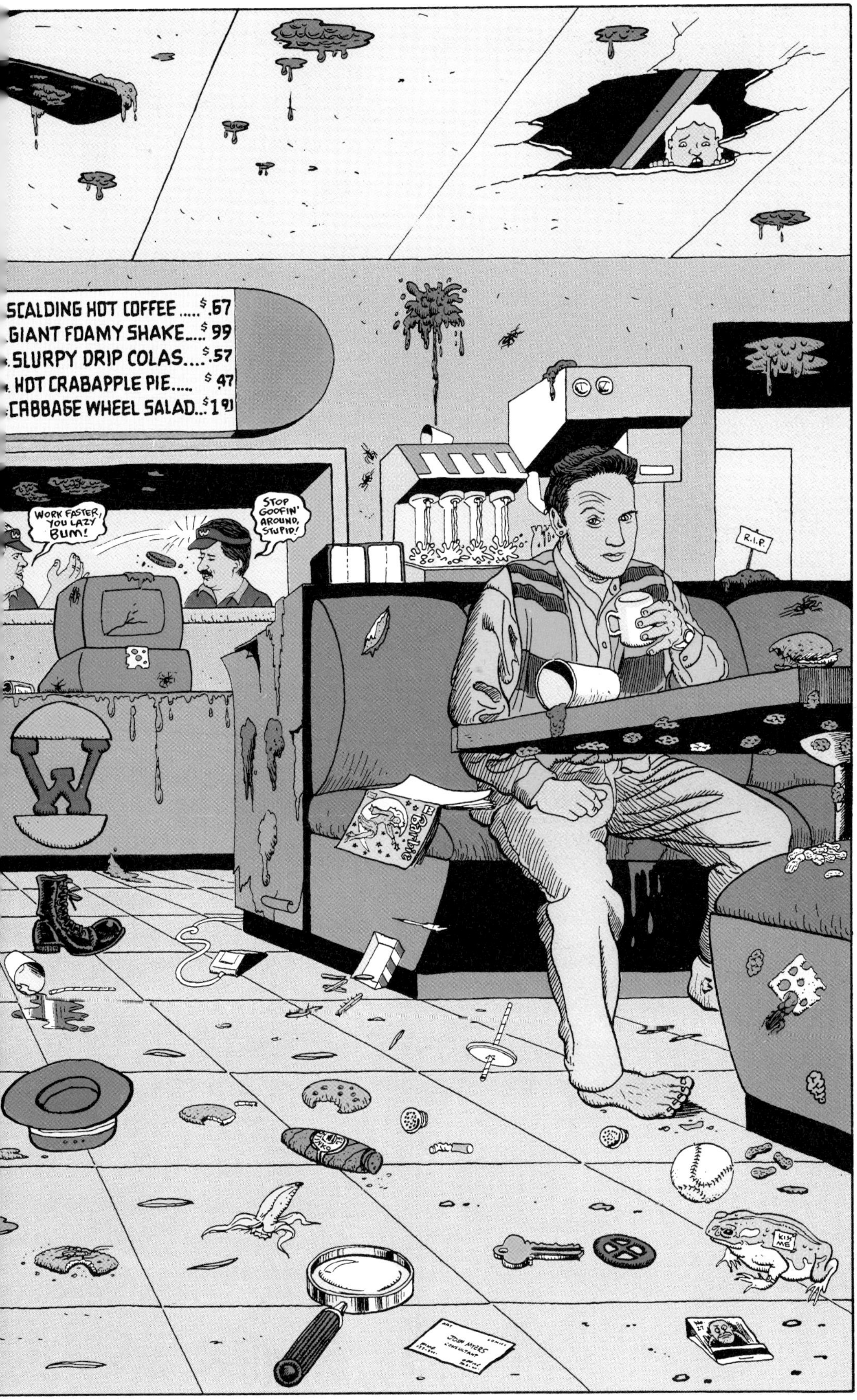
SCALDING HOT COFFEE ..... $.67
GIANT FOAMY SHAKE.... $.99
SLURPY DRIP COLAS.... $.57
HOT CRABAPPLE PIE..... $.47
CABBAGE WHEEL SALAD.. $1.91
WORK FASTER, YOU LAZY BUM!
STOP GOOFIN' AROUND, STUPID!
R.I.P.
Barbie
KISS ME
JOSH MYERS
CONSULTANT

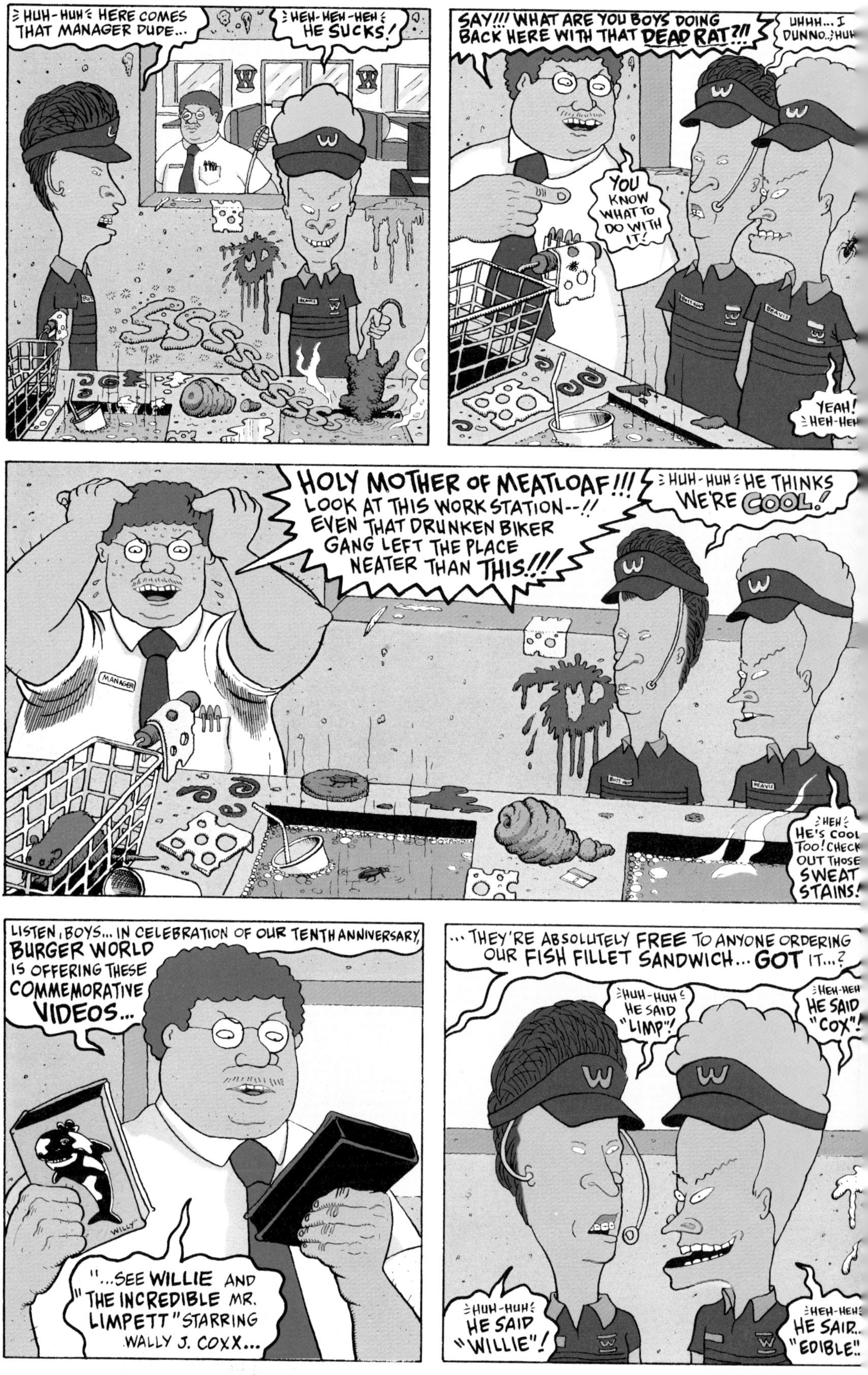
HUH-HUH HERE COMES THAT MANAGER DUDE...
HEH-HEH-HEH HE SUCKS!
SSSSSSSS
SAY!!! WHAT ARE YOU BOYS DOING BACK HERE WITH THAT DEAD RAT?!!
UHHH... I DUNNO..; HUH
YOU KNOW WHAT TO DO WITH IT!
YEAH! HEH-HEH
HOLY MOTHER OF MEATLOAF!!! LOOK AT THIS WORK STATION--!! EVEN THAT DRUNKEN BIKER GANG LEFT THE PLACE NEATER THAN THIS!!!
HUH-HUH HE THINKS WE'RE COOL!
HEH HE'S COOL TOO! CHECK OUT THOSE SWEAT STAINS!
MANAGER
LISTEN, BOYS... IN CELEBRATION OF OUR TENTH ANNIVERSARY, BURGER WORLD IS OFFERING THESE COMMEMORATIVE VIDEOS...
"...SEE WILLIE AND "THE INCREDIBLE MR. LIMPETT" STARRING WALLY J. COXX...
WILLY
...THEY'RE ABSOLUTELY FREE TO ANYONE ORDERING OUR FISH FILLET SANDWICH... GOT IT...?
HUH-HUH HE SAID "LIMP"!
HEH-HEH HE SAID "COX"!
HUH-HUH HE SAID "WILLIE"!
HEH-HEH HE SAID.. "EDIBLE"!

EXCUSE ME... WHY...? ≈HUH-HUH≈ DID YOU, LIKE, CUT THE CHEESE OR SOMETHING?

EXIT

ER... NO... MY GIANT FOAMY HAS A LIVE SLUG IN IT...

THAT'S COOL! LEMME SEE!

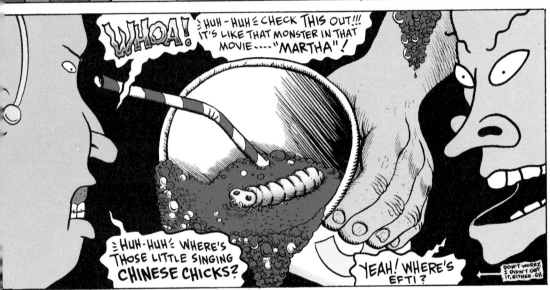

WHOA! ≈HUH-HUH≈ CHECK THIS OUT!!! IT'S LIKE THAT MONSTER IN THAT MOVIE..... "MARTHA"!

≈HUH-HUH≈ WHERE'S THOSE LITTLE SINGING CHINESE CHICKS?

YEAH! WHERE'S EFTI?

DON'T WORRY, I DIDN'T GET IT, EITHER.-GH.

I DEMAND ANOTHER GIANT FOAMY!!

BAM

UHHHHH...≈HUH-HUH≈ YA GOTTA ORDER BY NUMBER...

1 PUCK BURGER
2 GIANT FOAMY SHAR
3 CURLY FRIES
4 GRILLED FISH GILL FIL
5 PENICILLIN TURNOV

FINE!! GIMME A NICE THICK... NUMBER TWO!

HEY, BEAVIS... SHE JUST TOOK A NUMBER TWO...

YEAH! ≈HEH-HEH≈ ON US!

SLURP!

WIDE LOAD

HEH HEH HUH HUH HEH HEH

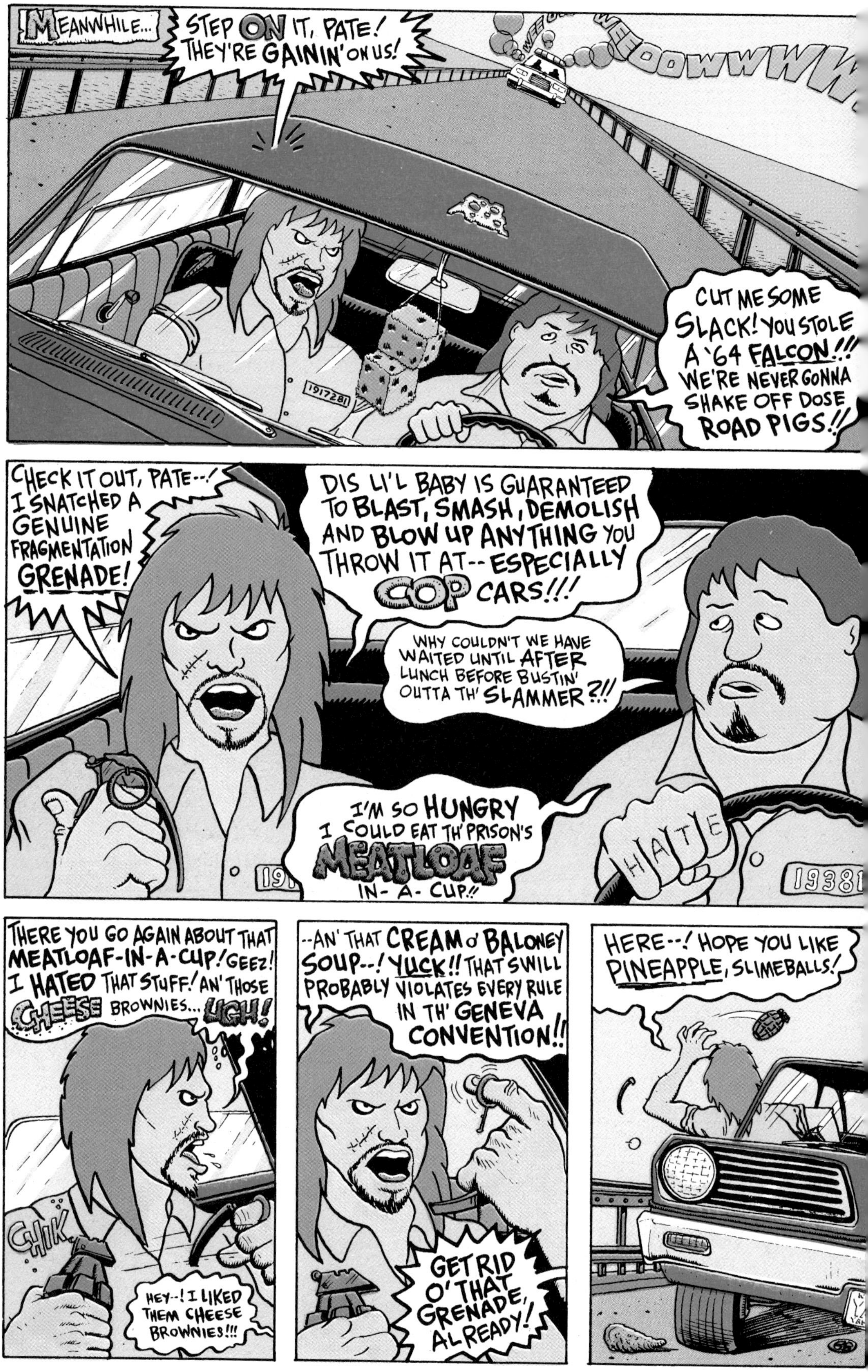
MEANWHILE...
STEP ON IT, PATE! THEY'RE GAININ' ON US!
WEEOOWWWWWW
1917281
CUT ME SOME SLACK! YOU STOLE A '64 FALCON!!! WE'RE NEVER GONNA SHAKE OFF DOSE ROAD PIGS!!!
CHECK IT OUT, PATE--! I SNATCHED A GENUINE FRAGMENTATION GRENADE!
DIS LI'L BABY IS GUARANTEED TO BLAST, SMASH, DEMOLISH AND BLOW UP ANYTHING YOU THROW IT AT--ESPECIALLY COP CARS!!!
WHY COULDN'T WE HAVE WAITED UNTIL AFTER LUNCH BEFORE BUSTIN' OUTTA TH' SLAMMER?!!
I'M SO HUNGRY I COULD EAT TH' PRISON'S MEATLOAF IN-A-CUP!!
HATE
THERE YOU GO AGAIN ABOUT THAT MEATLOAF-IN-A-CUP! GEEZ! I HATED THAT STUFF! AN' THOSE CHEESE BROWNIES... UGH!
CHIK
HEY--! I LIKED THEM CHEESE BROWNIES!!!
--AN' THAT CREAM o' BALONEY SOUP--! YUCK!! THAT SWILL PROBABLY VIOLATES EVERY RULE IN TH' GENEVA CONVENTION!!
GET RID O' THAT GRENADE, ALREADY!
HERE--! HOPE YOU LIKE PINEAPPLE, SLIMEBALLS!

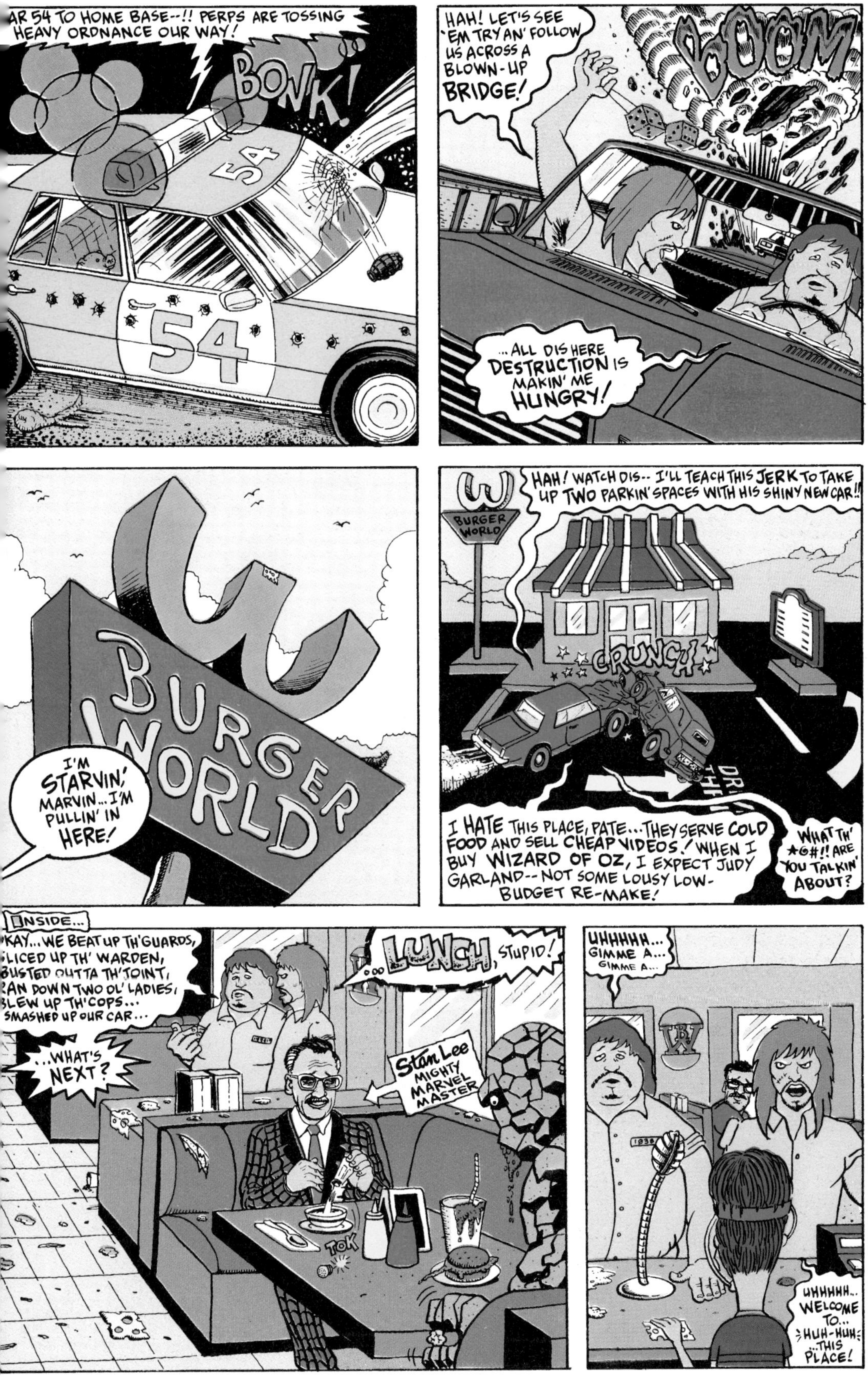

AR 54 TO HOME BASE--!! PERPS ARE TOSSING HEAVY ORDNANCE OUR WAY!
BONK!
54
54
HAH! LET'S SEE 'EM TRY AN' FOLLOW US ACROSS A BLOWN-UP BRIDGE!
BOOM
...ALL DIS HERE DESTRUCTION IS MAKIN' ME HUNGRY!
BURGER WORLD
I'M STARVIN', MARVIN... I'M PULLIN' IN HERE!
HAH! WATCH DIS-- I'LL TEACH THIS JERK TO TAKE UP TWO PARKIN' SPACES WITH HIS SHINY NEW CAR!!
BURGER WORLD
CRUNCH
I HATE THIS PLACE, PATE... THEY SERVE COLD FOOD AND SELL CHEAP VIDEOS! WHEN I BUY WIZARD OF OZ, I EXPECT JUDY GARLAND-- NOT SOME LOUSY LOW-BUDGET RE-MAKE!
WHAT TH' *@#!! ARE YOU TALKIN' ABOUT?
INSIDE...
KAY... WE BEAT UP TH' GUARDS, SLICED UP TH' WARDEN, BUSTED OUTTA TH' JOINT, RAN DOWN TWO OL' LADIES, BLEW UP TH' COPS... SMASHED UP OUR CAR...
...WHAT'S NEXT?
LUNCH, STUPID!
Stan Lee MIGHTY MARVEL MASTER
TOK
UHHHHH... GIMME A... GIMME A...
UHHHHH.. WELCOME TO... HUH-HUH ...THIS PLACE!

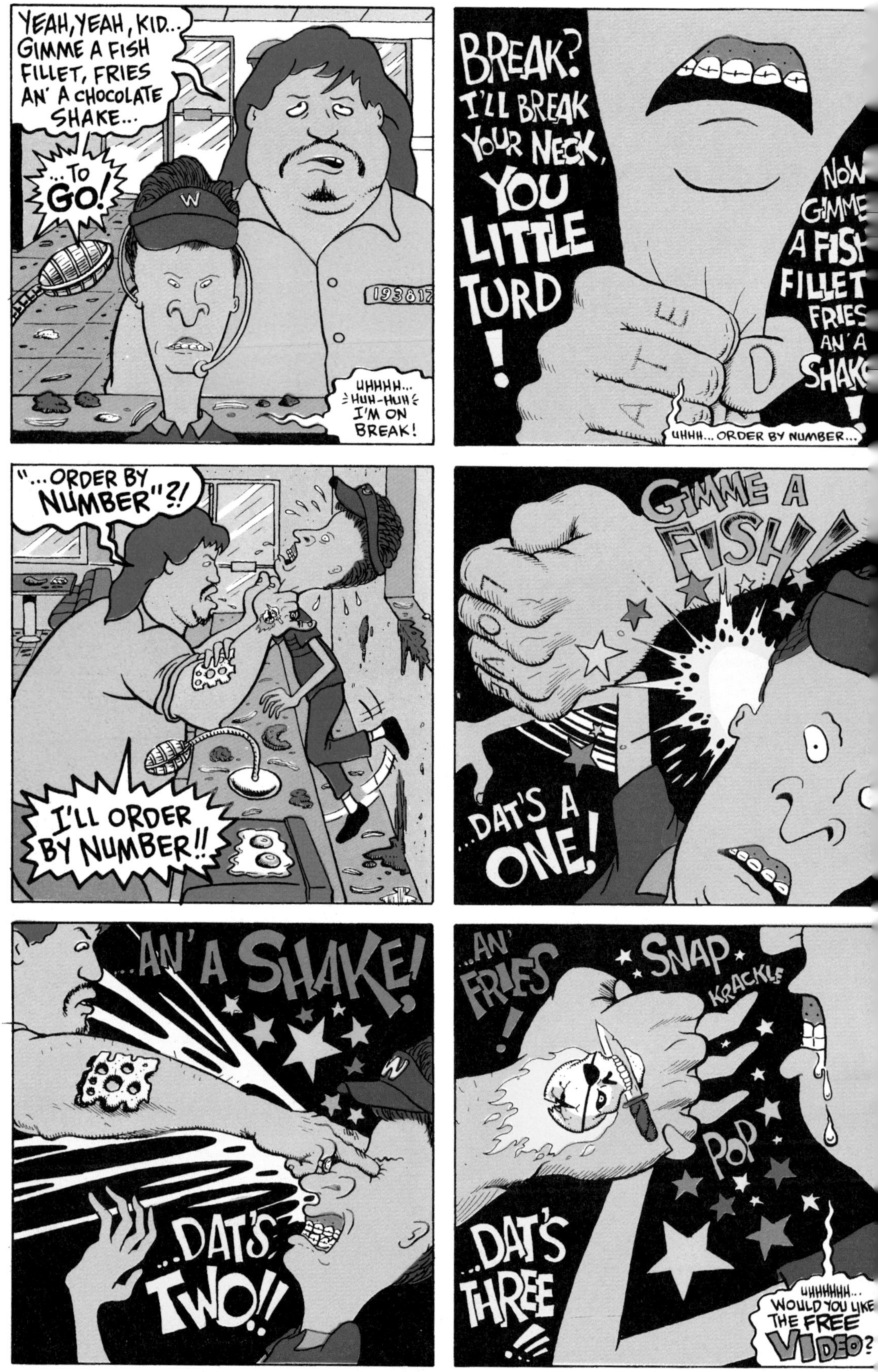
YEAH, YEAH, KID... GIMME A FISH FILLET, FRIES AN' A CHOCOLATE SHAKE...
...TO GO!
UHHHH... HUH-HUH I'M ON BREAK!
BREAK? I'LL BREAK YOUR NECK, YOU LITTLE TURD!
NOW GIMME A FISH FILLET FRIES AN' A SHAKE!
UHHH... ORDER BY NUMBER...
"...ORDER BY NUMBER"?!
I'LL ORDER BY NUMBER!!
GIMME A FISH!
...DAT'S A ONE!
...AN' A SHAKE!
...DAT'S TWO!!
...AN' FRIES!
SNAP
KRACKLE
POP
...DAT'S THREE!!!
UHHHHHH... WOULD YOU LIKE THE FREE VIDEO?

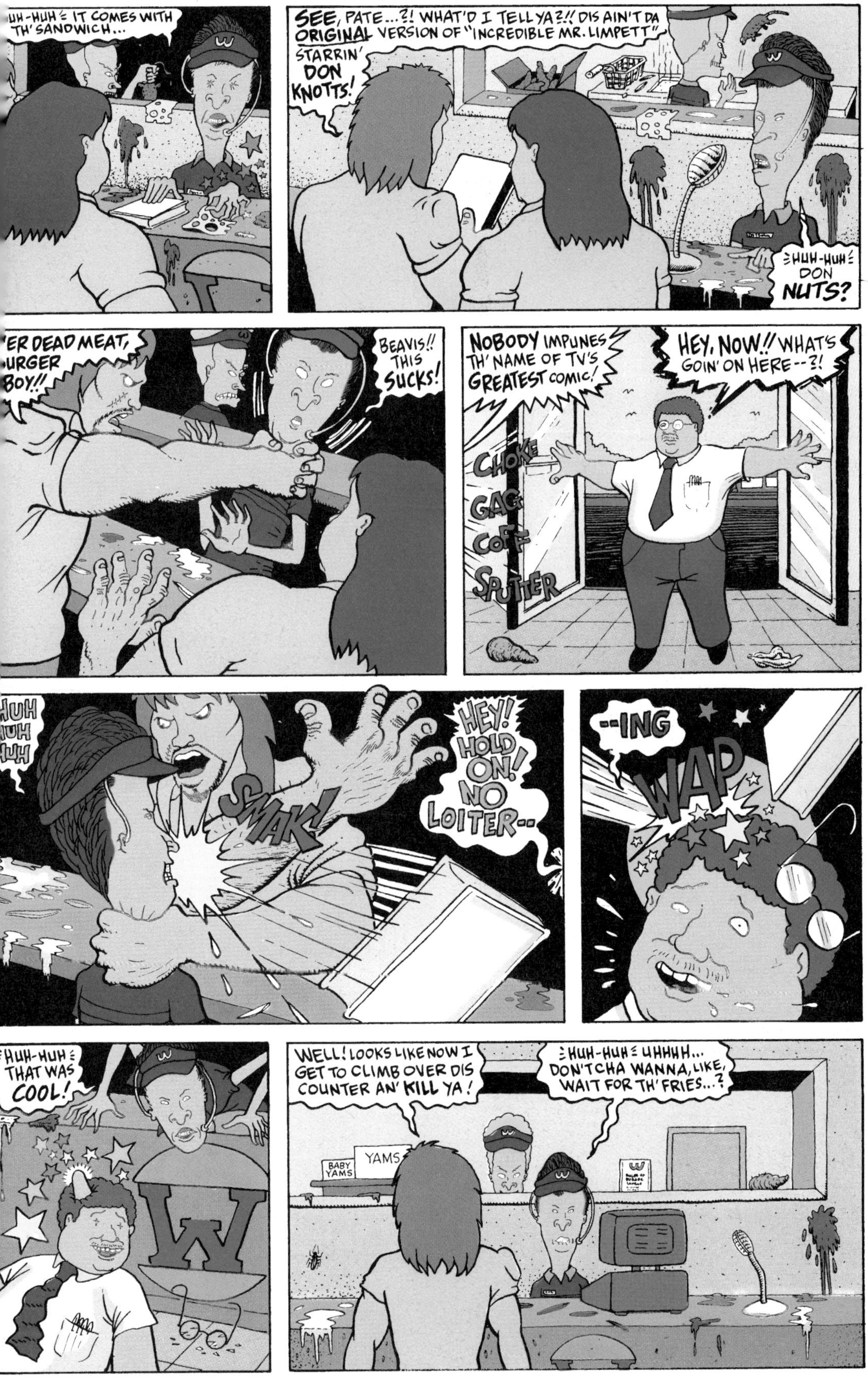
HUH-HUH IT COMES WITH TH' SANDWICH...
SEE, PATE...?! WHAT'D I TELL YA?!! DIS AIN'T DA ORIGINAL VERSION OF "INCREDIBLE MR. LIMPETT" STARRIN' DON KNOTTS!
HUH-HUH DON NUTS?
YER DEAD MEAT, BURGER BOY!!
BEAVIS!! THIS SUCKS!
NOBODY IMPUNES TH' NAME OF TV'S GREATEST COMIC!
HEY, NOW!! WHAT'S GOIN' ON HERE--?!
CHOKE
GAG
COFF
SPUTTER
HUH HUH HUH
SMAK!
HEY! HOLD ON! NO LOITER--
--ING
WAP
HUH-HUH THAT WAS COOL!
WELL! LOOKS LIKE NOW I GET TO CLIMB OVER DIS COUNTER AN' KILL YA!
HUH-HUH UHHHH... DON'TCHA WANNA, LIKE, WAIT FOR TH' FRIES...?
BABY YAMS
YAMS
R. PARKER

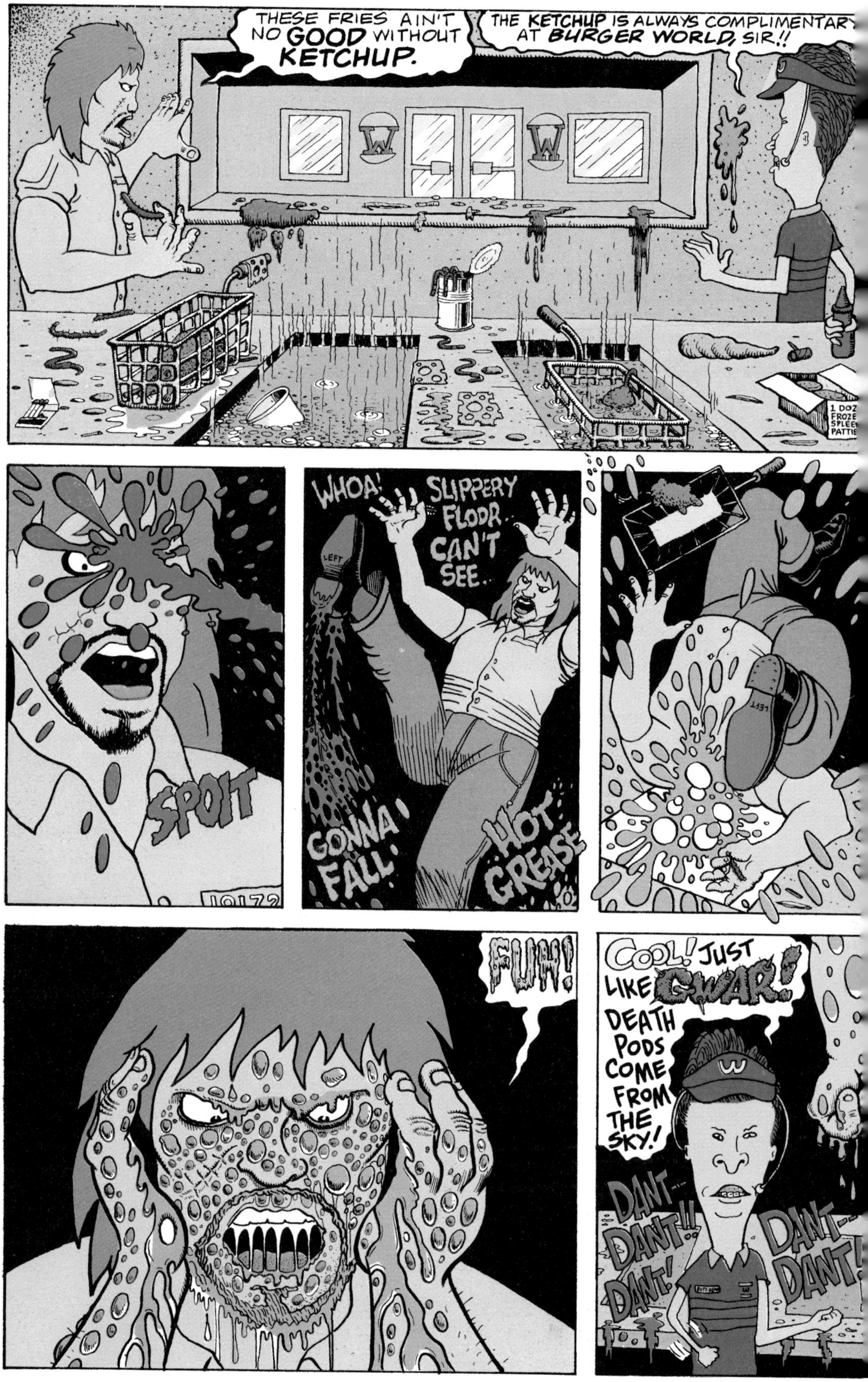
THESE FRIES AIN'T NO GOOD WITHOUT KETCHUP.
THE KETCHUP IS ALWAYS COMPLIMENTARY AT BURGER WORLD, SIR!!
1 DOZ FROZE SPLEE PATTIE
SPOIT
10172
WHOA! SLIPPERY FLOOR. CAN'T SEE..
LEFT
GONNA FALL
HOT GREASE
LEFT
FUH!
COOL! JUST LIKE GWAR! DEATH PODS COME FROM THE SKY!
DANT-DANT!! DANT! DANT!
DANT-DANT!

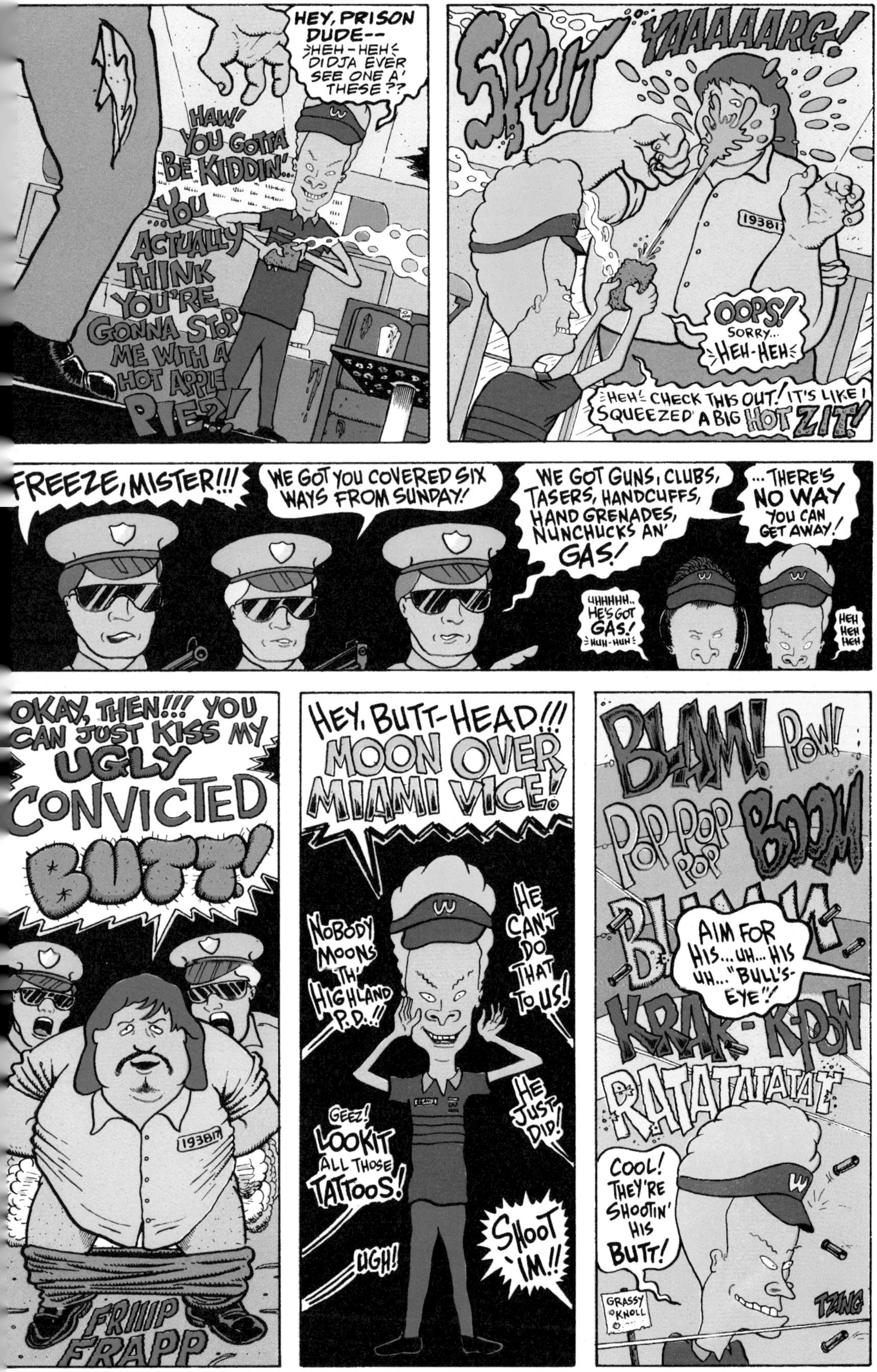
HEY, PRISON DUDE-- HEH-HEH DIDJA EVER SEE ONE A' THESE??
HAW! YOU GOTTA BE KIDDIN'... YOU ACTUALLY THINK YOU'RE GONNA STOP ME WITH A HOT APPLE PIE?!
SPUT
YAAAAARG!
OOPS! SORRY... HEH-HEH
HEH CHECK THIS OUT! IT'S LIKE I SQUEEZED A BIG HOT ZIT!
19381
FREEZE, MISTER!!!
WE GOT YOU COVERED SIX WAYS FROM SUNDAY!
WE GOT GUNS, CLUBS, TASERS, HANDCUFFS, HAND GRENADES, NUNCHUCKS AN' GAS!
...THERE'S NO WAY YOU CAN GET AWAY!
UHHHHH.. HE'S GOT GAS! HUH-HUH
HEH HEH HEH
OKAY, THEN!!! YOU CAN JUST KISS MY UGLY CONVICTED BUTT!
19381
FRIIIP FRAPP
HEY, BUTT-HEAD!!! MOON OVER MIAMI VICE!
NOBODY MOONS TH' HIGHLAND P.D.!!
HE CAN'T DO THAT TO US!
HE JUST DID!
GEEZ! LOOKIT ALL THOSE TATTOOS!
SHOOT 'IM!!
UGH!
BLAM! POW!
POP POP POP BOOM
AIM FOR HIS... UH... HIS UH... "BULL'S-EYE"!
KRAK-K-POW
RATATATATAT
COOL! THEY'RE SHOOTIN' HIS BUTT!
GRASSY KNOLL
TZING

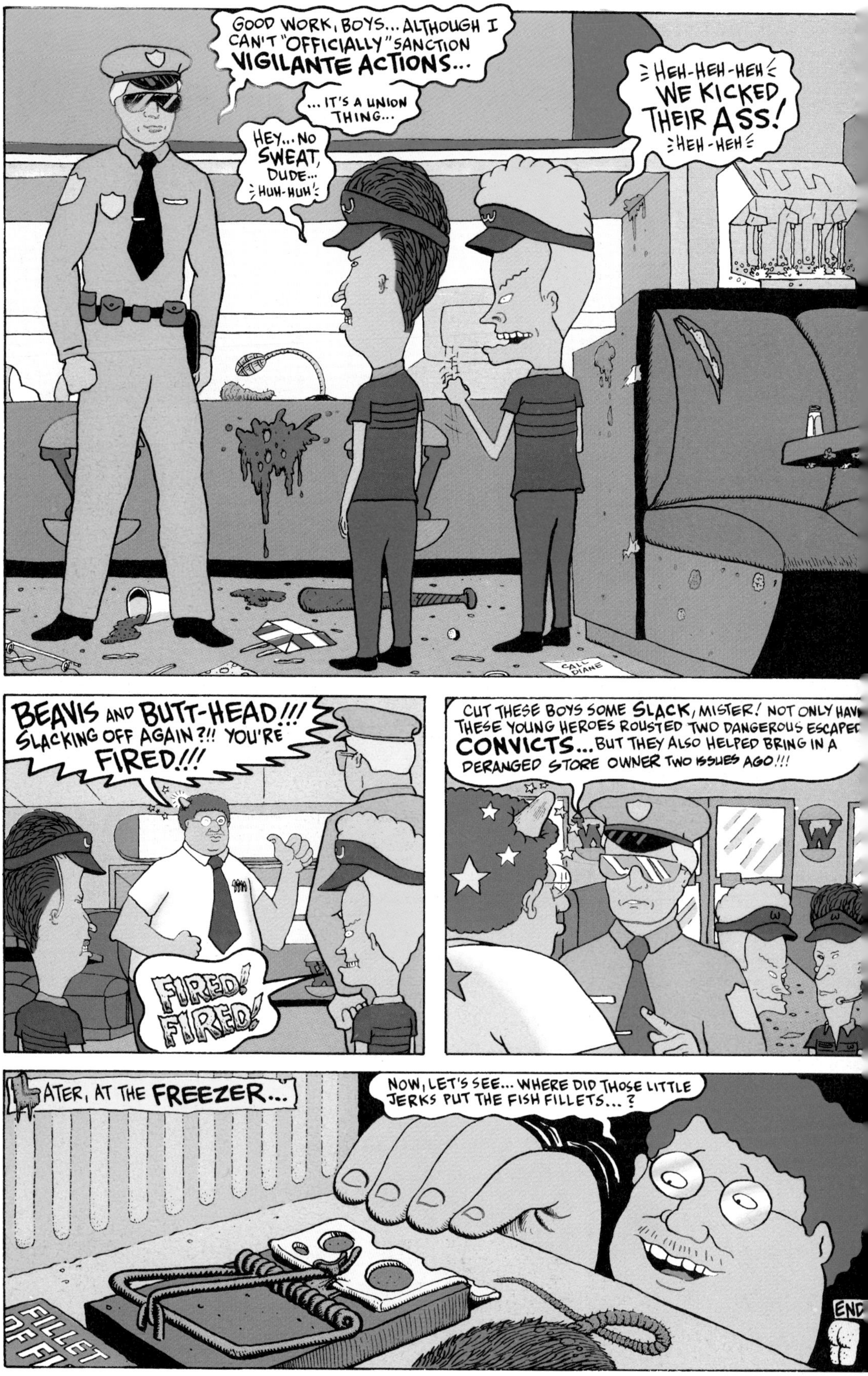
GOOD WORK, BOYS... ALTHOUGH I CAN'T "OFFICIALLY" SANCTION VIGILANTE ACTIONS...
... IT'S A UNION THING...
HEY... NO SWEAT, DUDE... HUH-HUH
HEH-HEH-HEH WE KICKED THEIR ASS! HEH-HEH
CALL DIANE
BEAVIS AND BUTT-HEAD!!! SLACKING OFF AGAIN?!! YOU'RE FIRED!!!
FIRED! FIRED!
CUT THESE BOYS SOME SLACK, MISTER! NOT ONLY HAVE THESE YOUNG HEROES ROUSTED TWO DANGEROUS ESCAPED CONVICTS... BUT THEY ALSO HELPED BRING IN A DERANGED STORE OWNER TWO ISSUES AGO!!!
LATER, AT THE FREEZER...
NOW, LET'S SEE... WHERE DID THOSE LITTLE JERKS PUT THE FISH FILLETS...?
FILLET
END

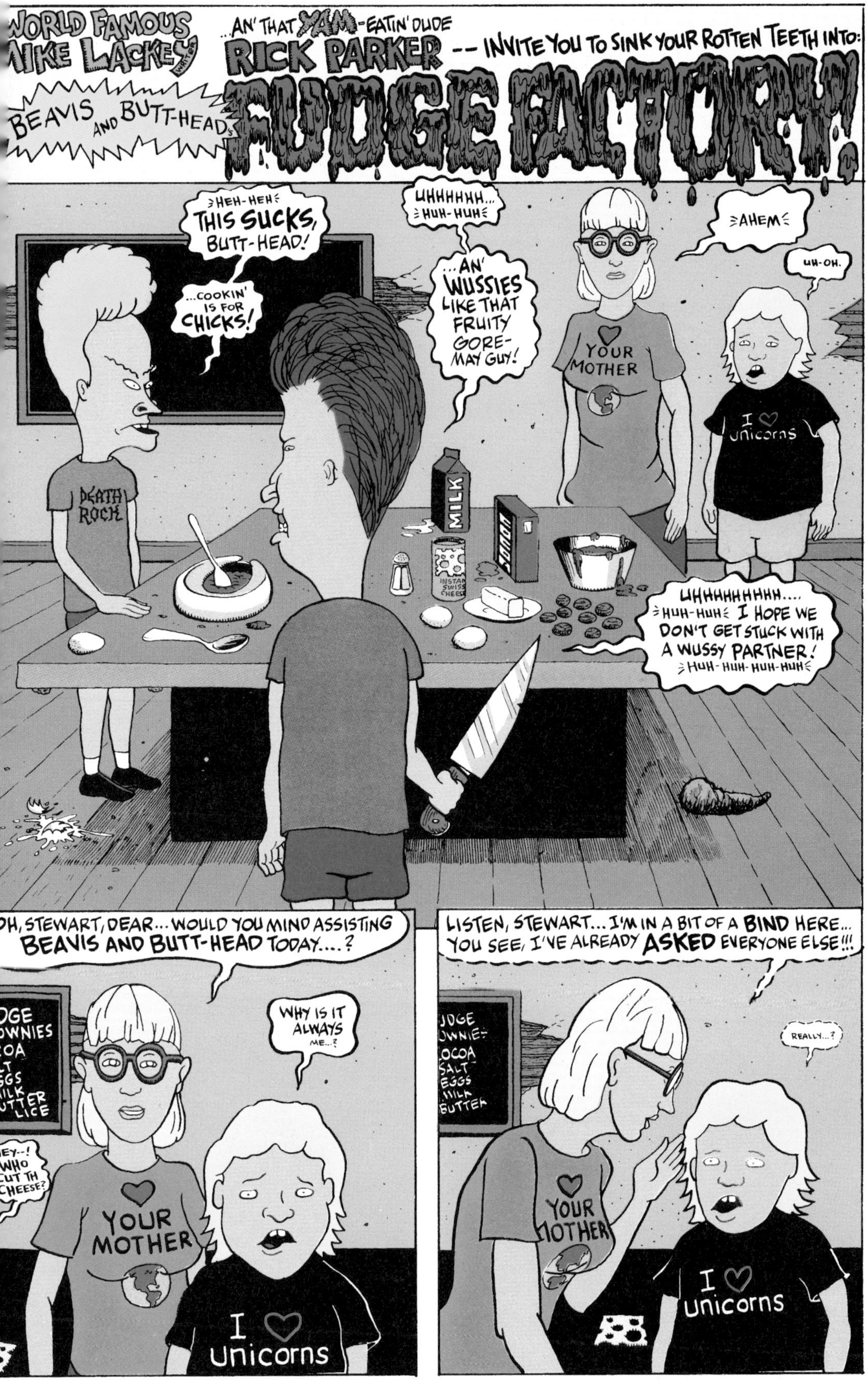

WORLD FAMOUS MIKE LACKEY (WRITER)
...AN' THAT YAM-EATIN' DUDE RICK PARKER -- INVITE YOU TO SINK YOUR ROTTEN TEETH INTO:
BEAVIS AND BUTT-HEAD'S FUDGE FACTORY!
HEH-HEH THIS SUCKS, BUTT-HEAD!
...COOKIN' IS FOR CHICKS!
UHHHHHH... HUH-HUH ...AN' WUSSIES LIKE THAT FRUITY GORE-MAY GUY!
AHEM
UH-OH.
UHHHHHHHHH.... HUH-HUH I HOPE WE DON'T GET STUCK WITH A WUSSY PARTNER! HUH-HUH-HUH-HUH
OH, STEWART, DEAR... WOULD YOU MIND ASSISTING BEAVIS AND BUTT-HEAD TODAY....?
WHY IS IT ALWAYS ME...?
HEY--! WHO CUT TH CHEESE?
LISTEN, STEWART... I'M IN A BIT OF A BIND HERE... YOU SEE, I'VE ALREADY ASKED EVERYONE ELSE!!!
REALLY...?

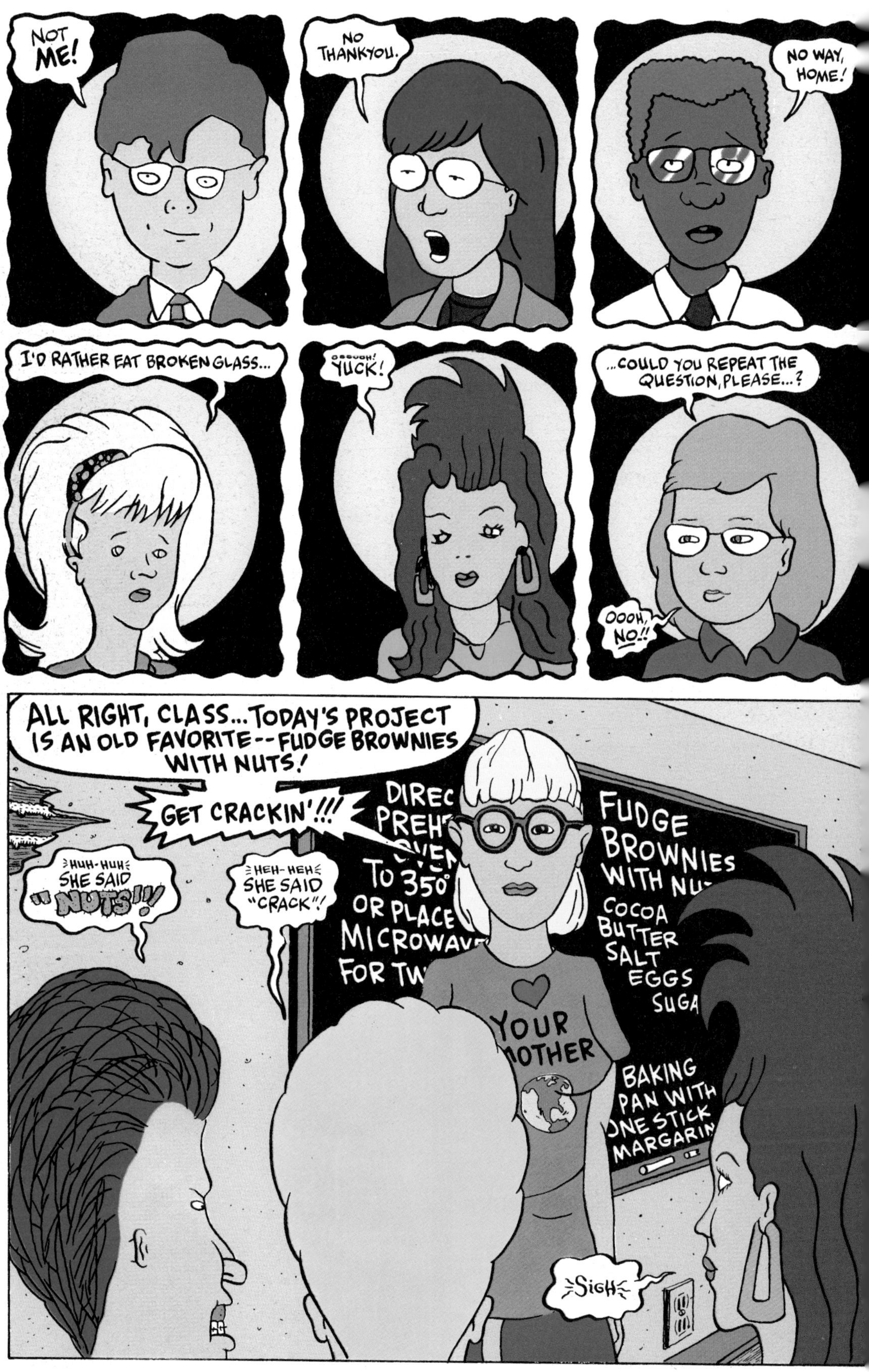

NOT ME!
NO THANKYOU.
NO WAY, HOME!
I'D RATHER EAT BROKEN GLASS...
OOOUOH! YUCK!
...COULD YOU REPEAT THE QUESTION, PLEASE...?
OOOH, NO!!
ALL RIGHT, CLASS... TODAY'S PROJECT IS AN OLD FAVORITE--FUDGE BROWNIES WITH NUTS!
GET CRACKIN'!!!
HUH-HUH SHE SAID "NUTS"!!
HEH-HEH SHE SAID "CRACK"!
FUDGE BROWNIES WITH NU
COCOA
BUTTER
SALT
EGGS
SUGA
BAKING PAN WITH ONE STICK MARGARIN
YOUR MOTHER
SIGH

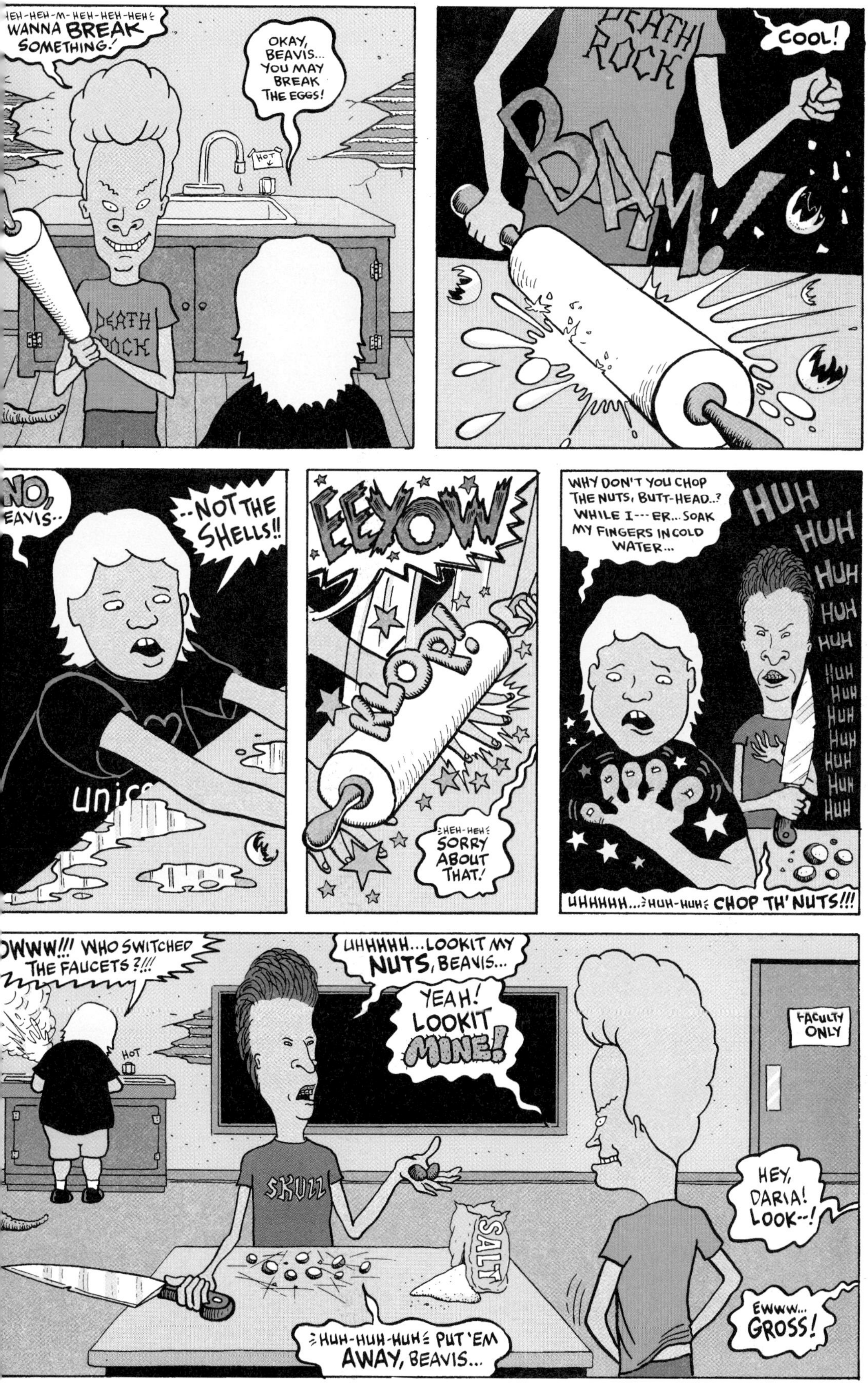
HEH-HEH-M-HEH-HEH-HEH WANNA BREAK SOMETHING!
OKAY, BEAVIS... YOU MAY BREAK THE EGGS!
HOT
DEATH ROCK
DEATH ROCK
BAM!
COOL!
NO, BEAVIS..
..NOT THE SHELLS!!
EEYOW
KLOP!
HEH-HEH SORRY ABOUT THAT!
WHY DON'T YOU CHOP THE NUTS, BUTT-HEAD..? WHILE I--- ER... SOAK MY FINGERS IN COLD WATER...
HUH HUH HUH HUH HUH HUH HUH HUH HUH HUH HUH HUH
UHHHHH... HUH-HUH CHOP TH' NUTS!!!
OWWW!!! WHO SWITCHED THE FAUCETS?!!!
HOT
UHHHHH... LOOKIT MY NUTS, BEAVIS...
YEAH! LOOKIT MINE!
FACULTY ONLY
SKULL
SALT
HEY, DARIA! LOOK--!
EWWW... GROSS!
HUH-HUH-HUH PUT 'EM AWAY, BEAVIS...

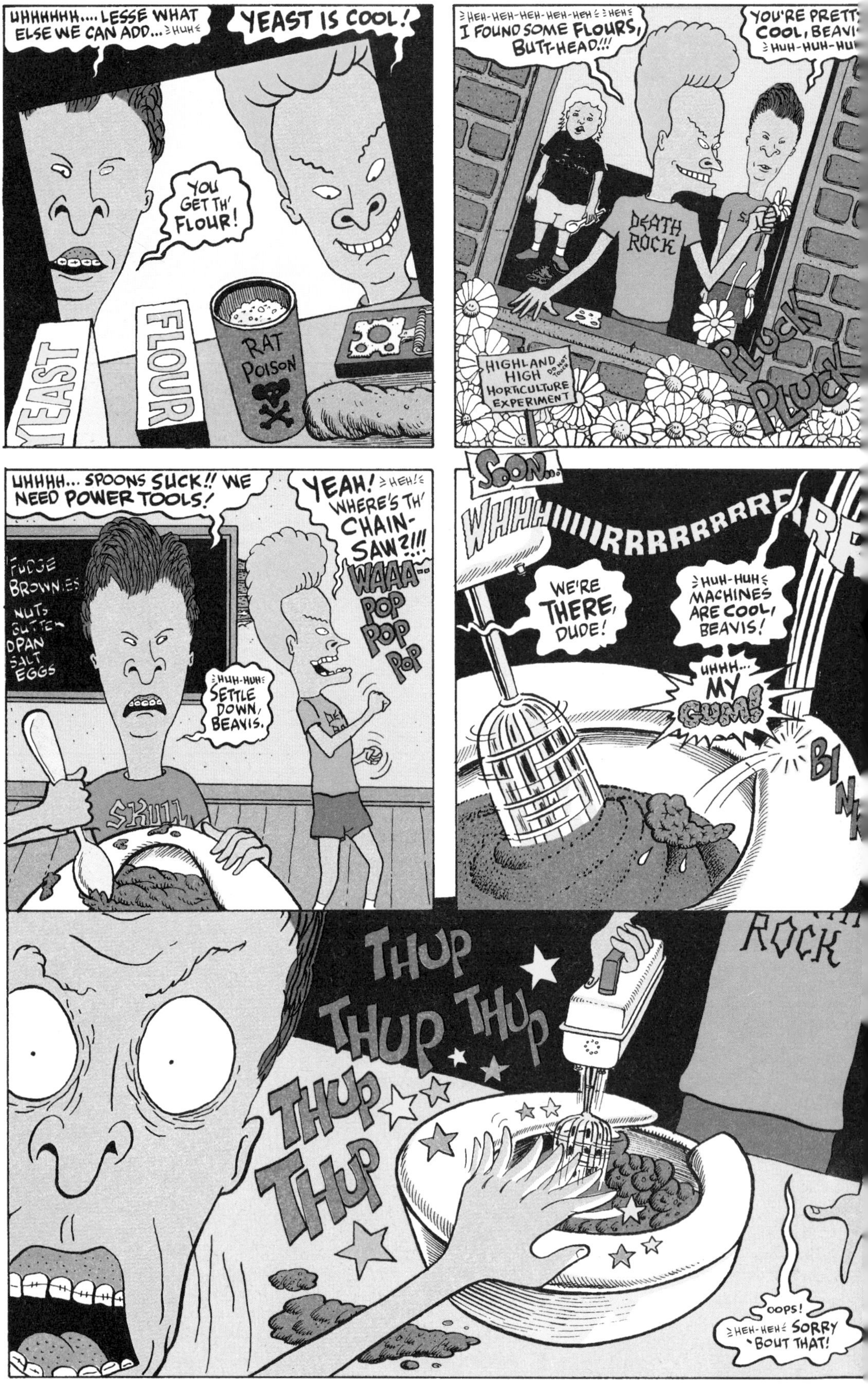

UHHHHHH.... LESSE WHAT ELSE WE CAN ADD... HUH
YEAST IS COOL!
YOU GET TH' FLOUR!
YEAST
FLOUR
RAT POISON
HEH-HEH-HEH-HEH-HEH HEH
I FOUND SOME FLOURS, BUTT-HEAD!!!
YOU'RE PRETT COOL, BEAVI HUH-HUH-HU
DEATH ROCK
HIGHLAND HIGH HORTICULTURE EXPERIMENT
DO NOT TOUCH
PLUCK
PLUCK
UHHHH... SPOONS SUCK!! WE NEED POWER TOOLS!
YEAH! HEH! WHERE'S TH' CHAIN-SAW?!!!
WAAA- POP POP POP
FUDGE BROWNIES NUTS BUTTER PAN SALT EGGS
HUH-HUH SETTLE DOWN, BEAVIS.
SKULL
SOON...
WHHHIIIIIRRRRRRRRRRR
WE'RE THERE, DUDE!
HUH-HUH MACHINES ARE COOL, BEAVIS!
UHHH... MY GUM!
BINK
THUP THUP THUP THUP THUP THUP
ROCK
OOPS! HEH-HEH SORRY 'BOUT THAT!

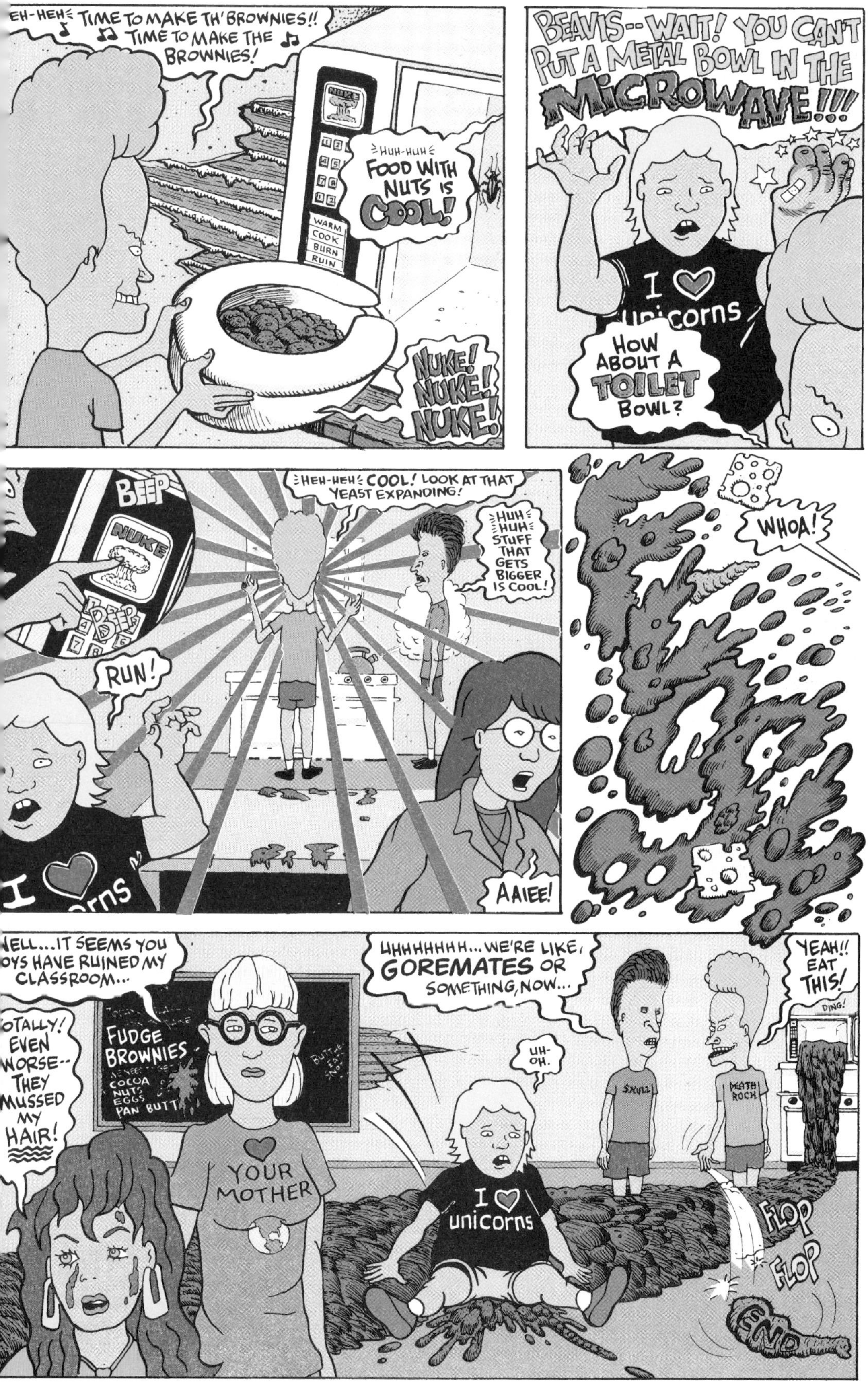
EH-HEH TIME TO MAKE TH' BROWNIES!! TIME TO MAKE THE BROWNIES!
NUKE
1 2
4 5
7 8
WARM
COOK
BURN
RUIN
HUH-HUH FOOD WITH NUTS IS COOL!
NUKE! NUKE! NUKE!
BEAVIS--WAIT! YOU CAN'T PUT A METAL BOWL IN THE MICROWAVE!!!
I ♥ unicorns
HOW ABOUT A TOILET BOWL?
BEEP
NUKE
BEEP
HEH-HEH COOL! LOOK AT THAT YEAST EXPANDING!
HUH HUH STUFF THAT GETS BIGGER IS COOL!
RUN!
AAIEE!
WHOA!
WELL...IT SEEMS YOU BOYS HAVE RUINED MY CLASSROOM...
TOTALLY! EVEN WORSE-- THEY MUSSED MY HAIR!
FUDGE BROWNIES
COCOA
NUTS
EGGS
PAN BUTT
YOUR MOTHER
UHHHHHHH... WE'RE LIKE, GOREMATES OR SOMETHING, NOW...
UH-OH.
I ♥ unicorns
SKULL
DEATH ROCK
YEAH!! EAT THIS!
DING!
FLOP
FLOP
END

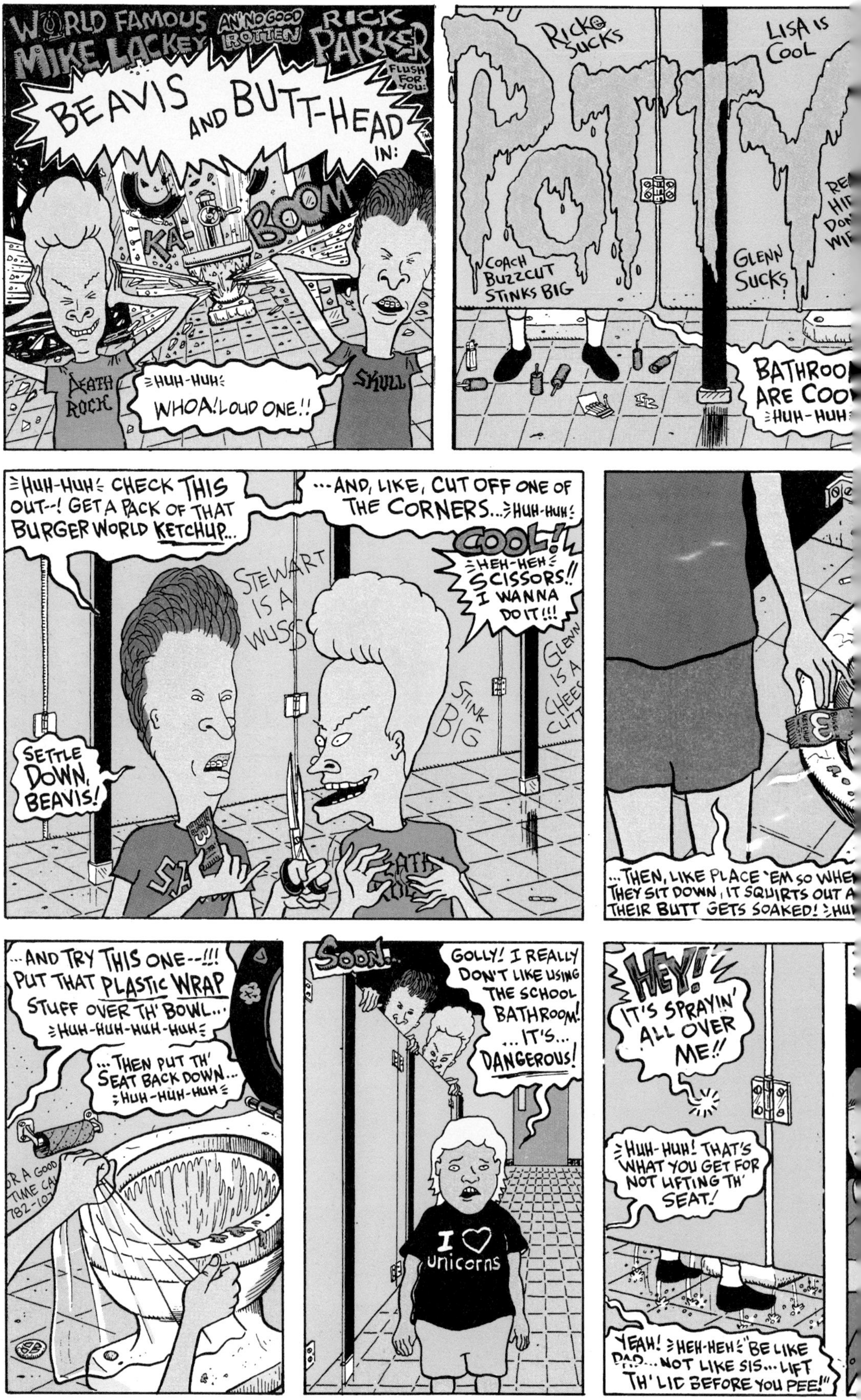
WORLD FAMOUS MIKE LACKEY
AN' NO GOOD ROTTEN
RICK PARKER
FLUSH FOR YOU:
BEAVIS AND BUTT-HEAD™ IN:
KA-BOOM
DEATH ROCK
SKULL
HUH-HUH WHOA! LOUD ONE!!
RICK SUCKS
LISA IS COOL
POTTY
COACH BUZZCUT STINKS BIG
GLENN SUCKS
BATHROO ARE COO HUH-HUH
HUH-HUH CHECK THIS OUT--! GET A PACK OF THAT BURGER WORLD KETCHUP...
...AND, LIKE, CUT OFF ONE OF THE CORNERS... HUH-HUH
COOL! HEH-HEH SCISSORS!! I WANNA DO IT!!!
STEWART IS A WUSS
STINK BIG
SETTLE DOWN, BEAVIS!
...THEN, LIKE PLACE 'EM SO WHE THEY SIT DOWN, IT SQUIRTS OUT A THEIR BUTT GETS SOAKED! HU
...AND TRY THIS ONE--!!! PUT THAT PLASTIC WRAP STUFF OVER TH' BOWL... HUH-HUH-HUH-HUH
...THEN PUT TH' SEAT BACK DOWN... HUH-HUH-HUH
SOON...
GOLLY! I REALLY DON'T LIKE USING THE SCHOOL BATHROOM! ...IT'S... DANGEROUS!
I ♥ unicorns
HEY! IT'S SPRAYIN' ALL OVER ME!!
HUH-HUH! THAT'S WHAT YOU GET FOR NOT LIFTING TH' SEAT!
YEAH! HEH-HEH "BE LIKE DAD... NOT LIKE SIS... LIFT TH' LID BEFORE YOU PEE!"

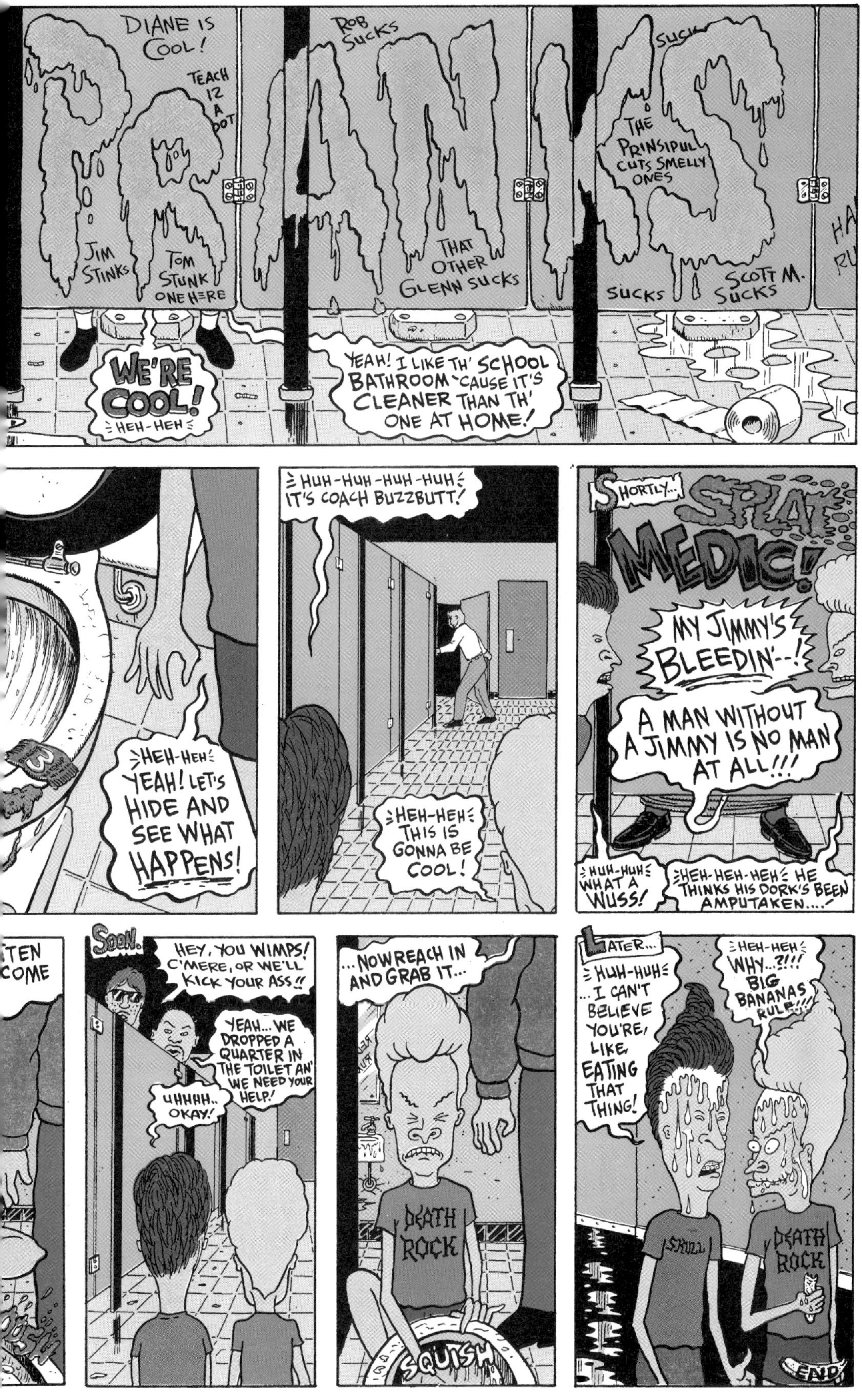

DIANE IS COOL!
TEACH IZ A DOT
ROB SUCKS
SUCK
THE PRINSIPUL CUTS SMELLY ONES
JIM STINKS
TOM STUNK ONE HERE
THAT OTHER GLENN SUCKS
SUCKS
SCOTT M. SUCKS
WE'RE COOL! HEH-HEH
YEAH! I LIKE TH' SCHOOL BATHROOM 'CAUSE IT'S CLEANER THAN TH' ONE AT HOME!
HEH-HEH YEAH! LET'S HIDE AND SEE WHAT HAPPENS!
HUH-HUH-HUH-HUH IT'S COACH BUZZBUTT!
HEH-HEH THIS IS GONNA BE COOL!
SHORTLY...
SPLAT
MEDIC!
MY JIMMY'S BLEEDIN'--!
A MAN WITHOUT A JIMMY IS NO MAN AT ALL!!!
HUH-HUH WHAT A WUSS!
HEH-HEH-HEH HE THINKS HIS DORK'S BEEN AMPUTAKEN...!
SOON.
HEY, YOU WIMPS! C'MERE, OR WE'LL KICK YOUR ASS!!
YEAH... WE DROPPED A QUARTER IN THE TOILET AN' WE NEED YOUR HELP!
UHHHH.. OKAY!
...NOW REACH IN AND GRAB IT...
DEATH ROCK
SQUISH
LATER...
HUH-HUH ...I CAN'T BELIEVE YOU'RE, LIKE, EATING THAT THING!
HEH-HEH WHY...?!!! BIG BANANAS RULE!!!
SKULL
DEATH ROCK
END

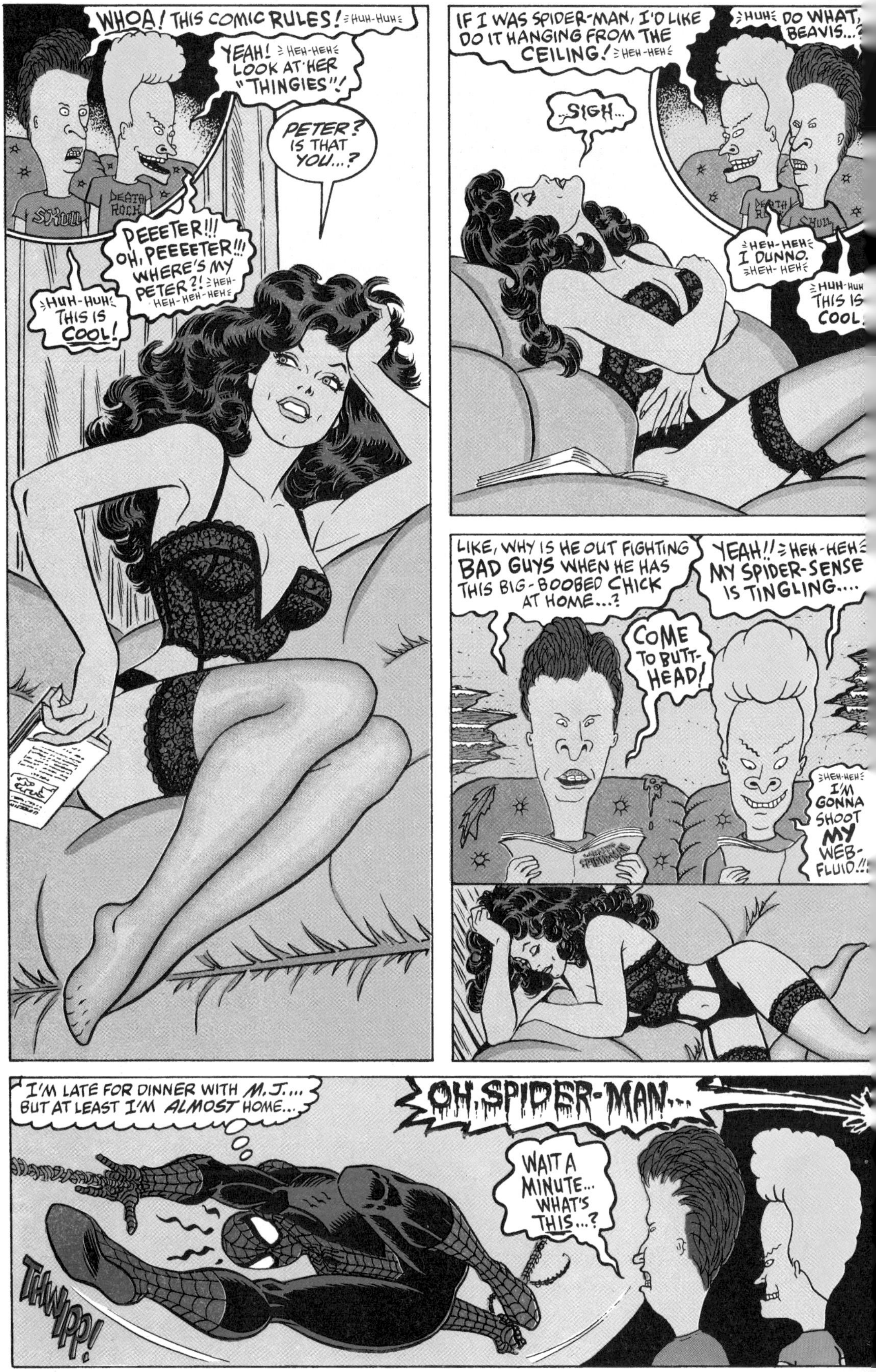

WHOA! THIS COMIC RULES! HUH-HUH
YEAH! HEH-HEH LOOK AT HER "THINGIES"!
PETER? IS THAT YOU...?
PEEEETER!!! OH, PEEEEETER!!! WHERE'S MY PETER?! HEH-HEH-HEH-HEH
HUH-HUH THIS IS COOL!
IF I WAS SPIDER-MAN, I'D LIKE DO IT HANGING FROM THE CEILING! HEH-HEH
HUH DO WHAT, BEAVIS...?
...SIGH...
HEH-HEH I DUNNO. HEH-HEH
HUH-HUH THIS IS COOL.
LIKE, WHY IS HE OUT FIGHTING BAD GUYS WHEN HE HAS THIS BIG-BOOBED CHICK AT HOME...?
YEAH!! HEH-HEH MY SPIDER-SENSE IS TINGLING....
COME TO BUTT-HEAD!
HEH-HEH I'M GONNA SHOOT MY WEB-FLUID!!!
I'M LATE FOR DINNER WITH M.J.... BUT AT LEAST I'M ALMOST HOME...
OH, SPIDER-MAN...
WAIT A MINUTE... WHAT'S THIS...?
THWIPP!

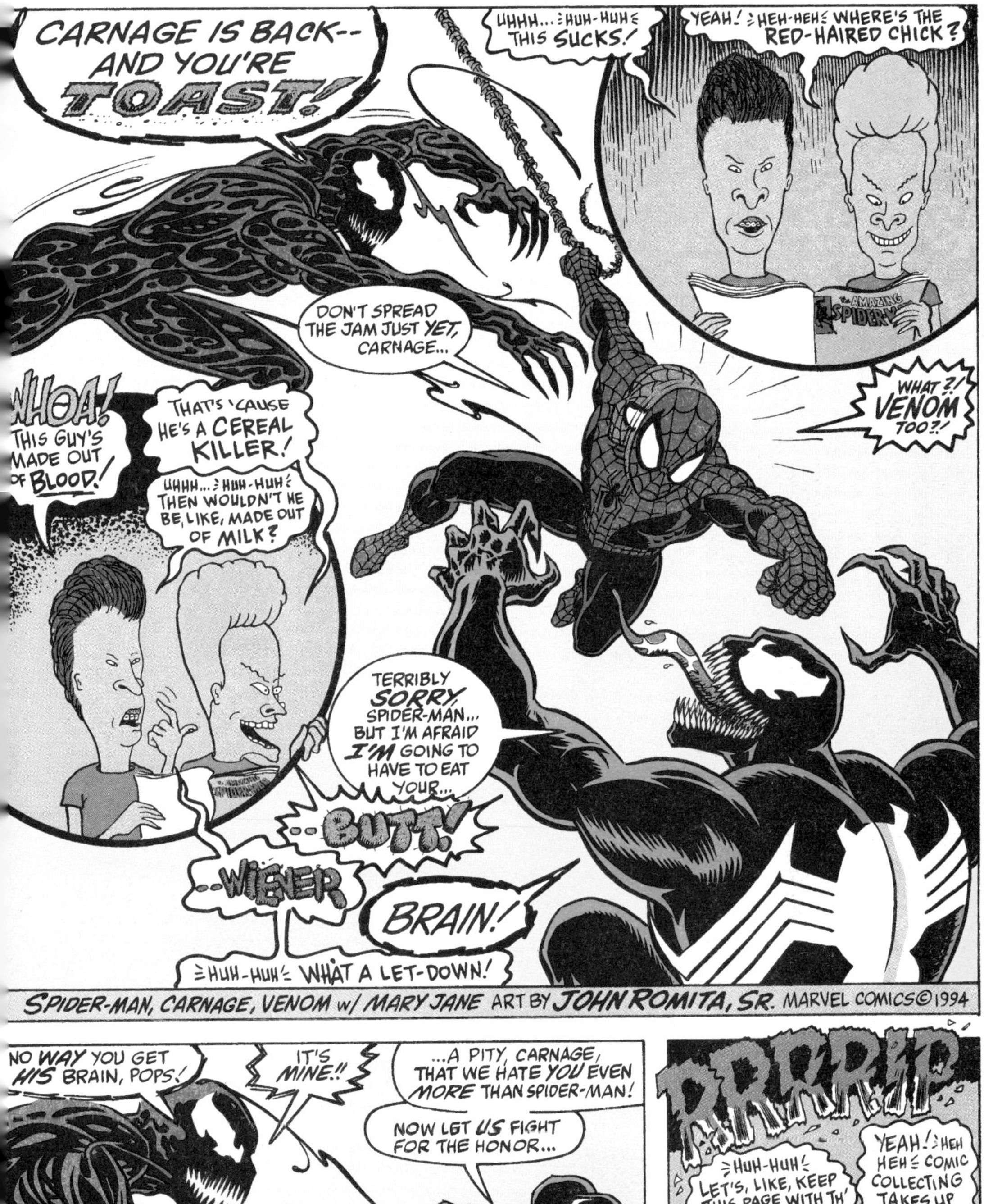
CARNAGE IS BACK-- AND YOU'RE TOAST!
UHHH... HUH-HUH THIS SUCKS!
YEAH! HEH-HEH WHERE'S THE RED-HAIRED CHICK?
THE AMAZING SPIDER
DON'T SPREAD THE JAM JUST YET, CARNAGE...
WHAT?! VENOM TOO?!
WHOA! THIS GUY'S MADE OUT OF BLOOD!
THAT'S 'CAUSE HE'S A CEREAL KILLER!
UHHH... HUH-HUH THEN WOULDN'T HE BE, LIKE, MADE OUT OF MILK?
TERRIBLY SORRY, SPIDER-MAN... BUT I'M AFRAID I'M GOING TO HAVE TO EAT YOUR...
--BUTT!
--WIENER
BRAIN!
HUH-HUH WHAT A LET-DOWN!

SPIDER-MAN, CARNAGE, VENOM w/ MARY JANE ART BY JOHN ROMITA, SR. MARVEL COMICS© 1994

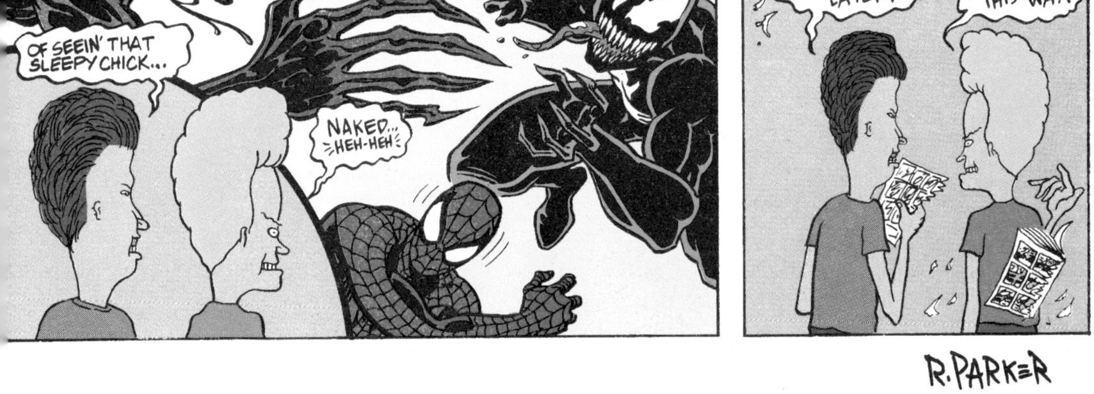
NO WAY YOU GET HIS BRAIN, POPS!
IT'S MINE!!
...A PITY, CARNAGE, THAT WE HATE YOU EVEN MORE THAN SPIDER-MAN!
NOW LET US FIGHT FOR THE HONOR...
OF SEEIN' THAT SLEEPY CHICK...
NAKED... HEH-HEH
DRRRIP
HUH-HUH LET'S, LIKE, KEEP THIS PAGE WITH TH' CHICK ON IT... FOR LATER!
YEAH! HEH HEH COMIC COLLECTING TAKES UP LESS ROOM THIS WAY!
R. PARKER

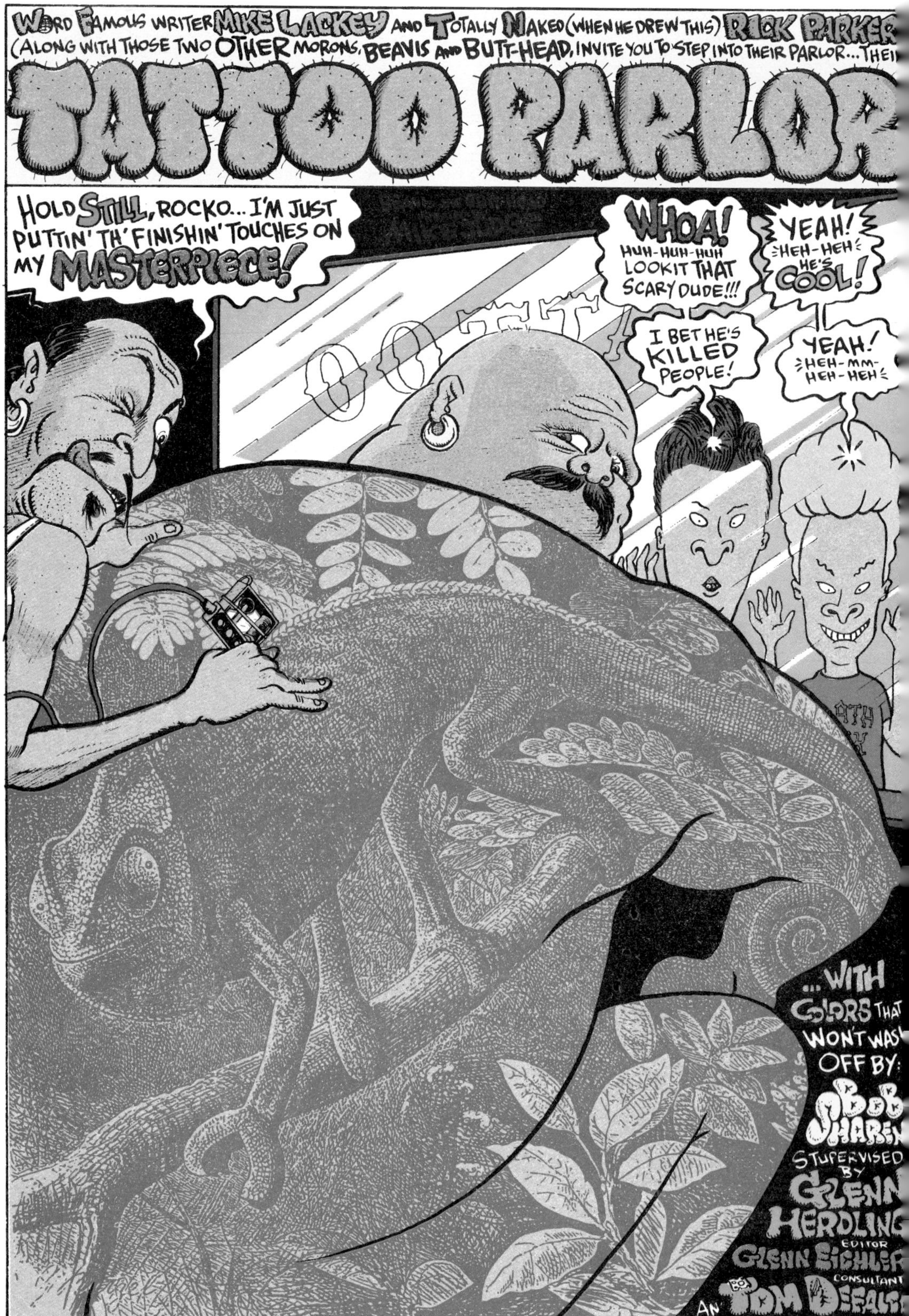
WORD FAMOUS WRITER MIKE LACKEY AND TOTALLY NAKED (WHEN HE DREW THIS) RICK PARKER
(ALONG WITH THOSE TWO OTHER MORONS, BEAVIS AND BUTT-HEAD, INVITE YOU TO STEP INTO THEIR PARLOR... THEI
TATTOO PARLOR
HOLD STILL, ROCKO... I'M JUST PUTTIN' TH' FINISHIN' TOUCHES ON MY MASTERPIECE!
WHOA! HUH-HUH-HUH LOOKIT THAT SCARY DUDE!!!
YEAH! HEH-HEH HE'S COOL!
I BET HE'S KILLED PEOPLE!
YEAH! HEH-MM-HEH-HEH
...WITH COLORS THAT WON'T WAS OFF BY:
BOB SHAREN
STUPERVISED BY
GLENN HERDLING
EDITOR
GLENN EICHLER
CONSULTANT
AN BO TOM DEFALC
EDITOR IN CHEESE

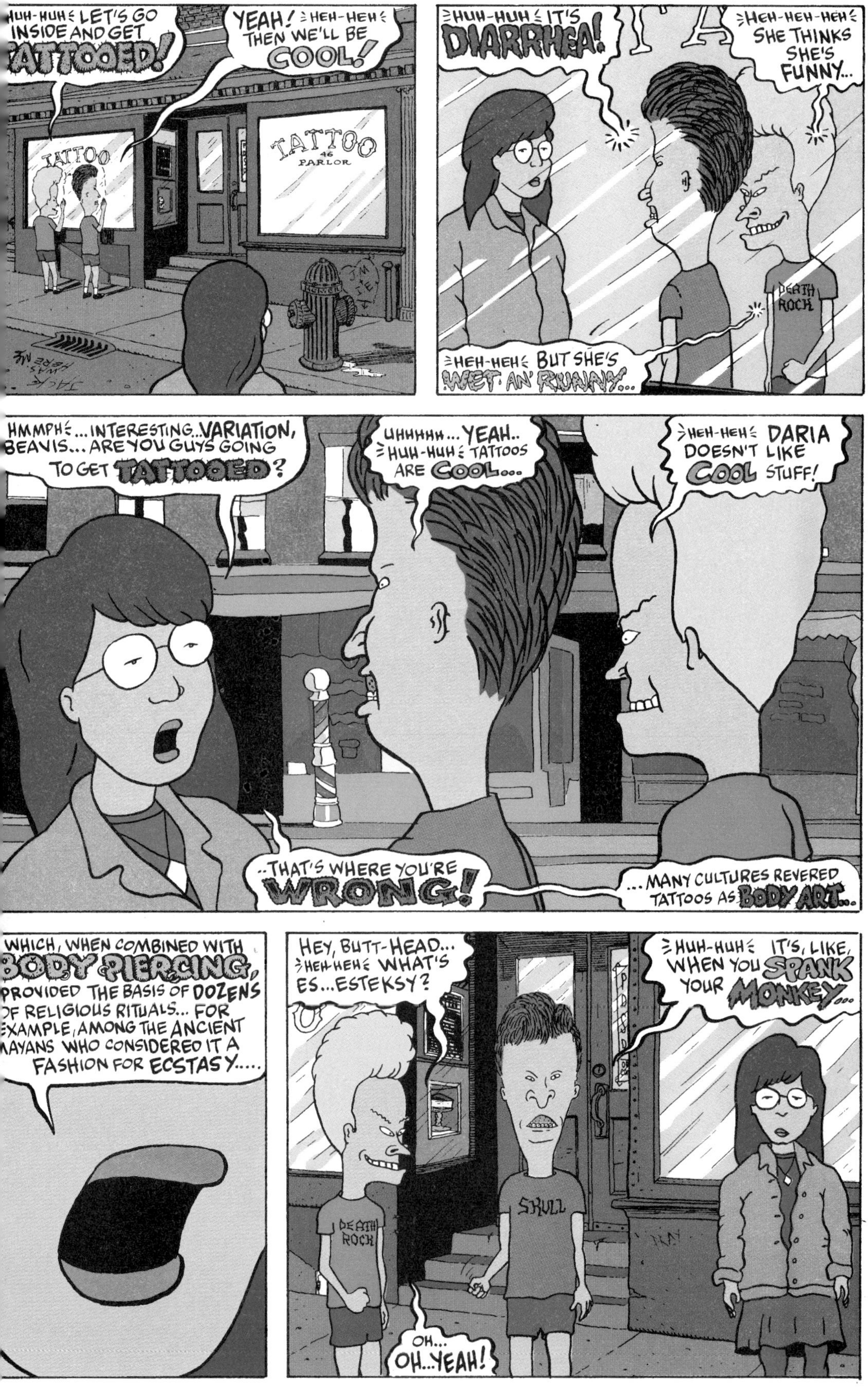
HUH-HUH LET'S GO INSIDE AND GET TATTOOED!
YEAH! HEH-HEH THEN WE'LL BE COOL!
TATTOO
TATTOO 46 PARLOR
HUH-HUH IT'S DIARRHEA!
HEH-HEH-HEH SHE THINKS SHE'S FUNNY...
DEATH ROCK
HEH-HEH BUT SHE'S WET AN' RUNNY...
HMMPH ... INTERESTING...VARIATION, BEAVIS... ARE YOU GUYS GOING TO GET TATTOOED?
UHHHHH... YEAH.. HUH-HUH TATTOOS ARE COOL...
HEH-HEH DARIA DOESN'T LIKE COOL STUFF!
..THAT'S WHERE YOU'RE WRONG!
...MANY CULTURES REVERED TATTOOS AS BODY ART...
WHICH, WHEN COMBINED WITH BODY PIERCING, PROVIDED THE BASIS OF DOZENS OF RELIGIOUS RITUALS... FOR EXAMPLE, AMONG THE ANCIENT MAYANS WHO CONSIDERED IT A FASHION FOR ECSTASY.....
HEY, BUTT-HEAD... HEH-HEH WHAT'S ES...ESTEKSY?
HUH-HUH IT'S, LIKE, WHEN YOU SPANK YOUR MONKEY...
DEATH ROCK
SKULL
OH... OH...YEAH!

...JUST REMEMBER, GUYS... YOU'LL HAVE THOSE TATTOOS FOREVER!

≋HUH-HUH≋ ...FOREVER ISN'T THAT LONG...

PLEAS! DO NO SLA DOO OPE COM IN

YEAH! ≋HEH-HEH≋

BACK INSIDE...

...JUST A FEW MORE LINES, ROCKO...

...AN' EVERYTHING...

...WILL BE...

...PERFECT...

No. 73 C.P.

No. 78 C.P.

No. 31 C.P.

No. 32

HELP! I AM BEING HELD PRISONER IN A TATTOO

N.Y. TATTOO SOCIETY T.S. N.Y. C.P.

≋HUH-HUH HUH-HUH HUH-HUH-HUH HUH-HUH≋ ≋HEH HEH HEH HEH≋

No. 70 C.P.

OOPS

ZZZZZZZRIIIPP!

CLAY PA

UHH... NO CHARGE, ROCKO!

WHO SLAMMED TH' DOOR?!

UH... ≋HUH-HUH≋ DO YOU WANT US TO, LIKE, SLAM IT AGAIN...?

YEAH! I CAN SLAM IT ALL DAY! ≋HEH! HEH!≋

NO!

RO SKULLY

YOU PUNKS MUST BE HERE FOR MY UNDER-AGE SPECIAL... "TATTOOS BY EIGHT...OR ELSE IT'S TOO LATE"...

FREE TICKETS TO AMERICAN AMAZONS WITH EVERY TATTOO OR BODY PIERCING

HEY, BUTT-HEAD... WHAT'S IT SAY...?

IT SAYS "FREE ASS-WIPE!

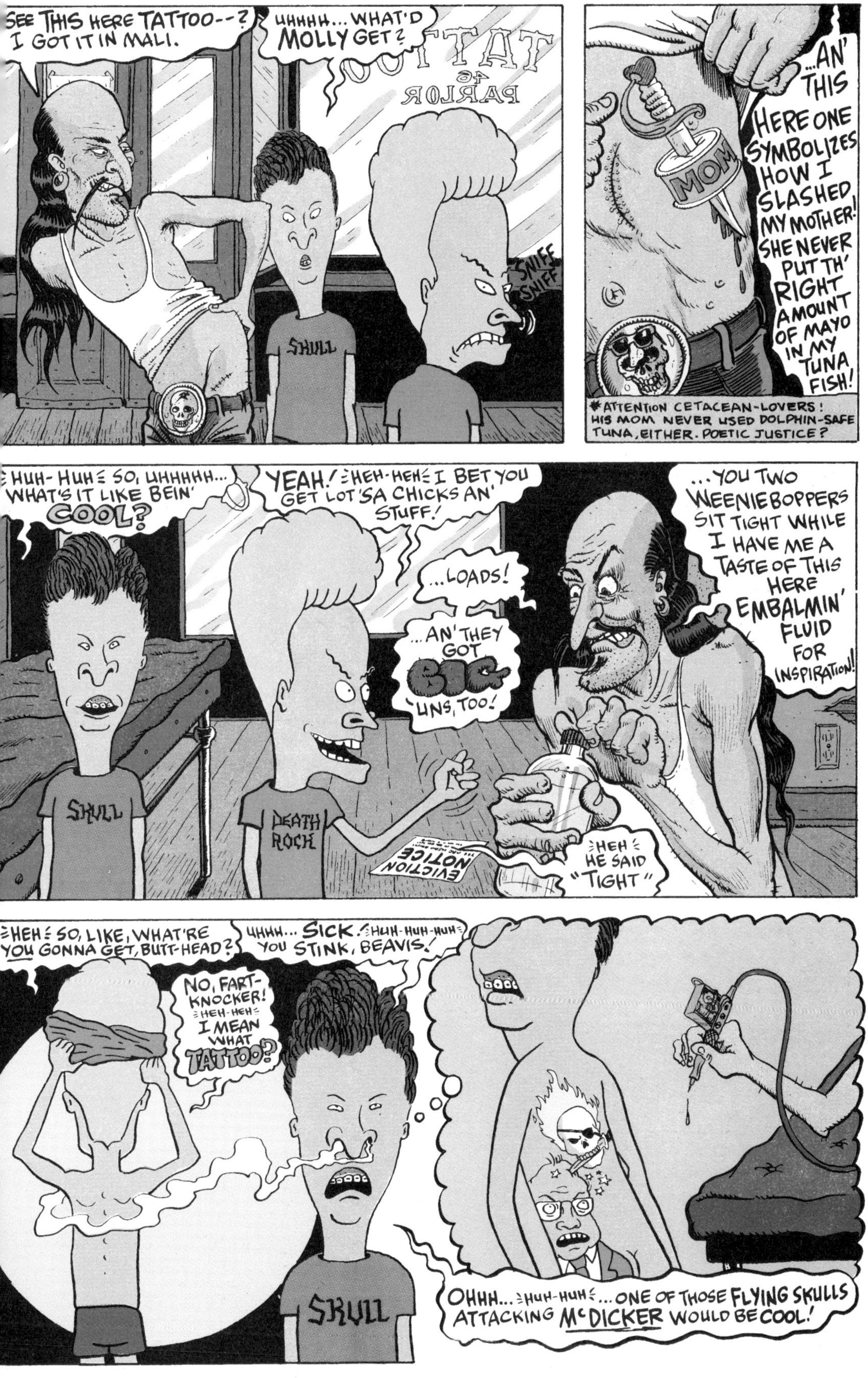
SEE THIS HERE TATTOO--? I GOT IT IN MALI.
UHHHH... WHAT'D MOLLY GET?
TATTOO PARLOR
SNIFF SNIFF
SKULL
...AN' THIS HERE ONE SYMBOLIZES HOW I SLASHED MY MOTHER! SHE NEVER PUT TH' RIGHT AMOUNT OF MAYO IN MY TUNA FISH!
MOM
*ATTENTION CETACEAN-LOVERS! HIS MOM NEVER USED DOLPHIN-SAFE TUNA, EITHER. POETIC JUSTICE?
HUH-HUH SO, UHHHHH... WHAT'S IT LIKE BEIN' COOL?
YEAH! HEH-HEH I BET YOU GET LOT'SA CHICKS AN' STUFF!
...LOADS!
...AN' THEY GOT BIG 'UNS, TOO!
...YOU TWO WEENIEBOPPERS SIT TIGHT WHILE I HAVE ME A TASTE OF THIS HERE EMBALMIN' FLUID FOR INSPIRATION!
HEH HE SAID "TIGHT"
SKULL
DEATH ROCK
EVICTION NOTICE
HEH SO, LIKE, WHAT'RE YOU GONNA GET, BUTT-HEAD?
UHHH... SICK. HUH-HUH-HUH YOU STINK, BEAVIS!
NO, FART-KNOCKER! HEH-HEH I MEAN WHAT TATTOO?
SKULL
OHHH... HUH-HUH ...ONE OF THOSE FLYING SKULLS ATTACKING McDICKER WOULD BE COOL!

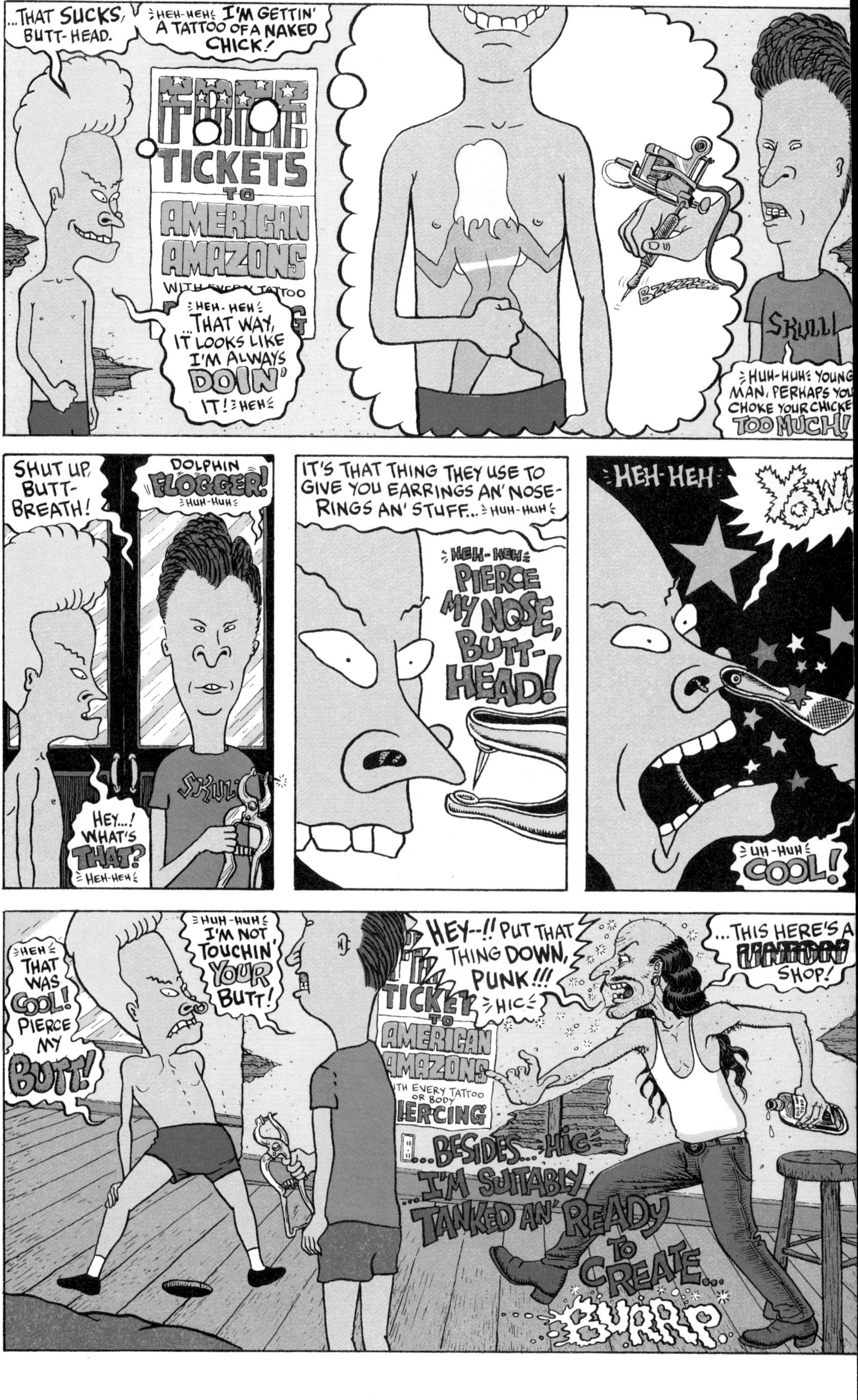

...THAT SUCKS, BUTT-HEAD.
HEH-HEH I'M GETTIN' A TATTOO OF A NAKED CHICK!
TICKETS TO AMERICAN AMAZONS
HEH-HEH ...THAT WAY, IT LOOKS LIKE I'M ALWAYS DOIN' IT! HEH
SKULL
HUH-HUH YOUNG MAN, PERHAPS YOU CHOKE YOUR CHICKE TOO MUCH!
SHUT UP, BUTT-BREATH!
DOLPHIN FLOGGER! HUH-HUH
HEY...! WHAT'S THAT? HEH-HEH
IT'S THAT THING THEY USE TO GIVE YOU EARRINGS AN' NOSE-RINGS AN' STUFF... HUH-HUH
HEH-HEH PIERCE MY NOSE, BUTT-HEAD!
HEH-HEH
UH-HUH COOL!
HEH THAT WAS COOL! PIERCE MY BUTT!
HUH-HUH I'M NOT TOUCHIN' YOUR BUTT!
HEY--!! PUT THAT THING DOWN, PUNK!!! HIC
...THIS HERE'S A SHOP!
TICKET TO AMERICAN AMAZONS
TH EVERY TATTOO OR BODY
IERCING
...BESIDES... HIC I'M SUITABLY TANKED AN' READY TO CREATE...
BURRP.

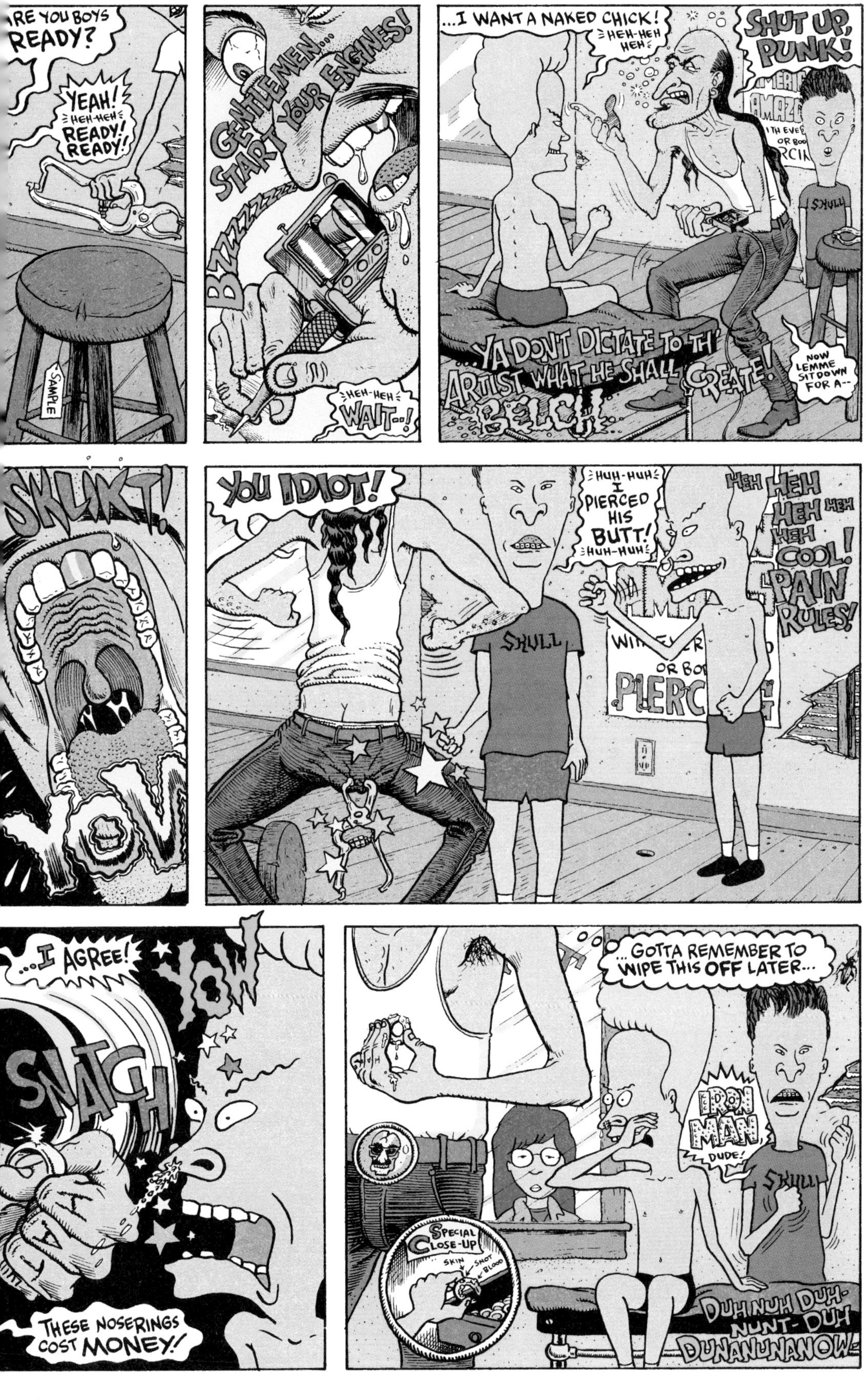
ARE YOU BOYS READY?
YEAH! HEH-HEH READY! READY!
SAMPLE
GENTLEMEN... START YOUR ENGINES!
BZZZZZZZ
HEH-HEH WAIT--!
...I WANT A NAKED CHICK! HEH-HEH HEH
SHUT UP, PUNK!
YA DON'T DICTATE TO TH' ARTIST WHAT HE SHALL CREATE!
BELCH
NOW LEMME SIT DOWN FOR A--
SKULL
SKLUKT!
YOW
YOU IDIOT!
HUH-HUH I PIERCED HIS BUTT! HUH-HUH
HEH HEH HEH HEH HEH COOL! PAIN RULES!
SKULL
PIERC
...I AGREE!
YOW
SNATCH
THESE NOSERINGS COST MONEY!
...GOTTA REMEMBER TO WIPE THIS OFF LATER...
IRON MAN, DUDE!
SKULL
SPECIAL CLOSE-UP
SKIN SNOT BLOOD
DUH NUH DUH-NUNT-DUH DUNANUNANOW

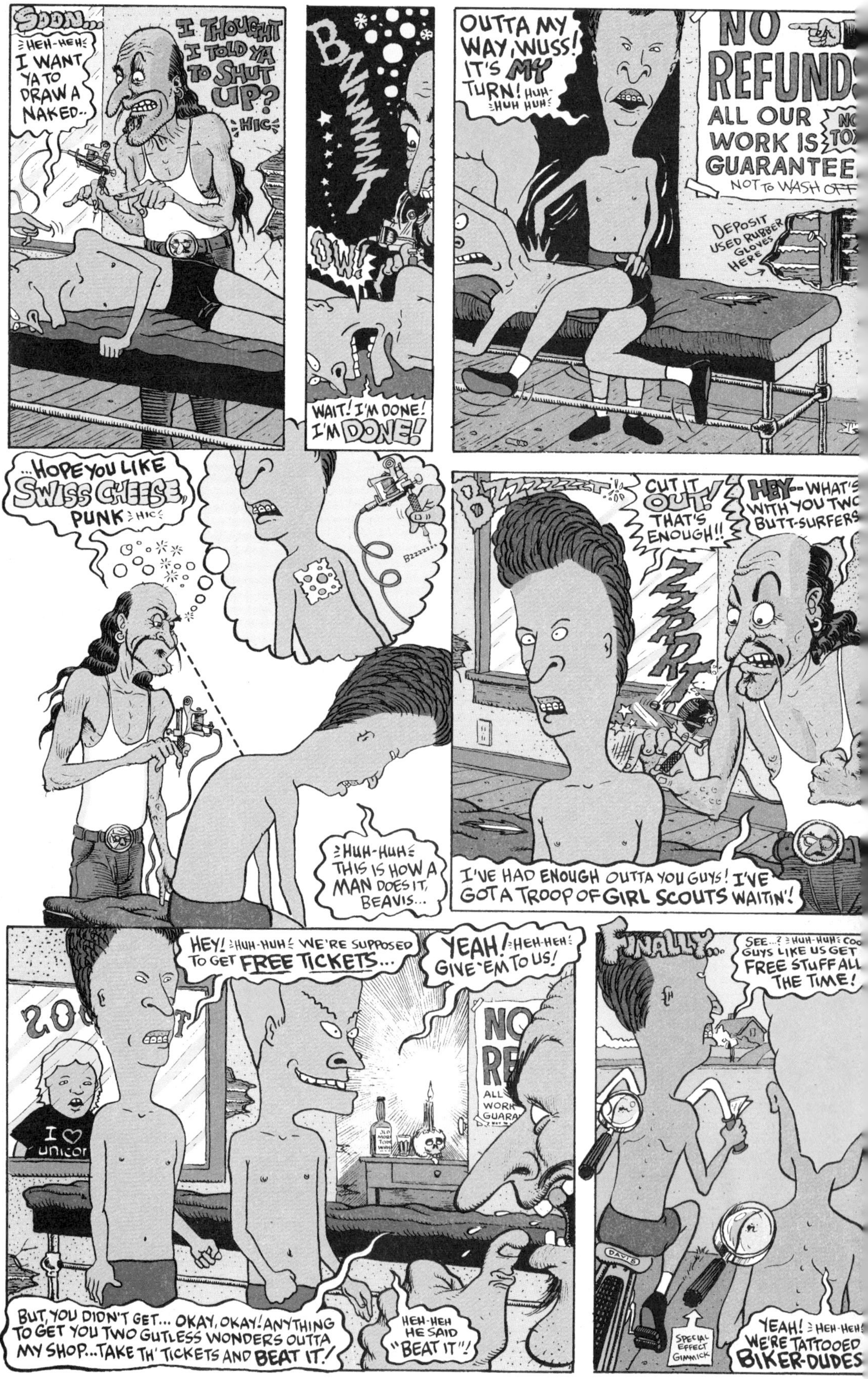
SOON...
HEH-HEH I WANT YA TO DRAW A NAKED..
I THOUGHT I TOLD YA TO SHUT UP? HIC
OW!
WAIT! I'M DONE! I'M DONE!
OUTTA MY WAY, WUSS! IT'S MY TURN! HUH-HUH HUH
NO REFUNDS ALL OUR WORK IS GUARANTEE
NOT TO WASH OFF
DEPOSIT USED RUBBER GLOVES HERE
...HOPE YOU LIKE SWISS CHEESE, PUNK HIC
HUH-HUH THIS IS HOW A MAN DOES IT, BEAVIS...
CUT IT OUT! THAT'S ENOUGH!!
HEY-- WHAT'S WITH YOU TWO BUTT-SURFERS
I'VE HAD ENOUGH OUTTA YOU GUYS! I'VE GOT A TROOP OF GIRL SCOUTS WAITIN'!
HEY! HUH-HUH WE'RE SUPPOSED TO GET FREE TICKETS...
YEAH! HEH-HEH GIVE 'EM TO US!
BUT, YOU DIDN'T GET... OKAY, OKAY! ANYTHING TO GET YOU TWO GUTLESS WONDERS OUTTA MY SHOP...TAKE TH' TICKETS AND BEAT IT!
HEH-HEH HE SAID "BEAT IT"!
FINALLY...
SEE...? HUH-HUH COO GUYS LIKE US GET FREE STUFF ALL THE TIME!
SPECIAL EFFECT GIMMICK
YEAH! HEH-HEH WE'RE TATTOOED BIKER-DUDES

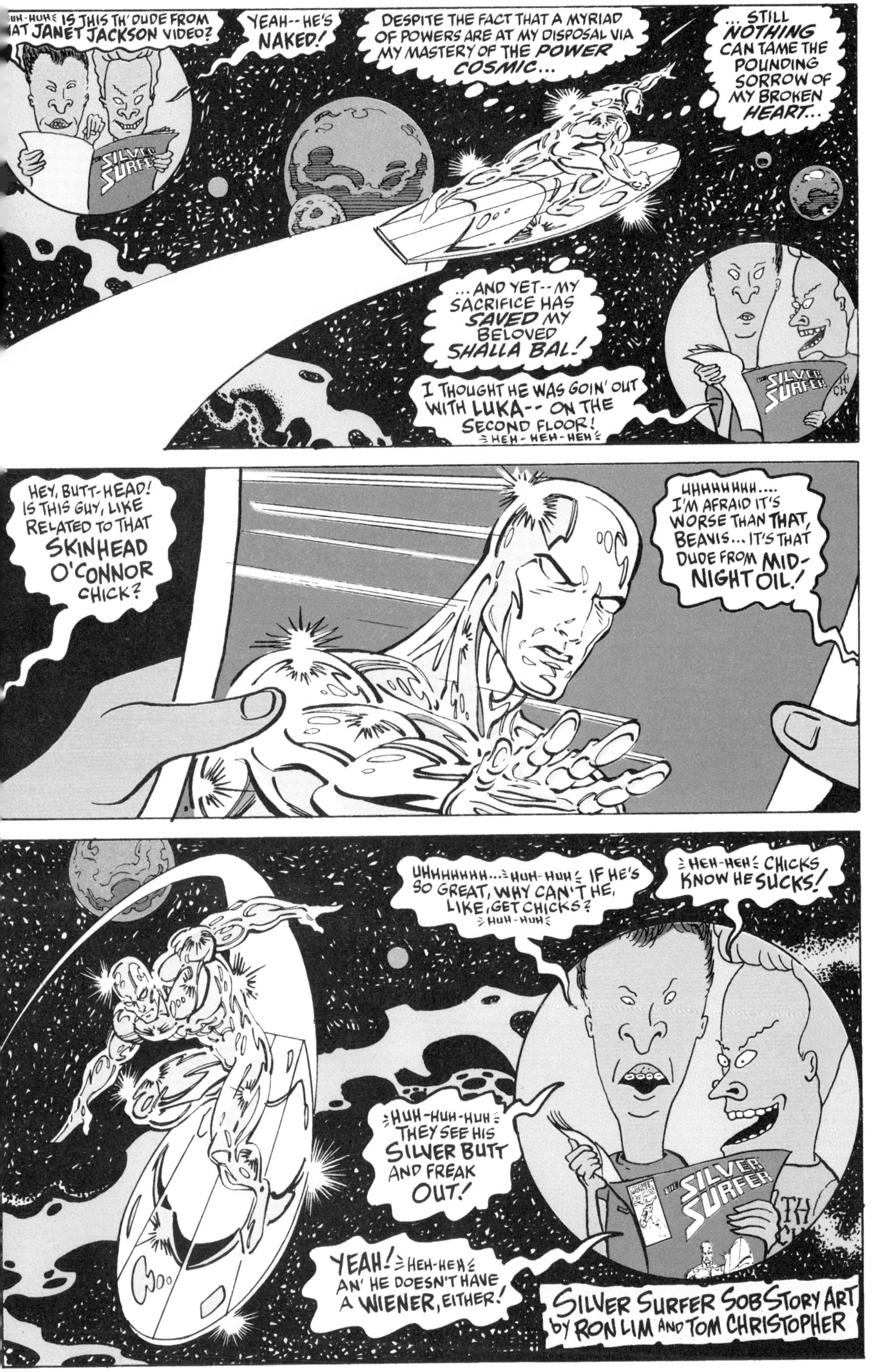
UH-HUH IS THIS TH' DUDE FROM AT JANET JACKSON VIDEO?
YEAH--HE'S NAKED!
DESPITE THE FACT THAT A MYRIAD OF POWERS ARE AT MY DISPOSAL VIA MY MASTERY OF THE POWER COSMIC...
...STILL NOTHING CAN TAME THE POUNDING SORROW OF MY BROKEN HEART...
...AND YET--MY SACRIFICE HAS SAVED MY BELOVED SHALLA BAL!
I THOUGHT HE WAS GOIN' OUT WITH LUKA-- ON THE SECOND FLOOR! HEH-HEH-HEH
SILVER SURFER
HEY, BUTT-HEAD! IS THIS GUY, LIKE RELATED TO THAT SKINHEAD O'CONNOR CHICK?
UHHHHHHH.... I'M AFRAID IT'S WORSE THAN THAT, BEAVIS... IT'S THAT DUDE FROM MID-NIGHT OIL!
UHHHHHHH... HUH-HUH IF HE'S SO GREAT, WHY CAN'T HE, LIKE, GET CHICKS? HUH-HUH
HEH-HEH CHICKS KNOW HE SUCKS!
HUH-HUH-HUH THEY SEE HIS SILVER BUTT AND FREAK OUT!
YEAH! HEH-HEH AN' HE DOESN'T HAVE A WIENER, EITHER!
THE SILVER SURFER
SILVER SURFER SOB STORY ART by RON LIM AND TOM CHRISTOPHER

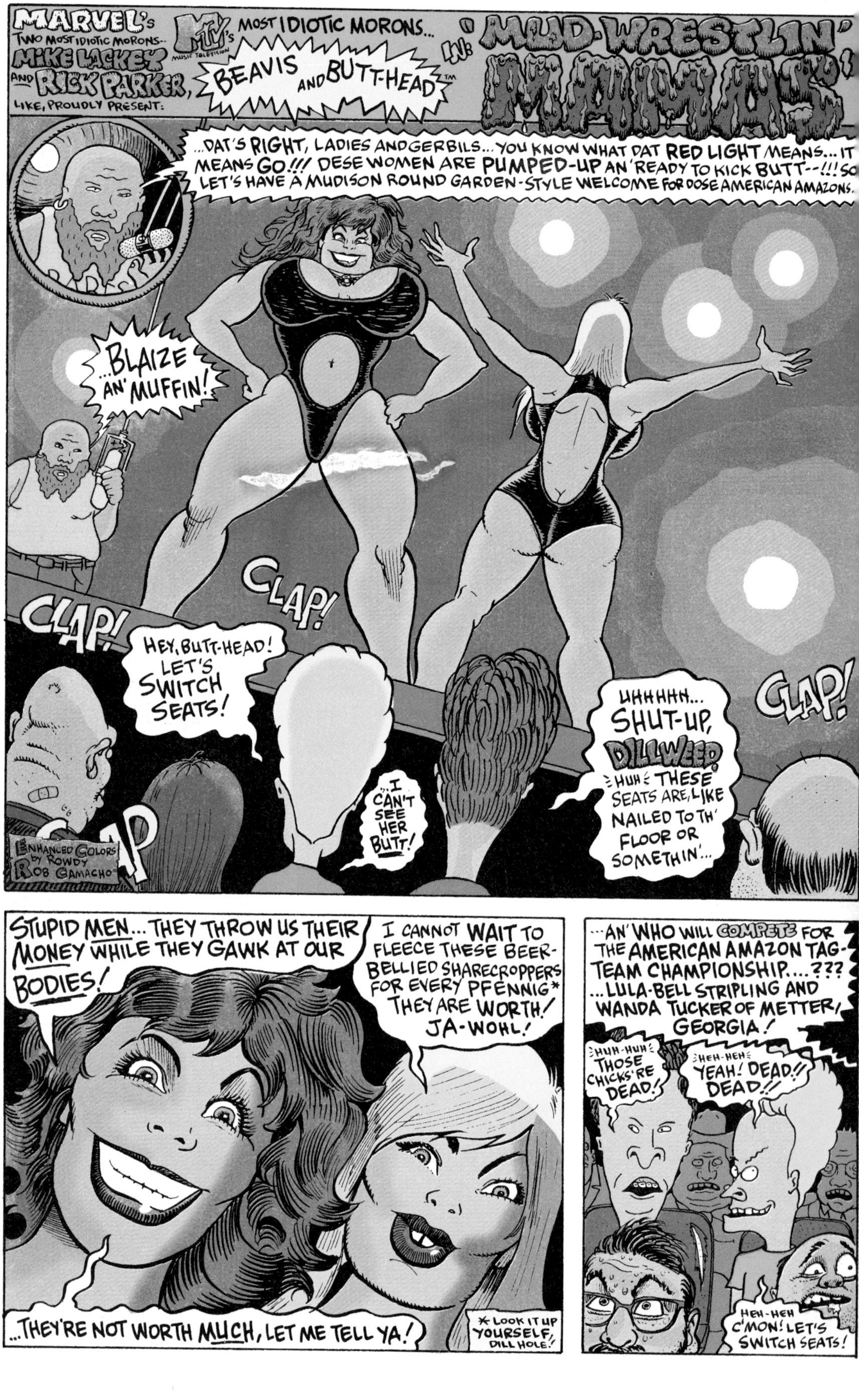
MARVEL's TWO MOST IDIOTIC MORONS... MIKE LACKEY AND RICK PARKER, LIKE, PROUDLY PRESENT:
MTV's MOST IDIOTIC MORONS... BEAVIS AND BUTT-HEAD™
IN: "MUD-WRESTLIN' MAMMAS"
...DAT'S RIGHT, LADIES AND GERBILS... YOU KNOW WHAT DAT RED LIGHT MEANS... IT MEANS GO!!! DESE WOMEN ARE PUMPED-UP AN' READY TO KICK BUTT--!!! SO LET'S HAVE A MUDISON ROUND GARDEN-STYLE WELCOME FOR DOSE AMERICAN AMAZONS.
...BLAIZE AN' MUFFIN!
CLAP!
CLAP!
HEY, BUTT-HEAD! LET'S SWITCH SEATS!
CLAP!
UHHHHH... SHUT-UP, DILLWEED. HUH THESE SEATS ARE, LIKE NAILED TO TH' FLOOR OR SOMETHIN'...
...I CAN'T SEE HER BUTT!
CLAP
ENHANCED COLORS by ROWDY ROB CAMACHO
STUPID MEN... THEY THROW US THEIR MONEY WHILE THEY GAWK AT OUR BODIES!
I CANNOT WAIT TO FLEECE THESE BEER-BELLIED SHARECROPPERS FOR EVERY PFENNIG* THEY ARE WORTH! JA-WOHL!
...THEY'RE NOT WORTH MUCH, LET ME TELL YA!
*LOOK IT UP YOURSELF, DILL HOLE!
...AN' WHO WILL COMPETE FOR THE AMERICAN AMAZON TAG-TEAM CHAMPIONSHIP....??? ...LULA-BELL STRIPLING AND WANDA TUCKER OF METTER, GEORGIA!
HUH-HUH THOSE CHICKS'RE DEAD!
HEH-HEH YEAH! DEAD!! DEAD!!
HEH-HEH C'MON! LET'S SWITCH SEATS!

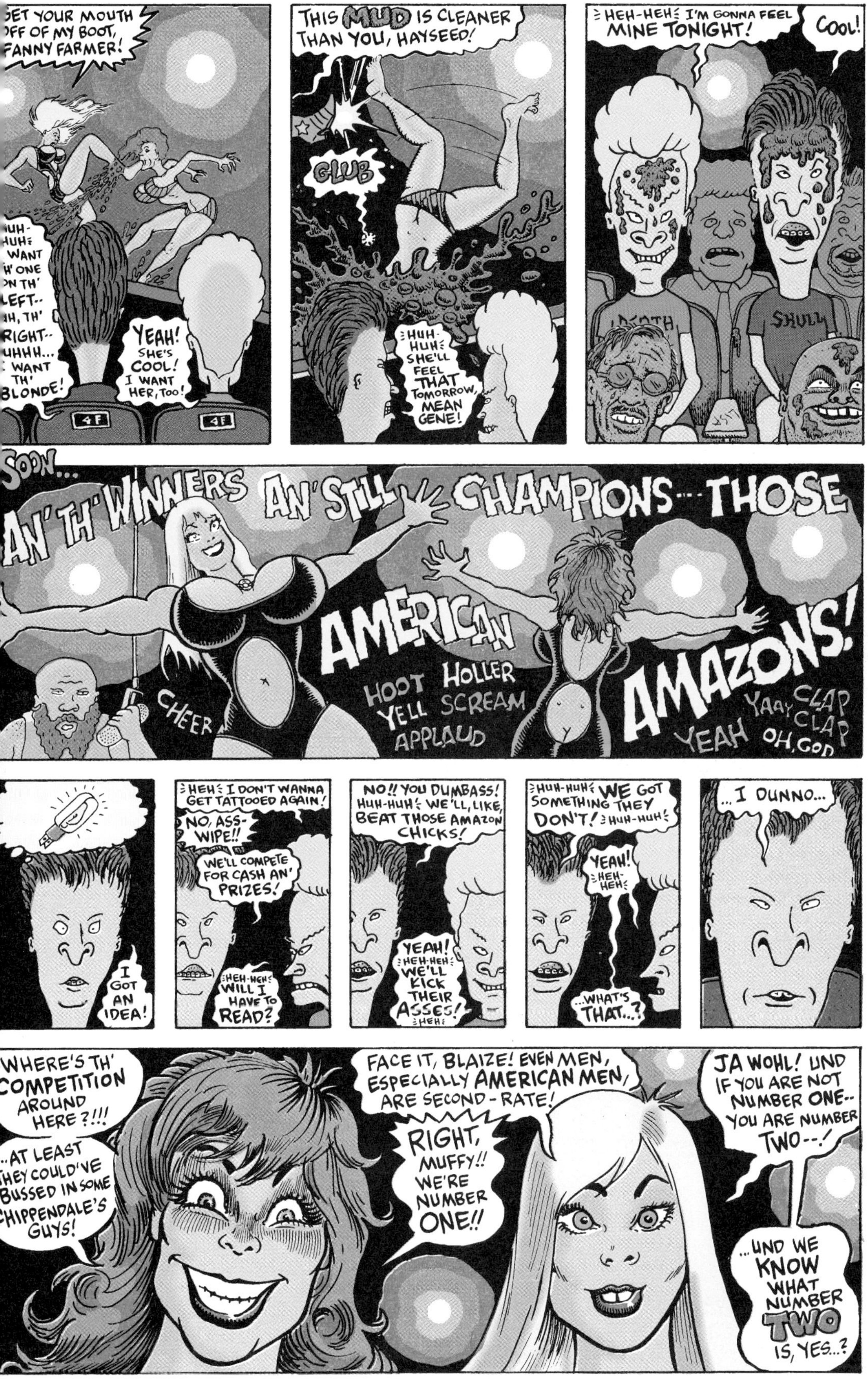

GET YOUR MOUTH OFF OF MY BOOT, FANNY FARMER!
HUH-HUH! WANT TH' ONE ON TH' LEFT-- UH, TH' RIGHT-- UHHH... I WANT TH' BLONDE!
YEAH! SHE'S COOL! I WANT HER, TOO!
4F
4F
THIS MUD IS CLEANER THAN YOU, HAYSEED!
GLUB
HUH-HUH! SHE'LL FEEL THAT TOMORROW, MEAN GENE!
HEH-HEH! I'M GONNA FEEL MINE TONIGHT!
COOL!
DEATH
SKULL
SOON...
AN' TH' WINNERS AN' STILL CHAMPIONS... THOSE
AMERICAN AMAZONS!
HOOT HOLLER YELL SCREAM APPLAUD CHEER
YAAY CLAP CLAP YEAH OH, GOD
I GOT AN IDEA!
HEH! I DON'T WANNA GET TATTOOED AGAIN!
NO, ASS-WIPE!!
WE'LL COMPETE FOR CASH AN' PRIZES!
HEH-HEH! WILL I HAVE TO READ?
NO!! YOU DUMBASS! HUH-HUH! WE'LL, LIKE, BEAT THOSE AMAZON CHICKS!
YEAH! HEH-HEH WE'LL KICK THEIR ASSES! HEH
HUH-HUH! WE GOT SOMETHING THEY DON'T! HUH-HUH!
YEAH! HEH-HEH
...WHAT'S THAT...?
... I DUNNO...
WHERE'S TH' COMPETITION AROUND HERE?!!!
...AT LEAST THEY COULD'VE BUSSED IN SOME CHIPPENDALE'S GUYS!
FACE IT, BLAIZE! EVEN MEN, ESPECIALLY AMERICAN MEN, ARE SECOND-RATE!
RIGHT, MUFFY!! WE'RE NUMBER ONE!!
JA WOHL! UND IF YOU ARE NOT NUMBER ONE-- YOU ARE NUMBER TWO--!
...UND WE KNOW WHAT NUMBER TWO IS, YES...?

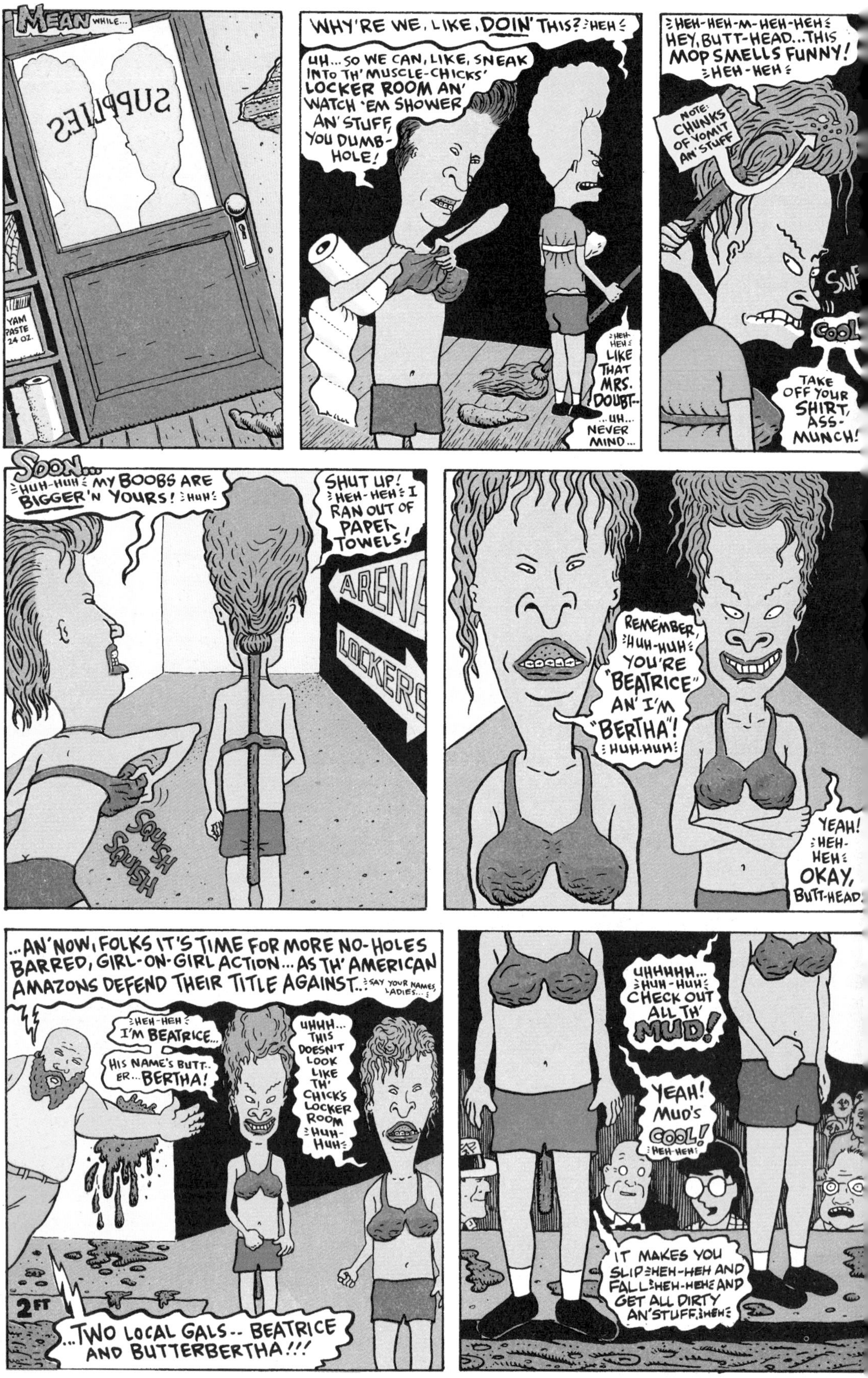
MEANWHILE...
SUPPLIES
YAM PASTE 24 OZ.
WHY'RE WE, LIKE, DOIN' THIS? HEH
UH... SO WE CAN, LIKE, SNEAK INTO TH' MUSCLE-CHICKS' LOCKER ROOM AN' WATCH 'EM SHOWER AN' STUFF, YOU DUMB-HOLE!
HEH-HEH LIKE THAT MRS. DOUBT-- ...UH... NEVER MIND...
HEH-HEH-M-HEH-HEH HEY, BUTT-HEAD...THIS MOP SMELLS FUNNY! HEH-HEH
NOTE: CHUNKS OF VOMIT AN' STUFF
SNIF
COOL
TAKE OFF YOUR SHIRT, ASS-MUNCH!
SOON...
HUH-HUH MY BOOBS ARE BIGGER'N YOURS! HUH
SHUT UP! HEH-HEH I RAN OUT OF PAPER TOWELS!
ARENA
LOCKERS
SQUISH SQUISH
REMEMBER, HUH-HUH YOU'RE "BEATRICE" AN' I'M "BERTHA"! HUH-HUH
YEAH! HEH-HEH OKAY, BUTT-HEAD.
...AN' NOW, FOLKS IT'S TIME FOR MORE NO-HOLES BARRED, GIRL-ON-GIRL ACTION... AS TH' AMERICAN AMAZONS DEFEND THEIR TITLE AGAINST... SAY YOUR NAMES, LADIES...
HEH-HEH I'M BEATRICE...
HIS NAME'S BUTT-- ER... BERTHA!
UHHH... THIS DOESN'T LOOK LIKE TH' CHICK'S LOCKER ROOM HUH-HUH
2FT
...TWO LOCAL GALS-- BEATRICE AND BUTTERBERTHA!!!
UHHHHH... HUH-HUH CHECK OUT ALL TH' MUD!
YEAH! MUD'S COOL! HEH-HEH
IT MAKES YOU SLIP HEH-HEH AND FALL HEH-HEH AND GET ALL DIRTY AN' STUFF. HEH

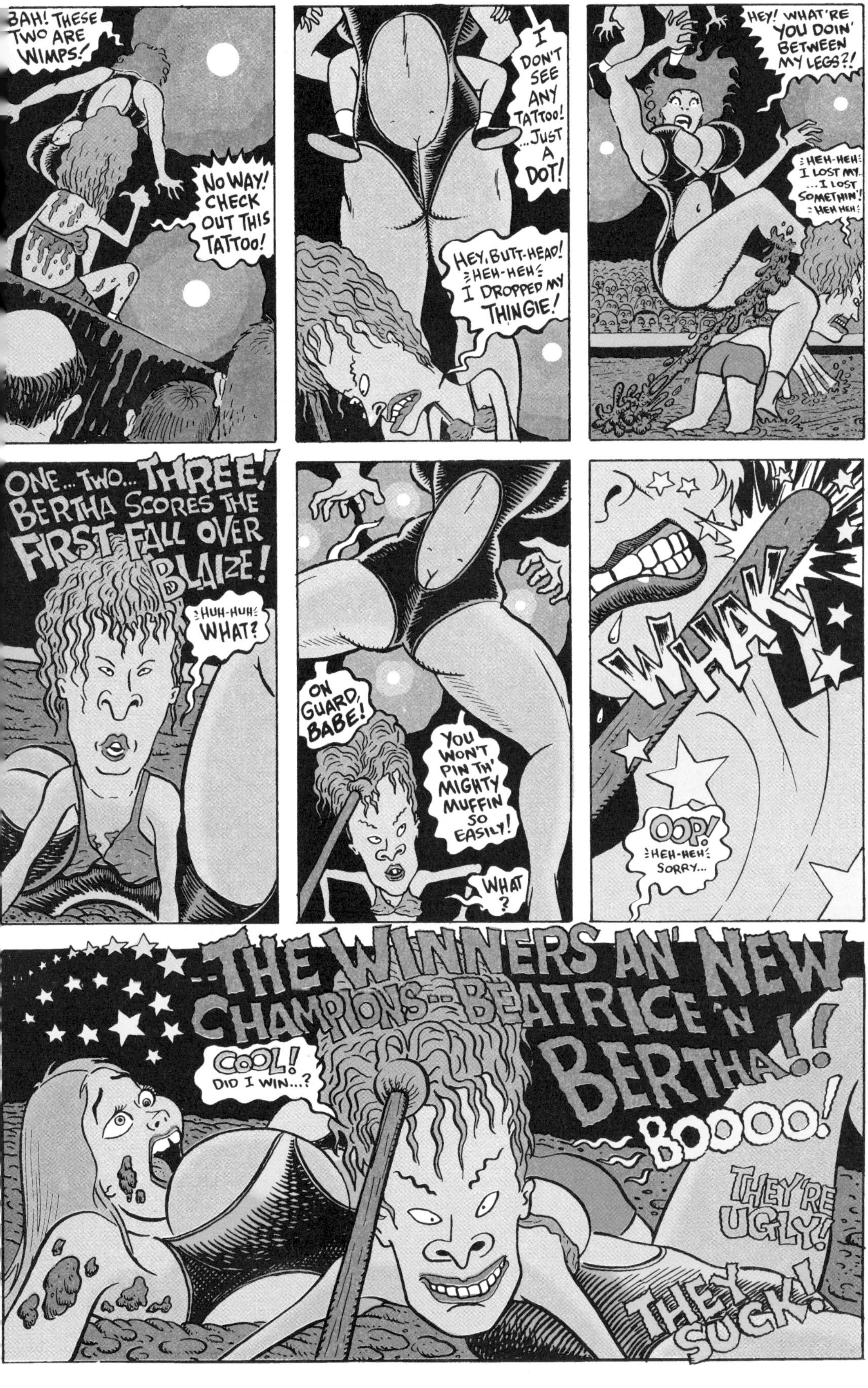

BAH! THESE TWO ARE WIMPS!
NO WAY! CHECK OUT THIS TATTOO!
I DON'T SEE ANY TATTOO! ...JUST A DOT!
HEY, BUTT-HEAD! HEH-HEH I DROPPED MY THINGIE!
HEY! WHAT'RE YOU DOIN' BETWEEN MY LEGS?!
HEH-HEH I LOST MY... I LOST SOMETHIN'! HEH HEH
ONE... TWO... THREE! BERTHA SCORES THE FIRST FALL OVER BLAIZE!
HUH-HUH WHAT?
ON GUARD, BABE!
YOU WON'T PIN TH' MIGHTY MUFFIN SO EASILY!
WHAT?
WHAK!
OOP! HEH-HEH SORRY...
..THE WINNERS AN' NEW CHAMPIONS.. BEATRICE 'N BERTHA!!
COOL! DID I WIN...?
BOOOO!
THEY'RE UGLY!
THEY SUCK!

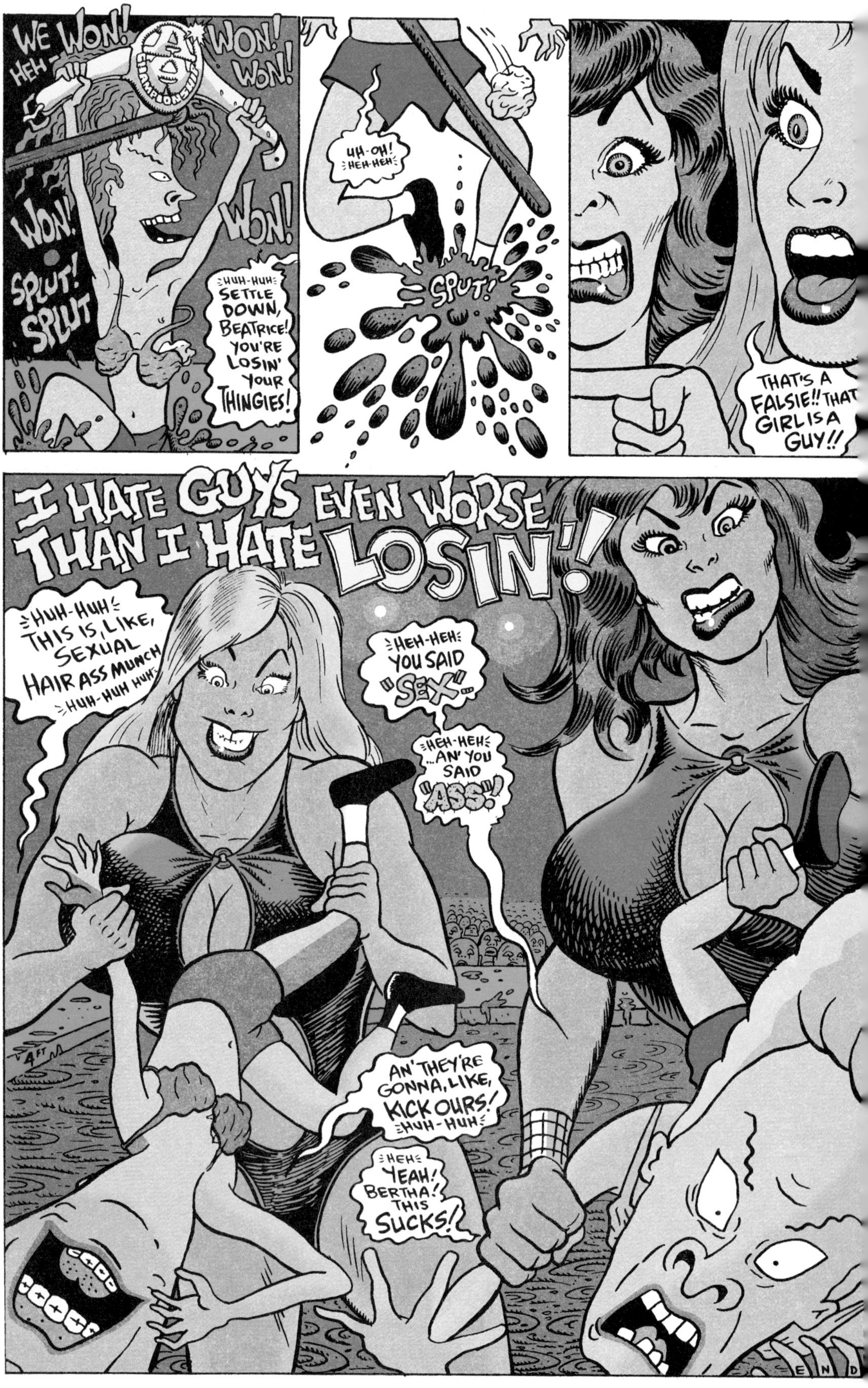
WE WON! HEH-
CHAMPIONSHIP
WON! WON!
WON!
WON!
SPLUT! SPLUT
HUH-HUH SETTLE DOWN, BEATRICE! YOU'RE LOSIN' YOUR THINGIES!
UH-OH! HEH-HEH
SPUT!
THAT'S A FALSIE!! THAT GIRL IS A GUY!!
I HATE GUYS EVEN WORSE THAN I HATE LOSIN'!!
HUH-HUH THIS IS, LIKE, SEXUAL HAIR ASS MUNCH HUH-HUH HUH
HEH-HEH YOU SAID "SEX"...
HEH-HEH ...AN' YOU SAID "ASS"!
4 FT
AN' THEY'RE GONNA, LIKE, KICK OURS! HUH-HUH
HEH YEAH! BERTHA! THIS SUCKS!
END

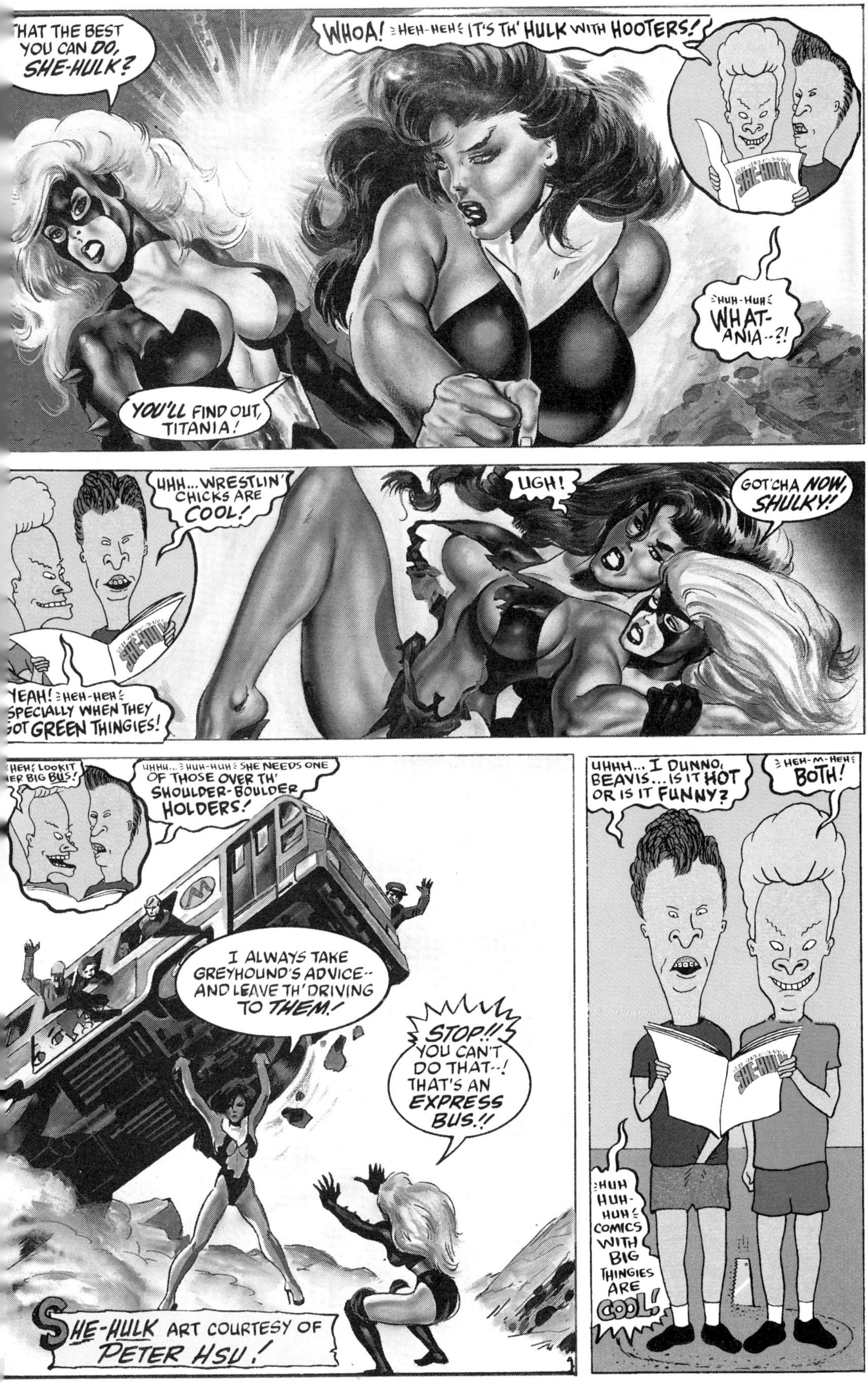
THAT THE BEST YOU CAN DO, SHE-HULK?
WHOA! HEH-HEH IT'S TH' HULK WITH HOOTERS!
SHE-HULK
HUH-HUH WHAT-ANIA--?!
YOU'LL FIND OUT, TITANIA!
UHH... WRESTLIN' CHICKS ARE COOL!
UGH!
GOT'CHA NOW, SHULKY!
SHE-HULK
YEAH! HEH-HEH SPECIALLY WHEN THEY GOT GREEN THINGIES!
HEH! LOOKIT ER BIG BUS!
UHHH... HUH-HUH SHE NEEDS ONE OF THOSE OVER TH' SHOULDER-BOULDER HOLDERS!
I ALWAYS TAKE GREYHOUND'S ADVICE-- AND LEAVE TH' DRIVING TO THEM!
STOP!! YOU CAN'T DO THAT--! THAT'S AN EXPRESS BUS.!!
SHE-HULK ART COURTESY OF PETER HSU!
UHHH... I DUNNO, BEAVIS... IS IT HOT OR IS IT FUNNY?
HEH-M-HEH BOTH!
SHE-HULK
HUH HUH-HUH COMICS WITH BIG THINGIES ARE COOL!

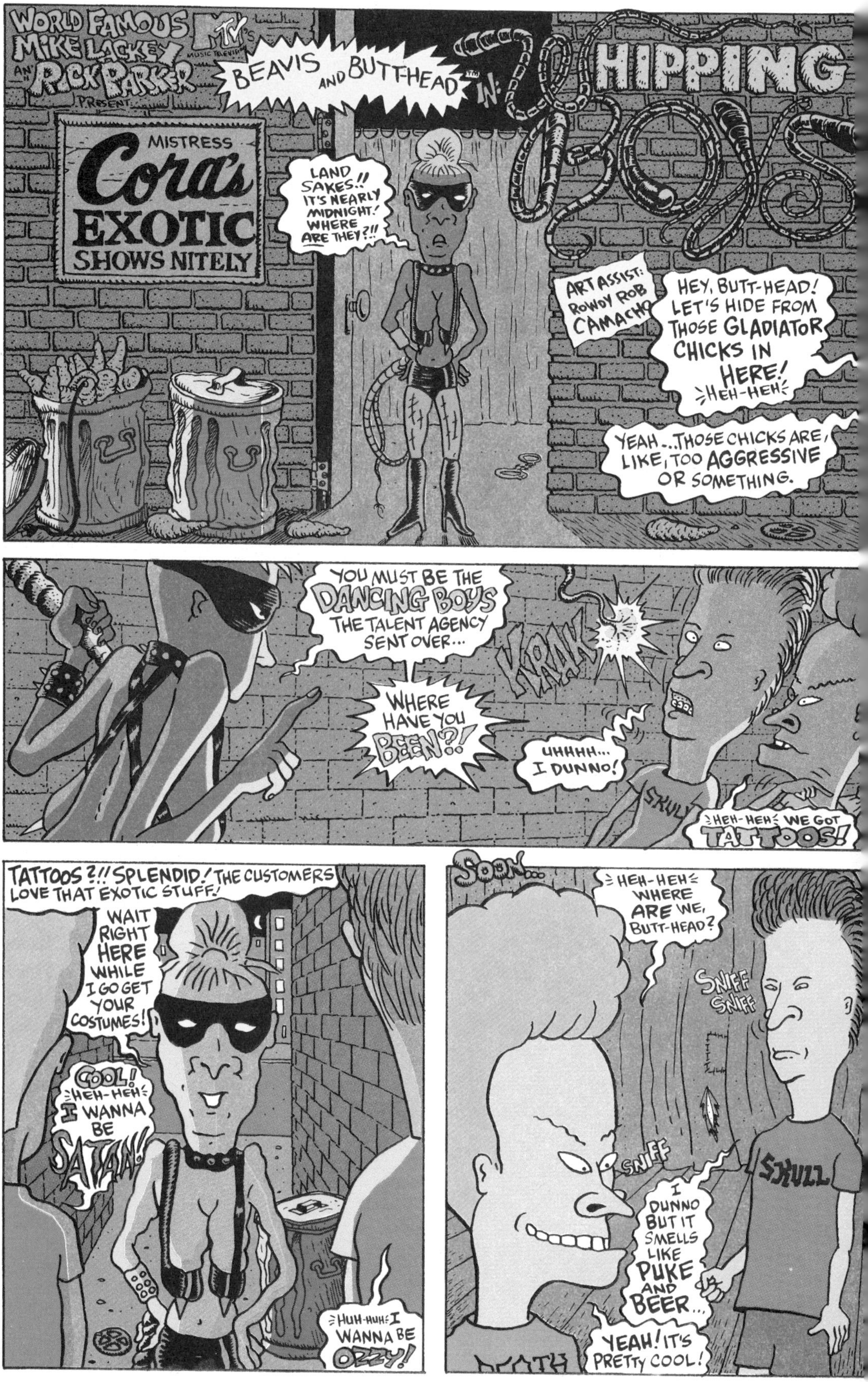
WORLD FAMOUS MIKE LACKEY AN' RICK PARKER PRESENT
MTV's MUSIC TELEVISION
BEAVIS AND BUTT-HEAD IN:
WHIPPING BOYS
MISTRESS Cora's EXOTIC SHOWS NITELY
LAND SAKES!! IT'S NEARLY MIDNIGHT! WHERE ARE THEY?!!
ART ASSIST: ROWDY ROB CAMACHO
HEY, BUTT-HEAD! LET'S HIDE FROM THOSE GLADIATOR CHICKS IN HERE! HEH-HEH
YEAH...THOSE CHICKS ARE, LIKE, TOO AGGRESSIVE OR SOMETHING.
YOU MUST BE THE DANCING BOYS THE TALENT AGENCY SENT OVER...
KRAK
WHERE HAVE YOU BEEN?!
UHHHH... I DUNNO!
SKULL
HEH-HEH WE GOT TATTOOS!
TATTOOS?!! SPLENDID! THE CUSTOMERS LOVE THAT EXOTIC STUFF!
WAIT RIGHT HERE WHILE I GO GET YOUR COSTUMES!
COOL! HEH-HEH I WANNA BE SATAN!
HUH-HUH I WANNA BE OZZY!
SOON...
HEH-HEH WHERE ARE WE, BUTT-HEAD?
SNIFF SNIFF
SNIFF
SKULL
I DUNNO BUT IT SMELLS LIKE PUKE AND BEER...
YEAH! IT'S PRETTY COOL!

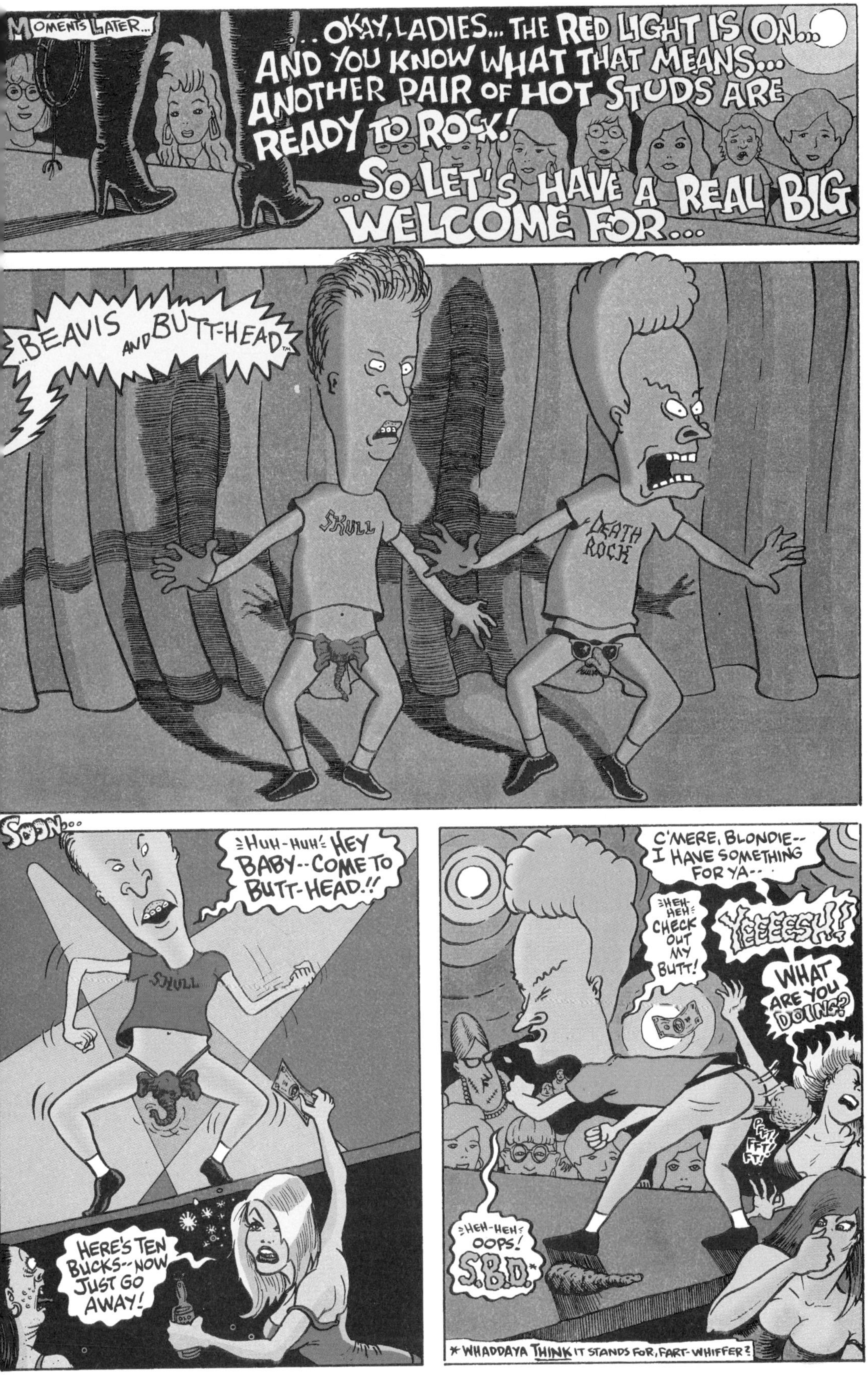
MOMENTS LATER...
...OKAY, LADIES... THE RED LIGHT IS ON... AND YOU KNOW WHAT THAT MEANS... ANOTHER PAIR OF HOT STUDS ARE READY TO ROCK!
...SO LET'S HAVE A REAL BIG WELCOME FOR...
...BEAVIS AND BUTT-HEAD™
SKULL
DEATH ROCK
SOON...
HUH-HUH! HEY BABY--COME TO BUTT-HEAD!!
SKULL
HERE'S TEN BUCKS--NOW JUST GO AWAY!
C'MERE, BLONDIE-- I HAVE SOMETHING FOR YA--
HEH-HEH CHECK OUT MY BUTT!
YEEEESH!?
WHAT ARE YOU DOING?
PFFT! FFT! FT!
HEH-HEH OOPS! S.B.D.*
* WHADDAYA THINK IT STANDS FOR, FART-WHIFFER?

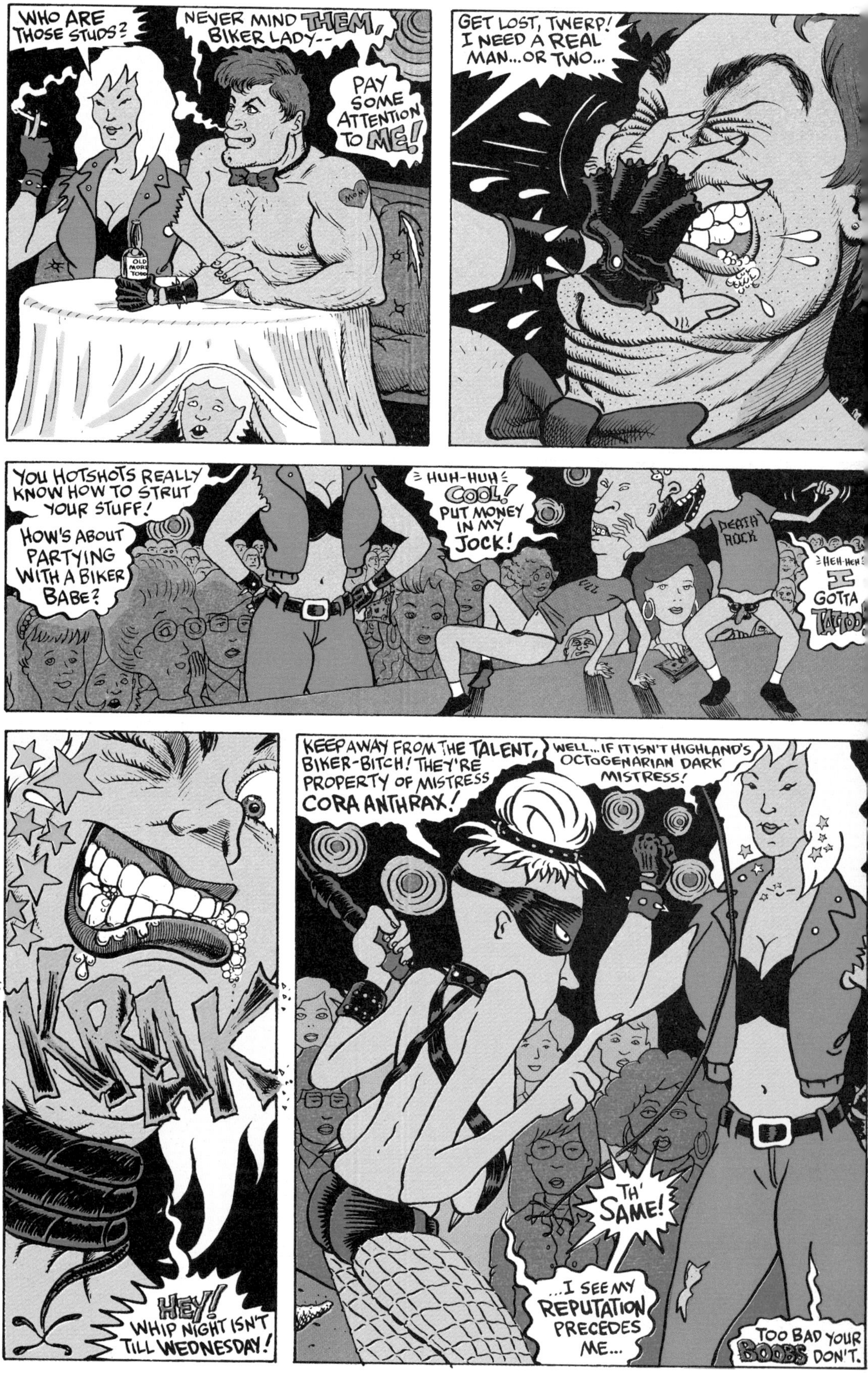
WHO ARE THOSE STUDS?
NEVER MIND THEM, BIKER LADY--
PAY SOME ATTENTION TO ME!
OLD MORD TODD
GET LOST, TWERP! I NEED A REAL MAN...OR TWO...
YOU HOTSHOTS REALLY KNOW HOW TO STRUT YOUR STUFF!
HOW'S ABOUT PARTYING WITH A BIKER BABE?
HUH-HUH COOL! PUT MONEY IN MY JOCK!
DEATH ROCK
HEH-HEH I GOTTA TATTOO!
KRAK
HEY! WHIP NIGHT ISN'T TILL WEDNESDAY!
KEEP AWAY FROM THE TALENT, BIKER-BITCH! THEY'RE PROPERTY OF MISTRESS CORA ANTHRAX!
WELL... IF IT ISN'T HIGHLAND'S OCTOGENARIAN DARK MISTRESS!
TH' SAME!
...I SEE MY REPUTATION PRECEDES ME...
TOO BAD YOUR BOOBS DON'T.

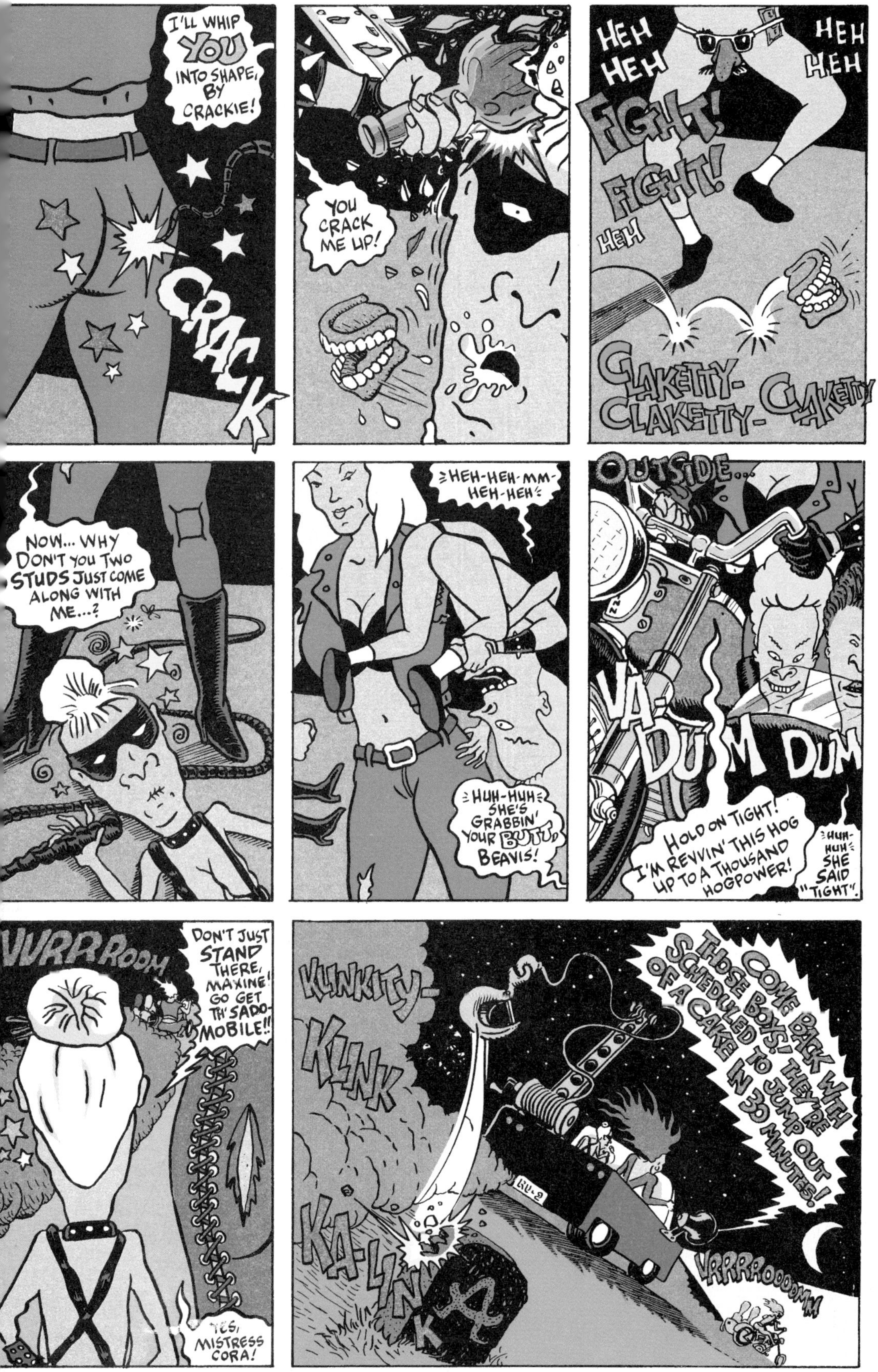
I'LL WHIP YOU INTO SHAPE, BY CRACKIE!
CRACK
YOU CRACK ME UP!
HEH HEH
HEH HEH
FIGHT! FIGHT!
HEH
CLAKETTY-CLAKETTY-CLAKETTY-CLAKETTY
NOW... WHY DON'T YOU TWO STUDS JUST COME ALONG WITH ME...?
HEH-HEH-MM-HEH-HEH
HUH-HUH SHE'S GRABBIN' YOUR BUTT, BEAVIS!
OUTSIDE...
VA-DUM DUM
HOLD ON TIGHT! I'M REVVIN' THIS HOG UP TO A THOUSAND HOGPOWER!
HUH-HUH SHE SAID "TIGHT".
VVRRROOM
DON'T JUST STAND THERE, MAXINE! GO GET TH' SADO-MOBILE!!
YES, MISTRESS CORA!
KLINKITY-KLINK
KA-LINK
COME BACK WITH THOSE BOYS! THEY'RE SCHEDULED TO JUMP OUT OF A CAKE IN 30 MINUTES!
VRRRROOOOMM

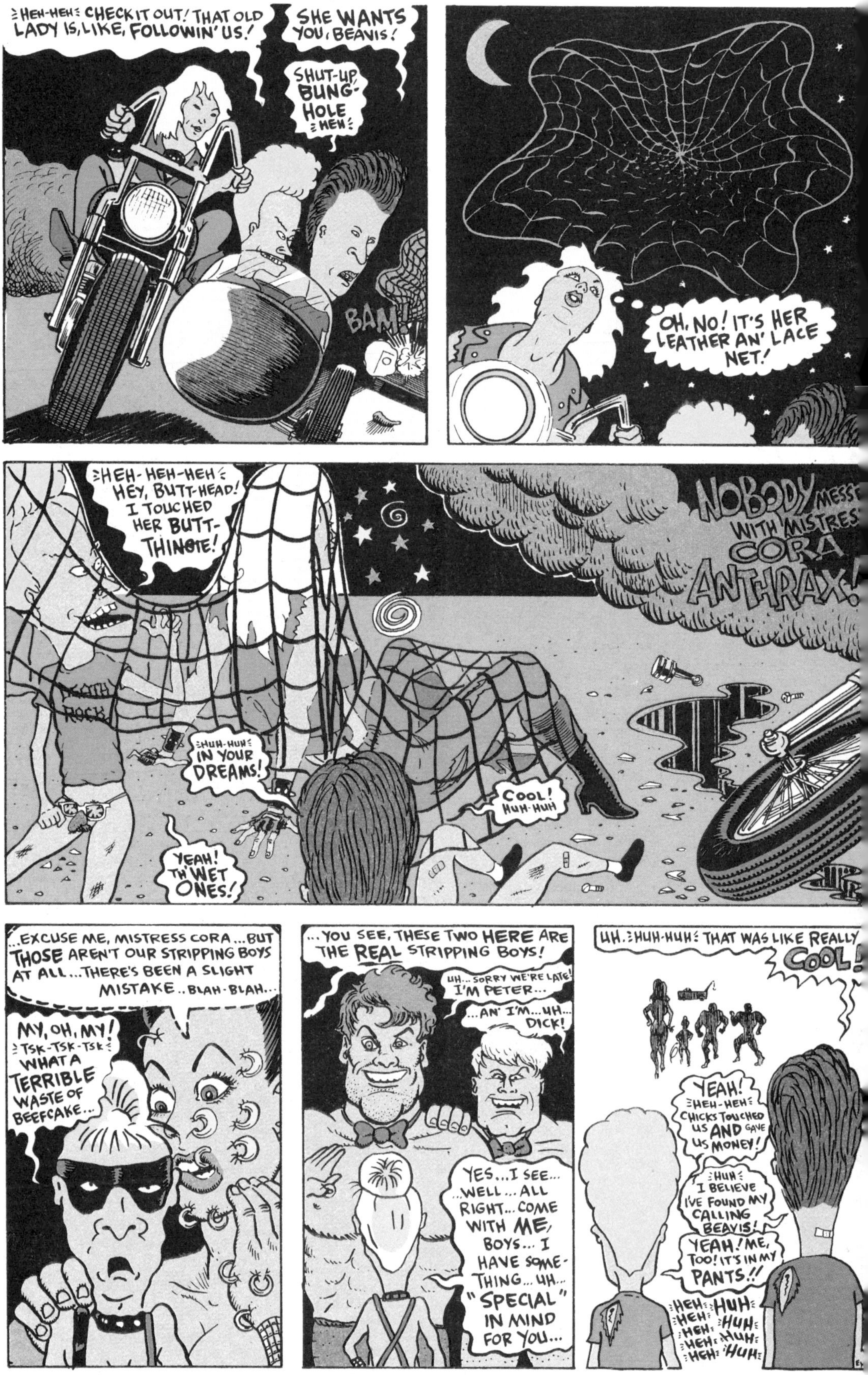

HEH-HEH CHECK IT OUT! THAT OLD LADY IS, LIKE, FOLLOWIN' US!
SHE WANTS YOU, BEAVIS!
SHUT-UP, BUNG-HOLE HEH
BAM!
OH, NO! IT'S HER LEATHER AN' LACE NET!
HEH-HEH-HEH HEY, BUTT-HEAD! I TOUCHED HER BUTT-THINGIE!
NOBODY MESSES WITH MISTRESS CORA ANTHRAX!
DEATH ROCK
HUH-HUH IN YOUR DREAMS!
COOL! HUH-HUH
YEAH! TH' WET ONES!
...EXCUSE ME, MISTRESS CORA ... BUT THOSE AREN'T OUR STRIPPING BOYS AT ALL ... THERE'S BEEN A SLIGHT MISTAKE .. BLAH-BLAH...
MY, OH, MY! TSK-TSK-TSK WHAT A TERRIBLE WASTE OF BEEFCAKE...
...YOU SEE, THESE TWO HERE ARE THE REAL STRIPPING BOYS!
UH... SORRY WE'RE LATE! I'M PETER...
...AN' I'M... UH... DICK!
YES ... I SEE... ...WELL ... ALL RIGHT ... COME WITH ME, BOYS ... I HAVE SOME-THING ... UH... "SPECIAL" IN MIND FOR YOU...
UH. HUH-HUH THAT WAS LIKE REALLY COOL!
YEAH! HEH-HEH CHICKS TOUCHED US AND GAVE US MONEY!
HUH I BELIEVE I'VE FOUND MY CALLING BEAVIS!
YEAH! ME, TOO! IT'S IN MY PANTS!!
HEH HEH HEH HEH HEH
HUH HUH HUH HUH

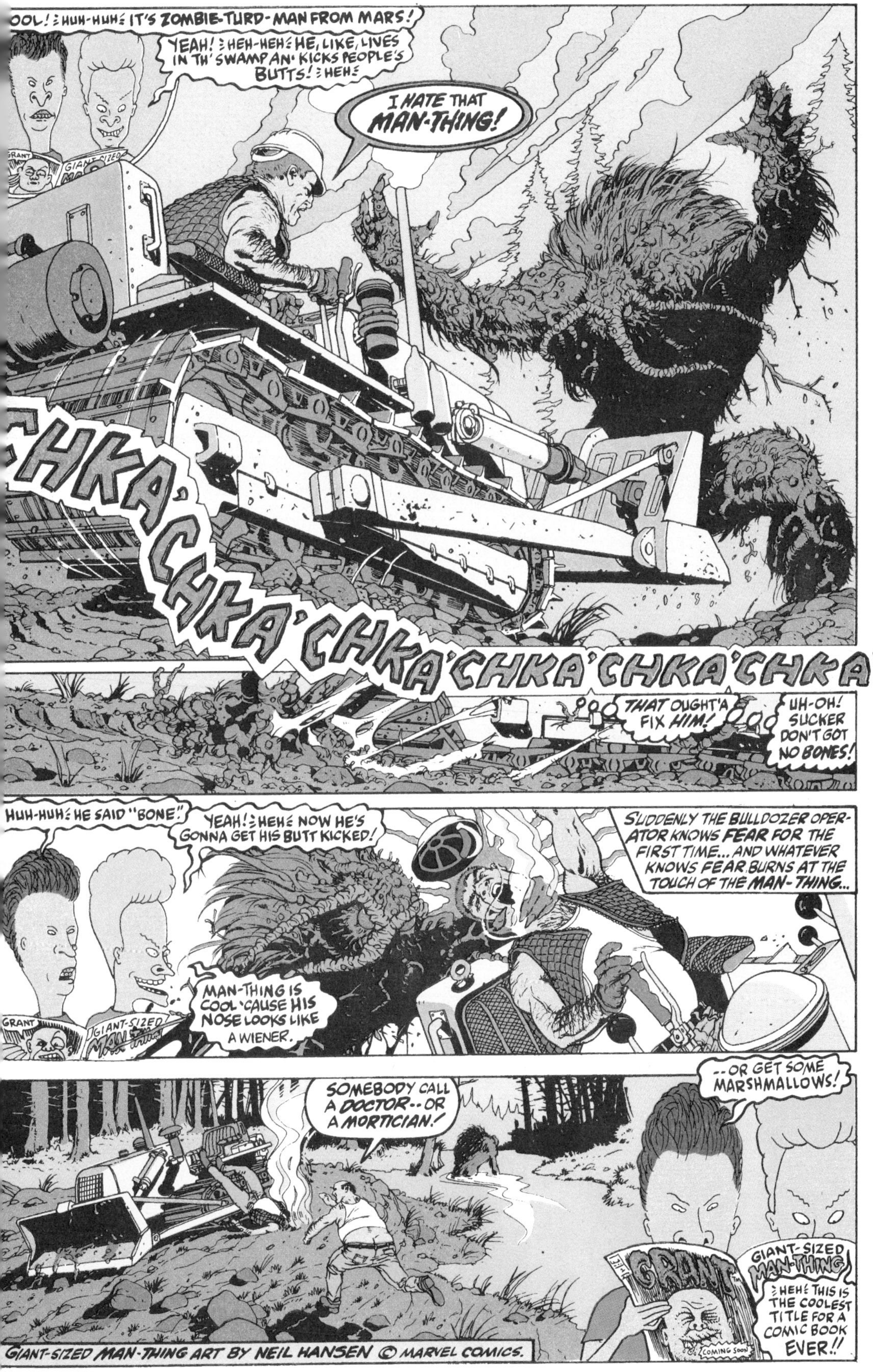
OOL! HUH-HUH IT'S ZOMBIE-TURD-MAN FROM MARS!
YEAH! HEH-HEH HE, LIKE, LIVES IN TH' SWAMP AN' KICKS PEOPLE'S BUTTS! HEH
I HATE THAT MAN-THING!
GIANT-SIZED
CHKA'CHKA'CHKA'CHKA'CHKA'CHKA'CHKA'
THAT OUGHT'A FIX HIM!
UH-OH! SUCKER DON'T GOT NO BONES!
HUH-HUH HE SAID "BONE."
YEAH! HEH NOW HE'S GONNA GET HIS BUTT KICKED!
SUDDENLY THE BULLDOZER OPERATOR KNOWS FEAR FOR THE FIRST TIME... AND WHATEVER KNOWS FEAR BURNS AT THE TOUCH OF THE MAN-THING...
MAN-THING IS COOL 'CAUSE HIS NOSE LOOKS LIKE A WIENER.
GRANT
GIANT-SIZED
SOMEBODY CALL A DOCTOR--OR A MORTICIAN!
--OR GET SOME MARSHMALLOWS!
GRANT
COMING SOON
GIANT-SIZED MAN-THING
HEH THIS IS THE COOLEST TITLE FOR A COMIC BOOK EVER!!
GIANT-SIZED MAN-THING ART BY NEIL HANSEN © MARVEL COMICS.

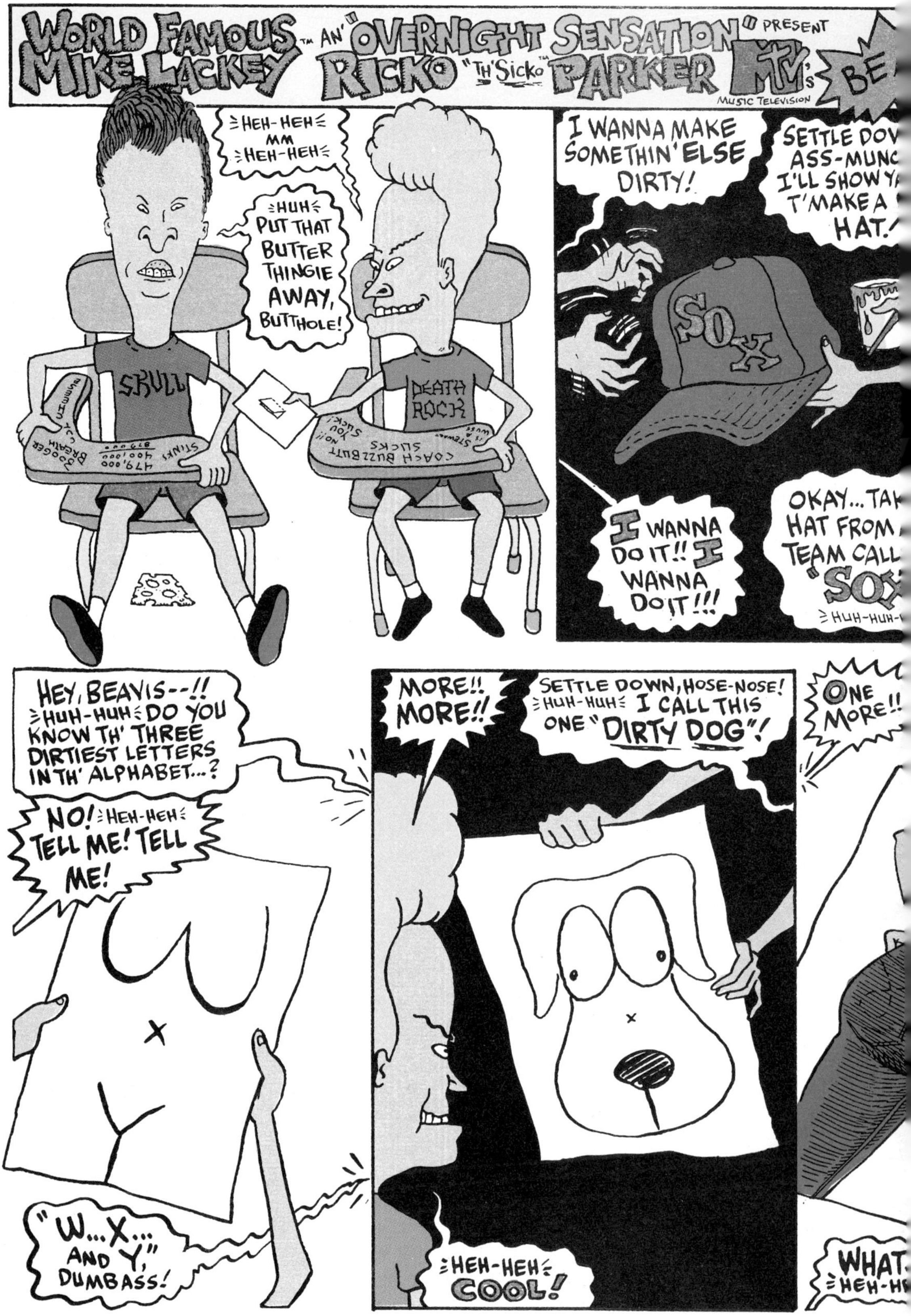

WORLD FAMOUS MIKE LACKEY™ AN' "OVERNIGHT SENSATION" RICKO "TH' SICKO"™ PARKER PRESENT MTV'S BE
MUSIC TELEVISION
HEH-HEH MM HEH-HEH
HUH PUT THAT BUTTER THINGIE AWAY, BUTTHOLE!
SKULL
DEATH ROCK
COACH BUZZCUT SUCKS
479,000
STINKS
BOOGER BREATH
I WANNA MAKE SOMETHIN' ELSE DIRTY!
SETTLE DOV ASS-MUNC I'LL SHOW YA T'MAKE A HAT!
SOX
I WANNA DO IT!! I WANNA DO IT!!!
OKAY... TAK HAT FROM TEAM CALL "SOX
HUH-HUH
HEY, BEAVIS--!! HUH-HUH DO YOU KNOW TH' THREE DIRTIEST LETTERS IN TH' ALPHABET...?
NO! HEH-HEH TELL ME! TELL ME!
"W...X... AND Y," DUMBASS!
MORE!! MORE!!
SETTLE DOWN, HOSE-NOSE! HUH-HUH I CALL THIS ONE "DIRTY DOG"!
HEH-HEH COOL!
ONE MORE!!
WHAT HEH-HE

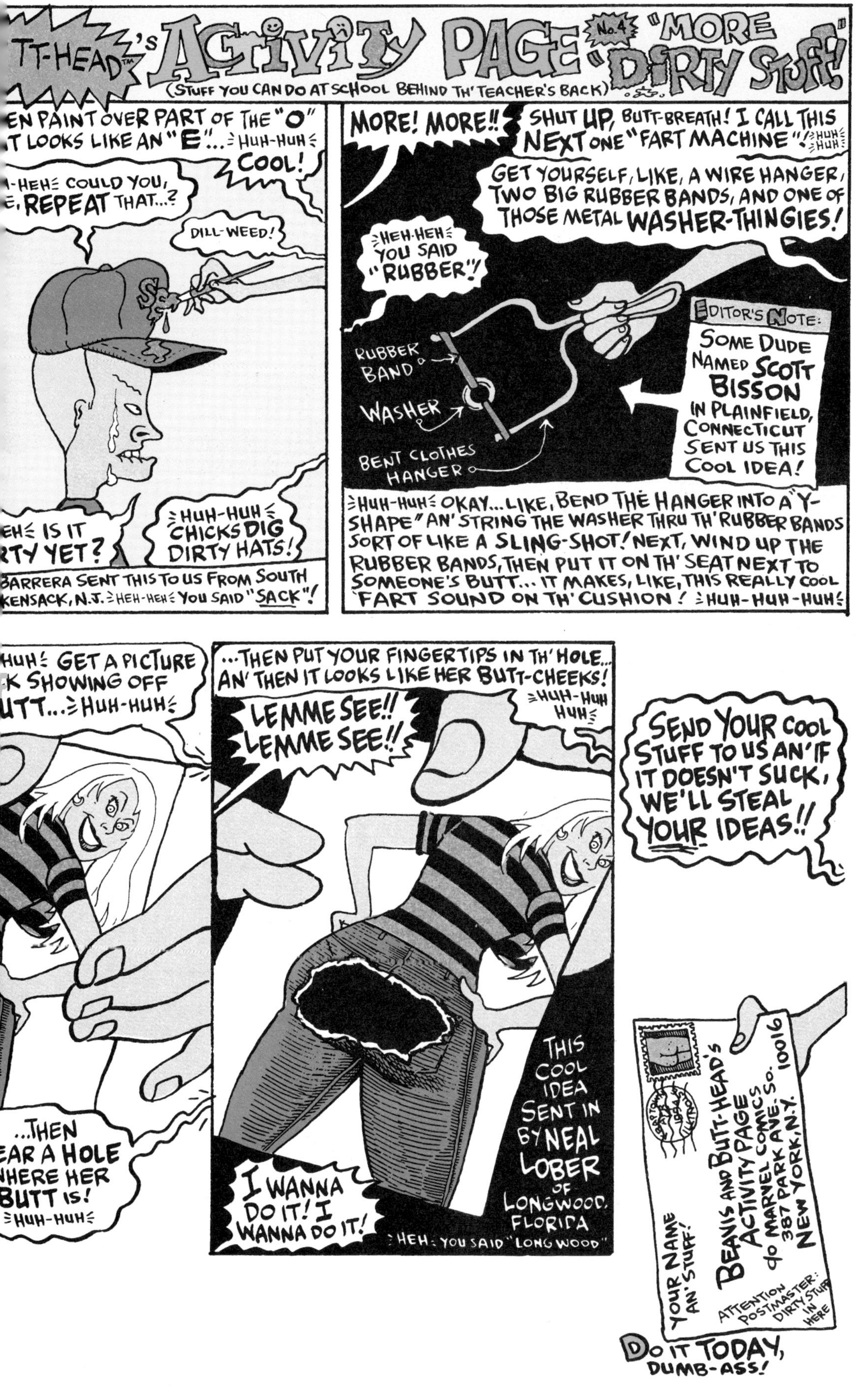

TT-HEAD™'s ACTIVITY PAGE No. 4 "MORE 'DIRTY STUFF'"
(STUFF YOU CAN DO AT SCHOOL BEHIND TH' TEACHER'S BACK)
EN PAINT OVER PART OF THE "O" T LOOKS LIKE AN "E"... HUH-HUH
COOL!
-HEH COULD YOU, E, REPEAT THAT...?
DILL-WEED!
EH IS IT RTY YET?
HUH-HUH CHICKS DIG DIRTY HATS!
BARRERA SENT THIS TO US FROM SOUTH KENSACK, N.J. HEH-HEH YOU SAID "SACK"!
MORE! MORE!!
SHUT UP, BUTT-BREATH! I CALL THIS NEXT ONE "FART MACHINE"! HUH HUH
GET YOURSELF, LIKE, A WIRE HANGER, TWO BIG RUBBER BANDS, AND ONE OF THOSE METAL WASHER-THINGIES!
HEH-HEH YOU SAID "RUBBER"!
RUBBER BAND
WASHER
BENT CLOTHES HANGER
EDITOR'S NOTE: SOME DUDE NAMED SCOTT BISSON IN PLAINFIELD, CONNECTICUT SENT US THIS COOL IDEA!
HUH-HUH OKAY... LIKE, BEND THE HANGER INTO A "Y-SHAPE" AN' STRING THE WASHER THRU TH' RUBBER BANDS SORT OF LIKE A SLING-SHOT! NEXT, WIND UP THE RUBBER BANDS, THEN PUT IT ON TH' SEAT NEXT TO SOMEONE'S BUTT... IT MAKES, LIKE, THIS REALLY COOL FART SOUND ON TH' CUSHION! HUH-HUH-HUH
HUH GET A PICTURE K SHOWING OFF UTT... HUH-HUH
...THEN EAR A HOLE HERE HER BUTT IS! HUH-HUH
...THEN PUT YOUR FINGERTIPS IN TH' HOLE... AN' THEN IT LOOKS LIKE HER BUTT-CHEEKS!
LEMME SEE!! LEMME SEE!!
HUH-HUH HUH
I WANNA DO IT! I WANNA DO IT!
THIS COOL IDEA SENT IN BY NEAL LOBER OF LONGWOOD, FLORIDA
HEH YOU SAID "LONGWOOD"
SEND YOUR COOL STUFF TO US AN' IF IT DOESN'T SUCK, WE'LL STEAL YOUR IDEAS!!
YOUR NAME AN' STUFF!
BEAVIS AND BUTT-HEAD'S ACTIVITY PAGE c/o MARVEL COMICS 387 PARK AVE. SO. NEW YORK, N.Y. 10016
ATTENTION POSTMASTER: DIRTY STUFF IN HERE
DO IT TODAY, DUMB-ASS!

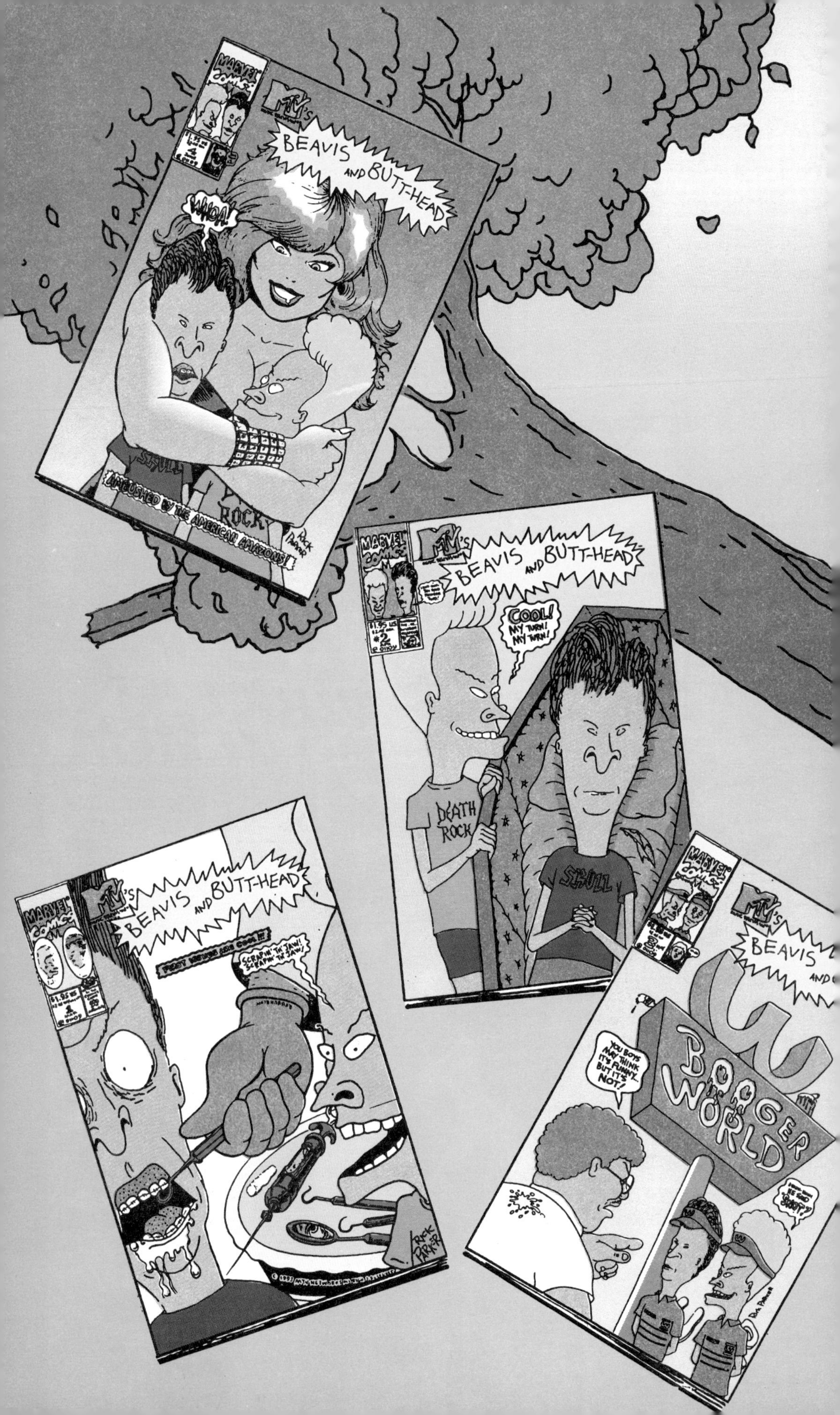
MARVEL COMICS
MTV's
BEAVIS AND BUTT-HEAD
WHOA!
SKULL
ROCKY
AMBUSHED BY THE AMERICAN AMAZONS!
RICK PARKER
MARVEL COMICS
MTV's
BEAVIS AND BUTT-HEAD
$1.95 US
#2
COOL! MY TURN! MY TURN!
DEATH ROCK
SKULL
MARVEL COMICS
MTV's
BEAVIS AND BUTT-HEAD
$1.95 US
1
SCRAPIN' TH' JAW! SCRAPIN' TH' JAW!
RICK PARKER
MARVEL COMICS
MTV's
BEAVIS AND
YOU BOYS MAY THINK IT'S FUNNY... BUT IT'S NOT!
BOOGER WORLD

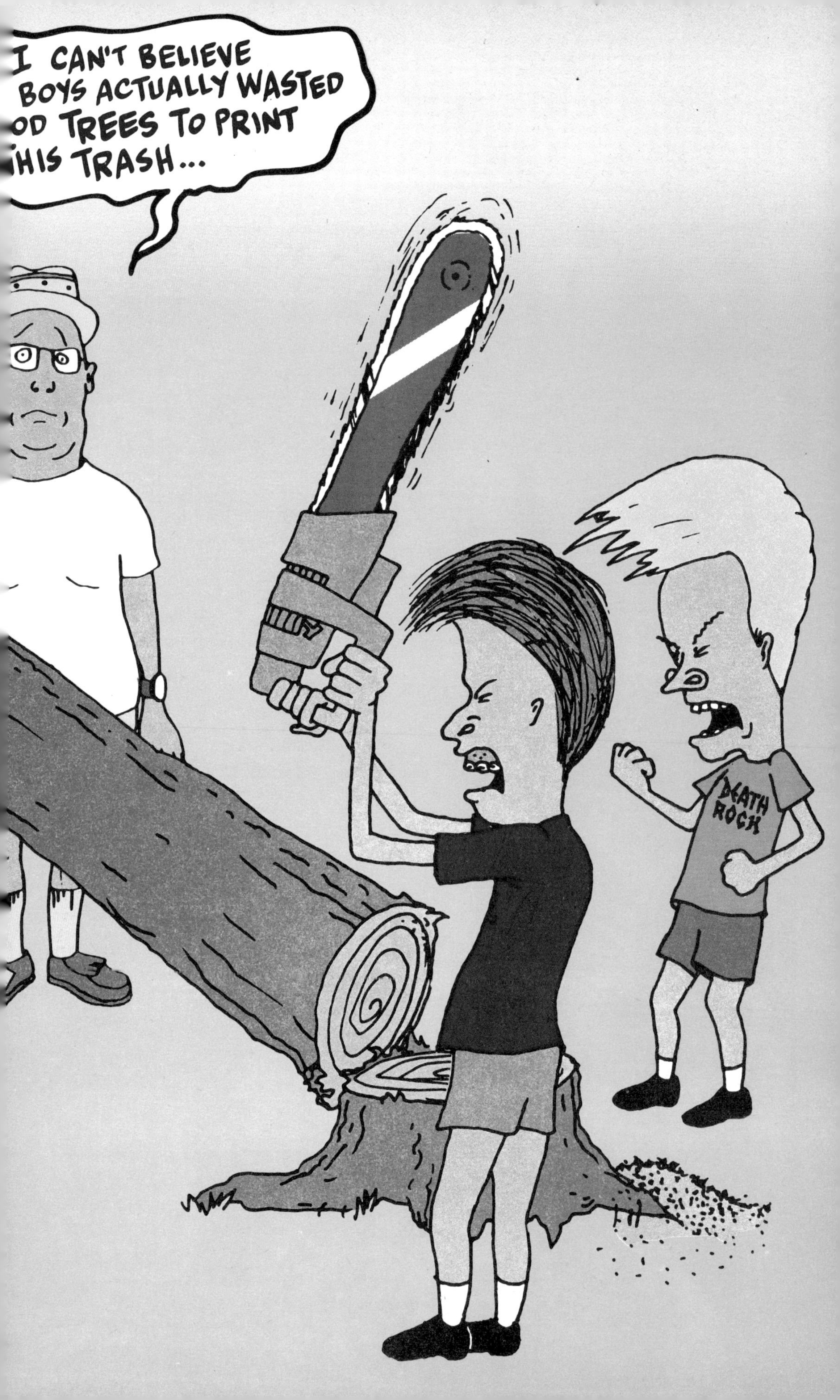
I CAN'T BELIEVE BOYS ACTUALLY WASTED OD TREES TO PRINT HIS TRASH...
DEATH ROCK

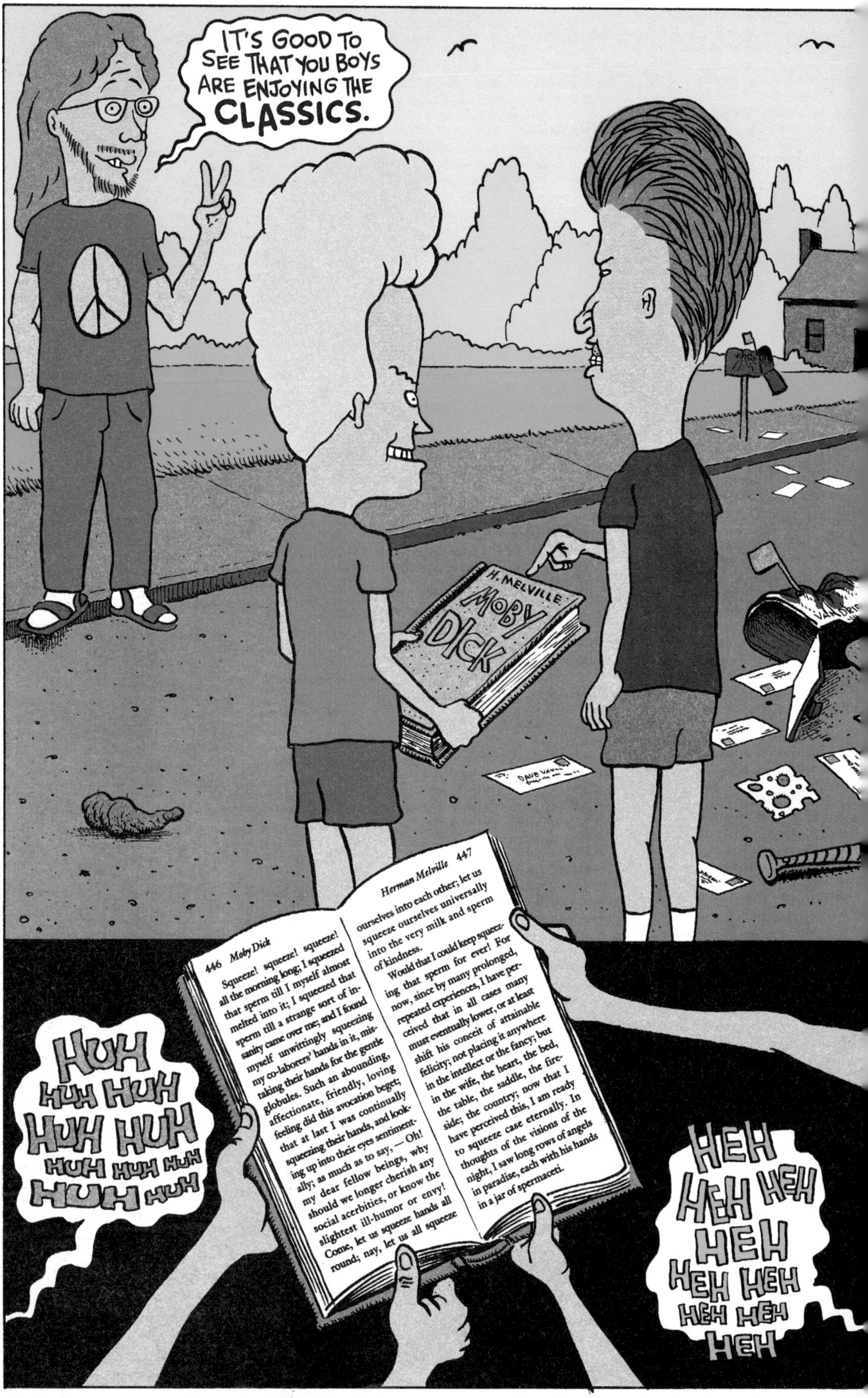
IT'S GOOD TO SEE THAT YOU BOYS ARE ENJOYING THE CLASSICS.
H. MELVILLE
MOBY DICK
446 Moby Dick
Squeeze! squeeze! squeeze! all the morning long; I squeezed that sperm till I myself almost melted into it; I squeezed that sperm till a strange sort of insanity came over me; and I found myself unwittingly squeezing my co-laborers' hands in it, mistaking their hands for the gentle globules. Such an abounding, affectionate, friendly, loving feeling did this avocation beget; that at last I was continually squeezing their hands, and looking up into their eyes sentimentally; as much as to say, — Oh! my dear fellow beings, why should we longer cherish any social acerbities, or know the slightest ill-humor or envy! Come, let us squeeze hands all round; nay, let us all squeeze
Herman Melville 447
ourselves into each other; let us squeeze ourselves universally into the very milk and sperm of kindness.
Would that I could keep squeezing that sperm for ever! For now, since by many prolonged, repeated experiences, I have perceived that in all cases many must eventually lower, or at least shift his conceit of attainable felicity; not placing it anywhere in the intellect or the fancy; but in the wife, the heart, the bed, the table, the saddle, the fire-side; the country; now that I have perceived this, I am ready to squeeze case eternally. In thoughts of the visions of the night, I saw long rows of angels in paradise, each with his hands in a jar of spermaceti.
HUH HUH HUH HUH HUH HUH HUH HUH HUH HUH
HEH HEH HEH HEH HEH HEH HEH HEH HEH